THERE'S TREASURE EVERYWHERE

Other Books by Bill Watterson

Calvin and Hobbes
Something Under the Bed Is Drooling
Yukon Ho!
Weirdos from Another Planet
The Revenge of the Baby-Sat
Scientific Progress Goes "Boink"
Attack of the Deranged Mutant Killer Monster Snow Goons
The Days Are Just Packed
Homicidal Psycho Jungle Cat

Treasury Collections

The Essential Calvin and Hobbes
The Calvin and Hobbes Lazy Sunday Book
The Authoritative Calvin and Hobbes
The Indispensable Calvin and Hobbes
The Calvin and Hobbes Tenth Anniversary Book

THERE'S TREASURE EVERYWHERE

A Calvin and Hobbes Collection by Bill Watterson

WHY ARE YOU DIGGING A HOLE?
I'M LOOKING FOR BURIED TREASURE!
WHAT HAVE YOU FOUND?
A FEW DIRTY ROCKS, A WEIRD ROOT, AND SOME DISGUSTING GRUBS.
ON YOUR FIRST TRY??
THERE'S TREASURE EVERYWHERE!

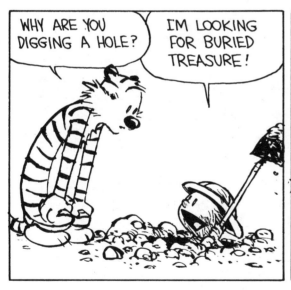

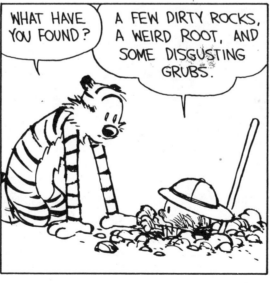

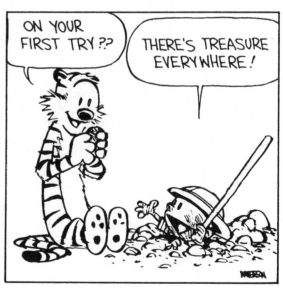

Andrews and McMeel
A Universal Press Syndicate Company
Kansas City

Printed in the United States of America. For information write Andrews and McMeel, a Universal Press Syndicate Company, 4900 Main Street, Kansas City, Missouri 64112.

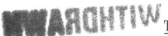

ISBN: 0-8362-1313-0 hardback
0-8362-1312-2 paperback

Library of Congress Catalog Card Number: 95-83102

IF I COULD JUST LEARN TO RIDE THAT BICYCLE, I COULD GO ALL SORTS OF PLACES.
I COULD COVER MILES IN NO TIME AT ALL! I COULD GO ANYWHERE! I COULD...
AAAAAAAAAA
I COULD GO TO HEAVEN.
YOU? I DOUBT IT.

OK BIKE, LISTEN UP! I DON'T LIKE YOU AND YOU DON'T LIKE ME.
BUT I'VE GOT THE TOOLS TO REDUCE YOU TO A PILE OF PIPES, SPROCKETS, AND BALL BEARINGS! DO WE UNDERSTAND EACH OTHER?
AAAAAAAA
MAYBE ALTOGETHER TOO WELL.

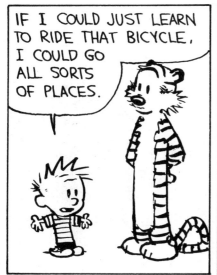

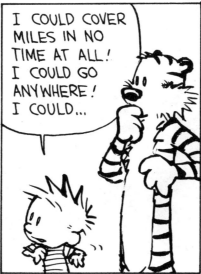

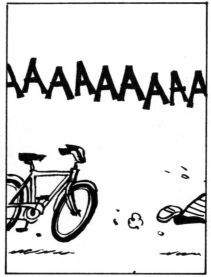

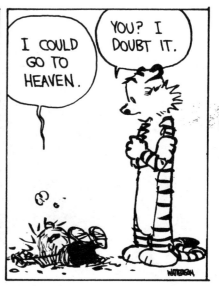

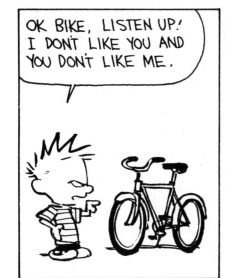

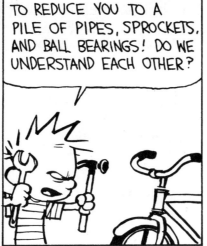

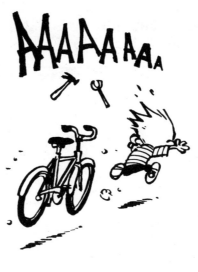

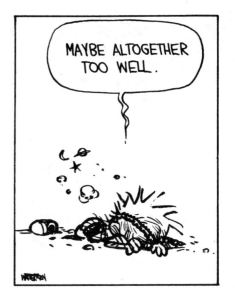

DAD, WILL YOU PUT A BELL ON MY BIKE?
I THINK YOU SHOULD LEARN HOW TO RIDE BEFORE YOU WORRY ABOUT HAVING A BELL TO RING.
NOT THAT KIND OF BELL! I WANT ONE THAT'LL WARN ME WHEN THE DARN BIKE'S SNEAKING UP ON ME!

I KNOW WHY DAD GOT ME THAT BIKE! HE'S TRYING TO BUMP ME OFF!
HE KNOWS THE BIKE WILL STOP AT NOTHING TO KILL ME.
DAD FIGURES PRETTY SOON I'LL HAVE MY HEAD THROUGH A TREE TRUNK AND HE'LL HAVE SOME PEACE AND QUIET! I'M ON TO HIM!
I SUPPOSE THAT'S EASIER THAN SENDING YOU TO CAMP AND MOVING.
WELL SURE. WHAT IF THE HOUSE DIDN'T SELL?

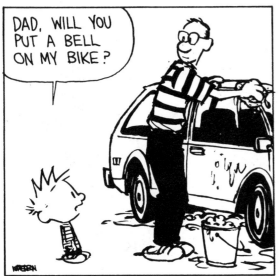

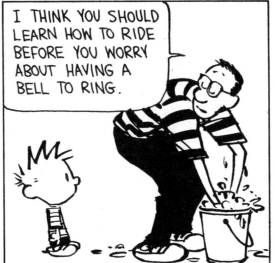

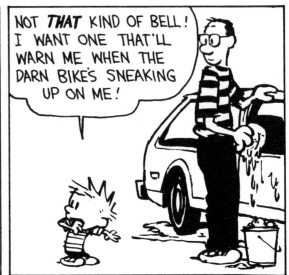

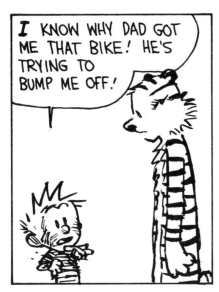

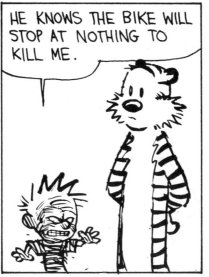

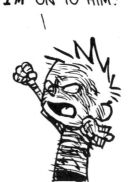

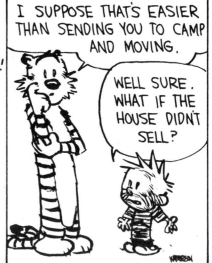

THAT CLOUD DOES IMPRESSIONS!

CALVIN, WOULD YOU SET THE TABLE FOR ME PLEASE?
MM... I DON'T THINK SO. I'M NOT ENTHUSIASTIC ABOUT SETTING THE TABLE.
I DON'T THINK YOU SHOULD HAVE TO DO SOMETHING UNLESS YOU'RE ENTHUSIASTIC ABOUT IT.

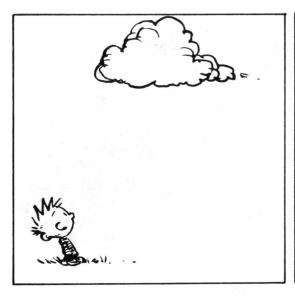

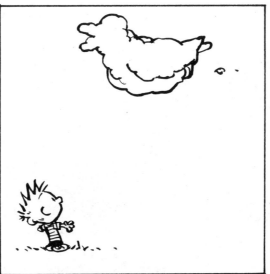

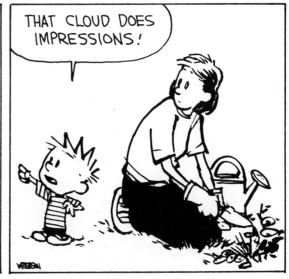

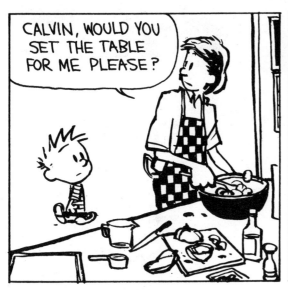

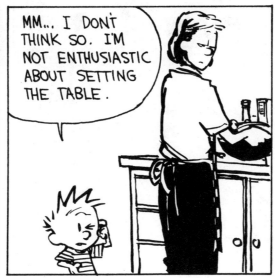

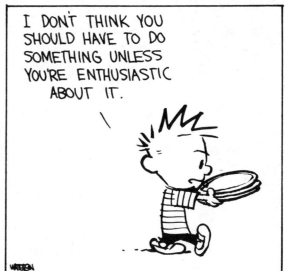

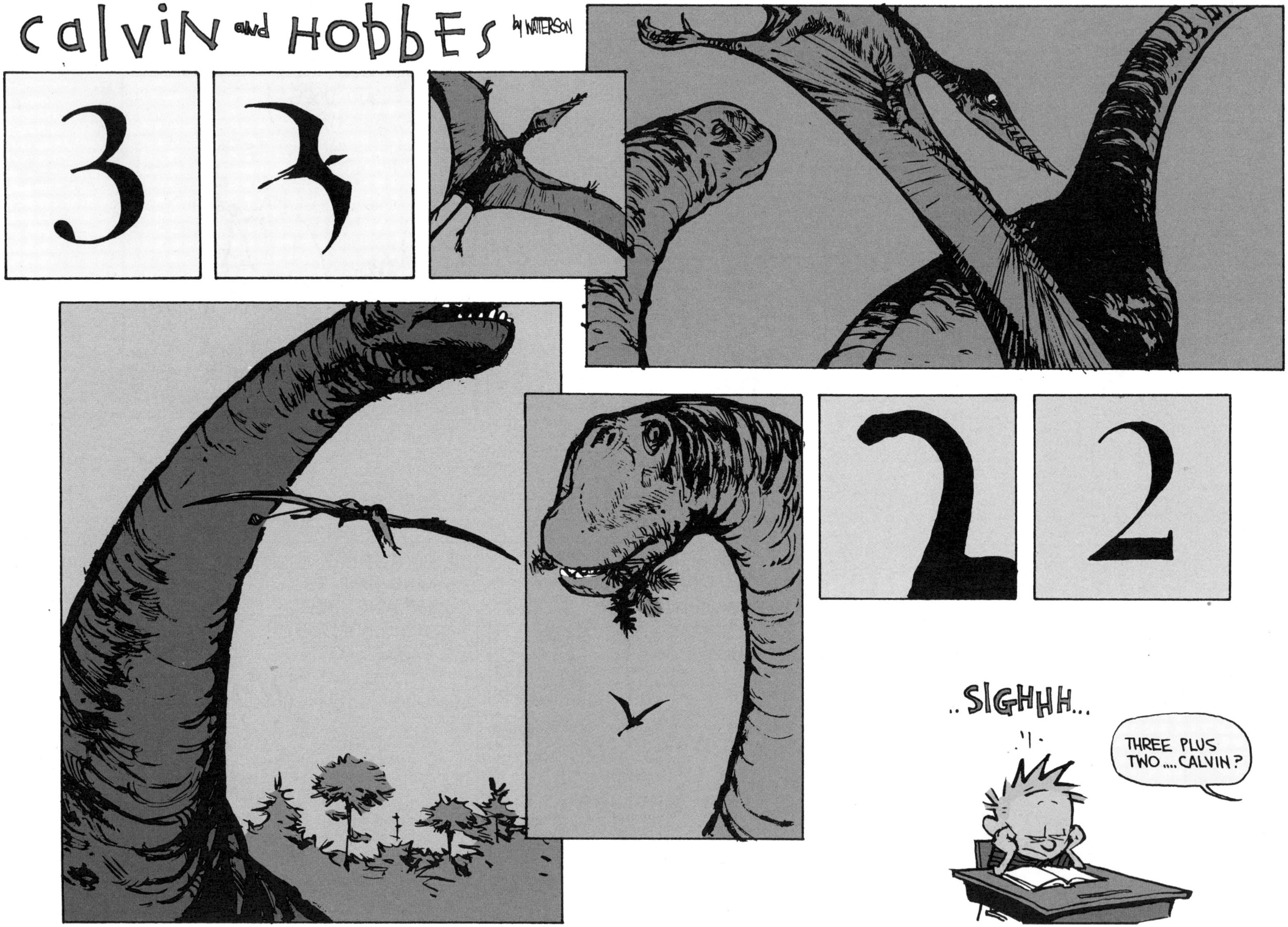
calvin and HOBBES by WATTERSON
3
2
..SIGHHH...
THREE PLUS TWO.... CALVIN?

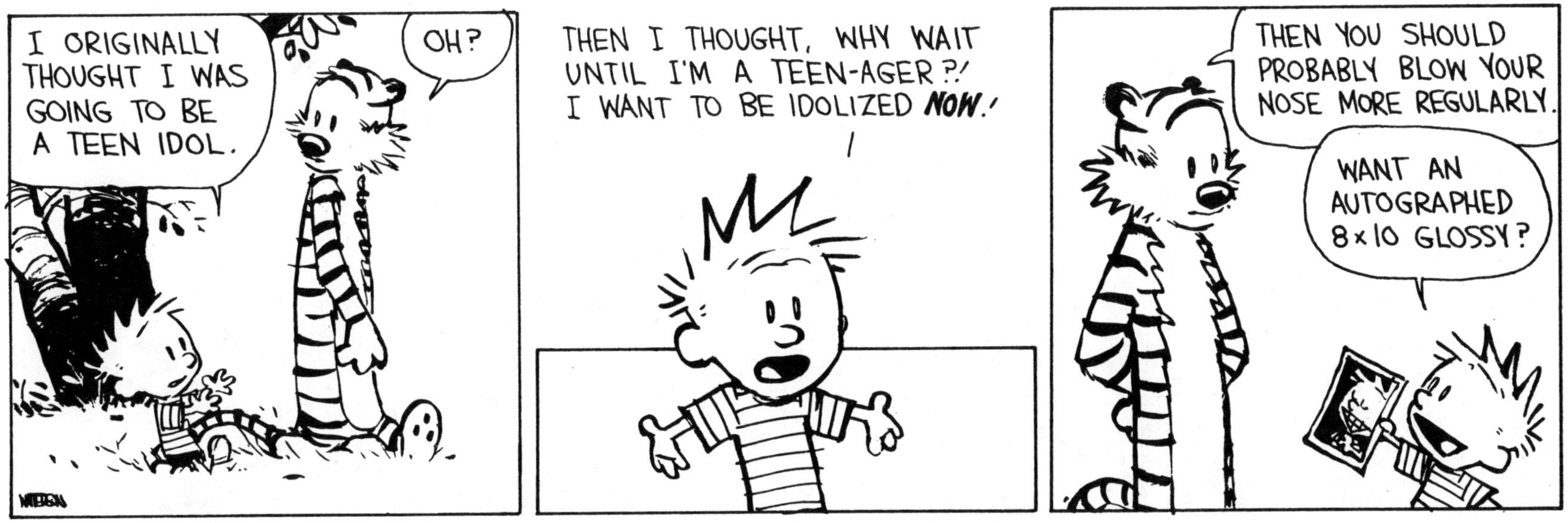
I ORIGINALLY THOUGHT I WAS GOING TO BE A TEEN IDOL.
OH?
THEN I THOUGHT, WHY WAIT UNTIL I'M A TEEN-AGER?! I WANT TO BE IDOLIZED **NOW**!
THEN YOU SHOULD PROBABLY BLOW YOUR NOSE MORE REGULARLY.
WANT AN AUTOGRAPHED 8×10 GLOSSY?

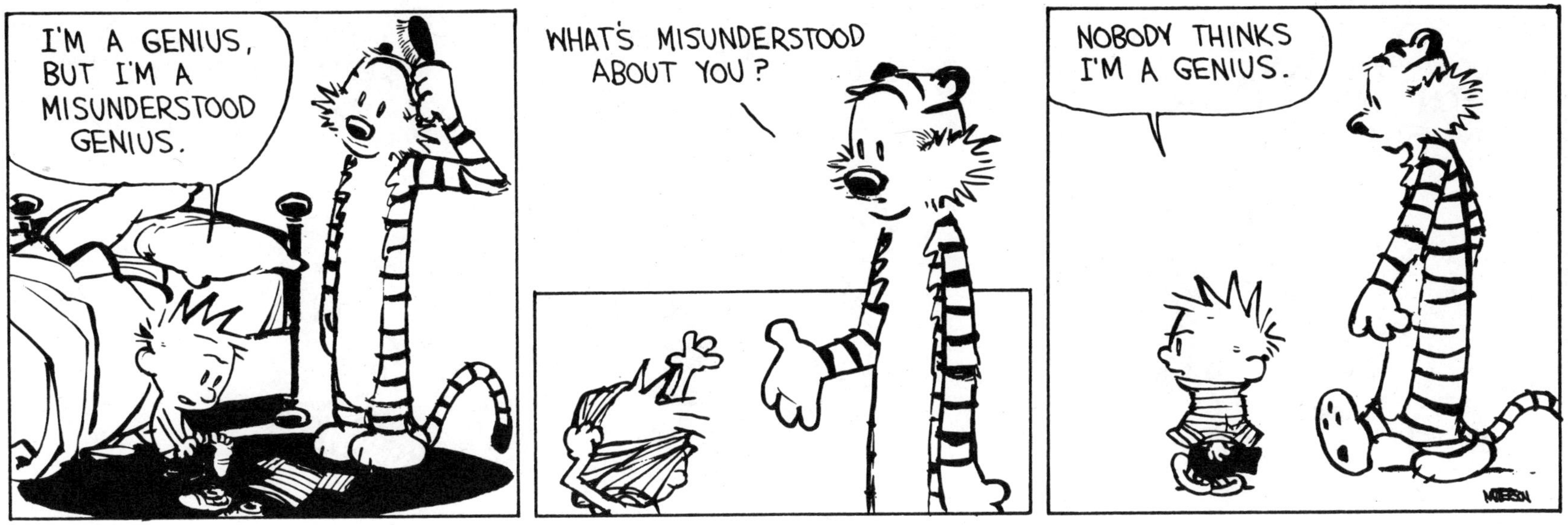
I'M A GENIUS, BUT I'M A MISUNDERSTOOD GENIUS.
WHAT'S MISUNDERSTOOD ABOUT YOU?
NOBODY THINKS I'M A GENIUS.

AT THIS ROOM, TIME ENTERS A NO-PASSING ZONE.

LET GO OF ME, YA BIG GALOOT! WHY DON'T YOU PICK ON SOMEBODY YOUR OWN SIZE?!
They'd hit back.
..I GUESS THAT HAS A CERTAIN UNETHICAL LOGIC TO IT...

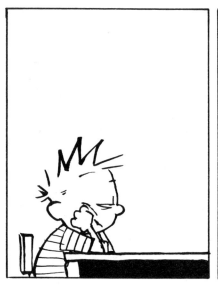

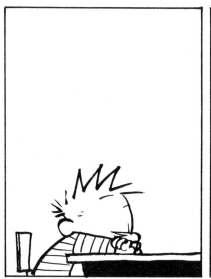

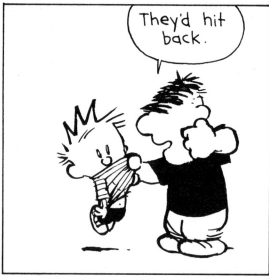

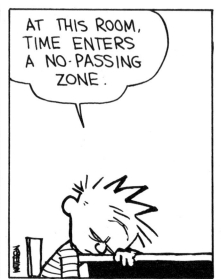

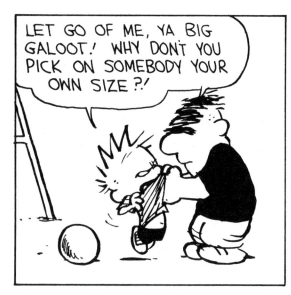

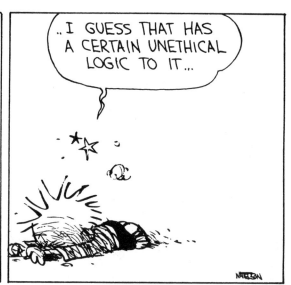

THAT'S IT! I'M THROUGH LEARNING TODAY!
SEE YOU ALL TOMORROW!
I THINK *I'M* A BETTER JUDGE OF WHEN I'M THROUGH.

DAD, WHAT'S IT LIKE BEING A GROWN-UP?
WELL, IT'S NOT TOO DIFFERENT FROM BEING A KID...
...EXCEPT YOU'RE MORE ATTACHED TO YOUR TOYS.

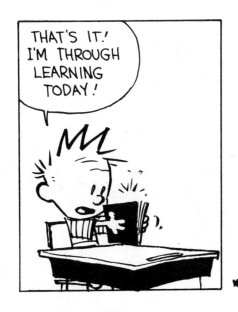

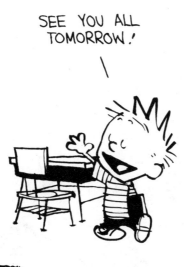

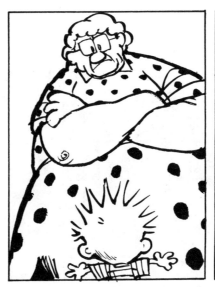

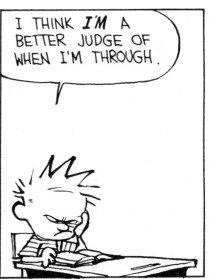

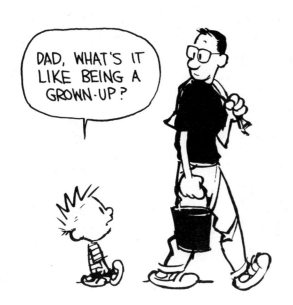

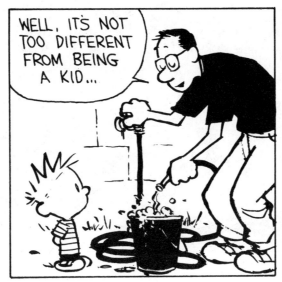

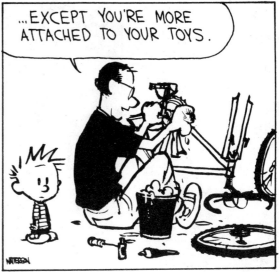

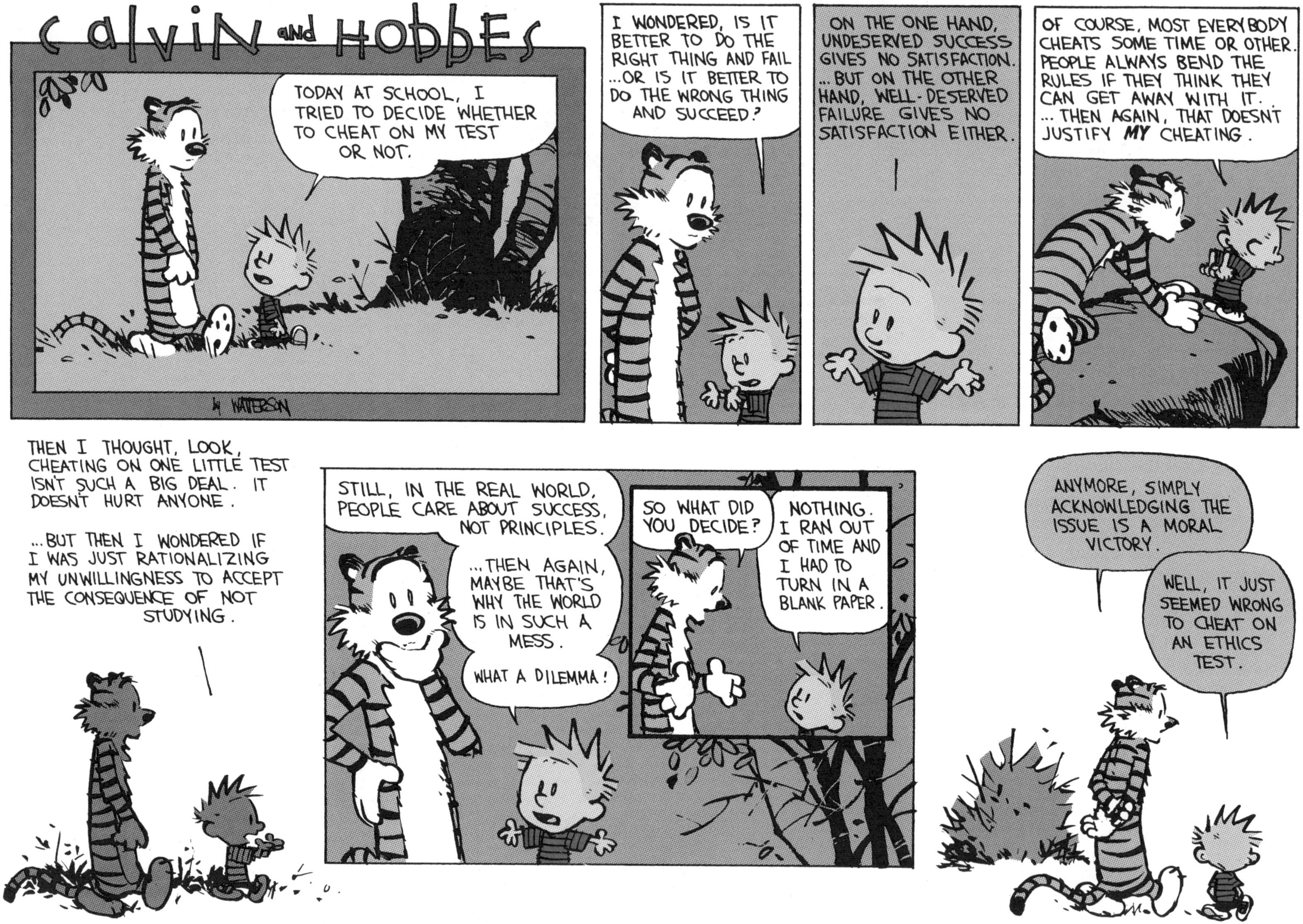

Calvin and HOBBES
TODAY AT SCHOOL, I TRIED TO DECIDE WHETHER TO CHEAT ON MY TEST OR NOT.
WATTERSON
I WONDERED, IS IT BETTER TO DO THE RIGHT THING AND FAIL ...OR IS IT BETTER TO DO THE WRONG THING AND SUCCEED?
ON THE ONE HAND, UNDESERVED SUCCESS GIVES NO SATISFACTION. ...BUT ON THE OTHER HAND, WELL-DESERVED FAILURE GIVES NO SATISFACTION EITHER.
OF COURSE, MOST EVERYBODY CHEATS SOME TIME OR OTHER. PEOPLE ALWAYS BEND THE RULES IF THEY THINK THEY CAN GET AWAY WITH IT. ... THEN AGAIN, THAT DOESN'T JUSTIFY MY CHEATING.
THEN I THOUGHT, LOOK, CHEATING ON ONE LITTLE TEST ISN'T SUCH A BIG DEAL. IT DOESN'T HURT ANYONE.
...BUT THEN I WONDERED IF I WAS JUST RATIONALIZING MY UNWILLINGNESS TO ACCEPT THE CONSEQUENCE OF NOT STUDYING.
STILL, IN THE REAL WORLD, PEOPLE CARE ABOUT SUCCESS, NOT PRINCIPLES.
...THEN AGAIN, MAYBE THAT'S WHY THE WORLD IS IN SUCH A MESS.
WHAT A DILEMMA!
SO WHAT DID YOU DECIDE?
NOTHING. I RAN OUT OF TIME AND I HAD TO TURN IN A BLANK PAPER.
ANYMORE, SIMPLY ACKNOWLEDGING THE ISSUE IS A MORAL VICTORY.
WELL, IT JUST SEEMED WRONG TO CHEAT ON AN ETHICS TEST.

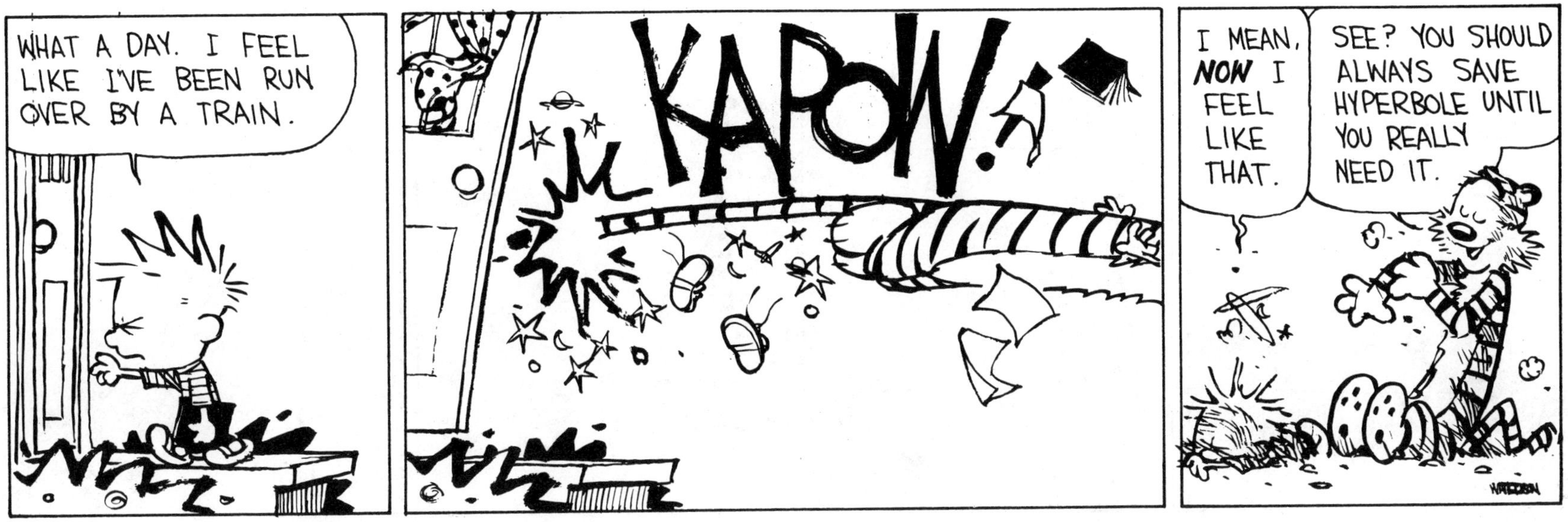
WHAT A DAY. I FEEL LIKE I'VE BEEN RUN OVER BY A TRAIN.
KAPOW!
I MEAN, NOW I FEEL LIKE THAT.
SEE? YOU SHOULD ALWAYS SAVE HYPERBOLE UNTIL YOU REALLY NEED IT.

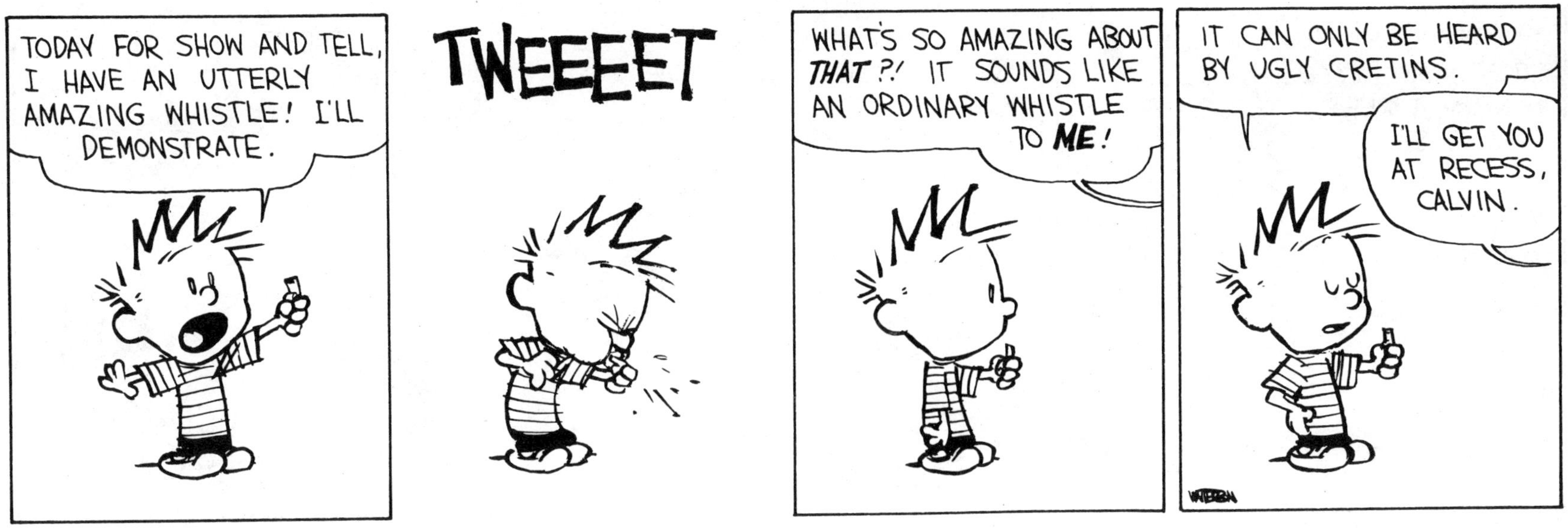
TODAY FOR SHOW AND TELL, I HAVE AN UTTERLY AMAZING WHISTLE! I'LL DEMONSTRATE.
TWEEEEET
WHAT'S SO AMAZING ABOUT THAT?! IT SOUNDS LIKE AN ORDINARY WHISTLE TO ME!
IT CAN ONLY BE HEARD BY UGLY CRETINS.
I'LL GET YOU AT RECESS, CALVIN.

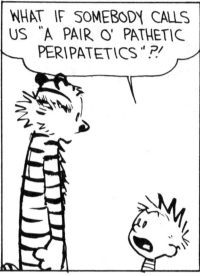

WHAT IF SOMEBODY CALLS US "A PAIR O' PATHETIC PERIPATETICS".?!

I'VE NEVER HEARD OF ANYONE TAKING THE TROUBLE TO RHYME WEIRD INSULTS.

BUT SHOULDN'T WE HAVE A READY RETORT?

I'M DOING A CROSSWORD PUZZLE. NUMBER THREE ACROSS SAYS "BIRD."

HMM..

I'VE GOT IT! "YELLOW-BELLIED SAPSUCKER"!

BUT THERE ARE ONLY FIVE BOXES.

I KNOW. THESE IDIOTS MAKE YOU WRITE REAL SMALL.

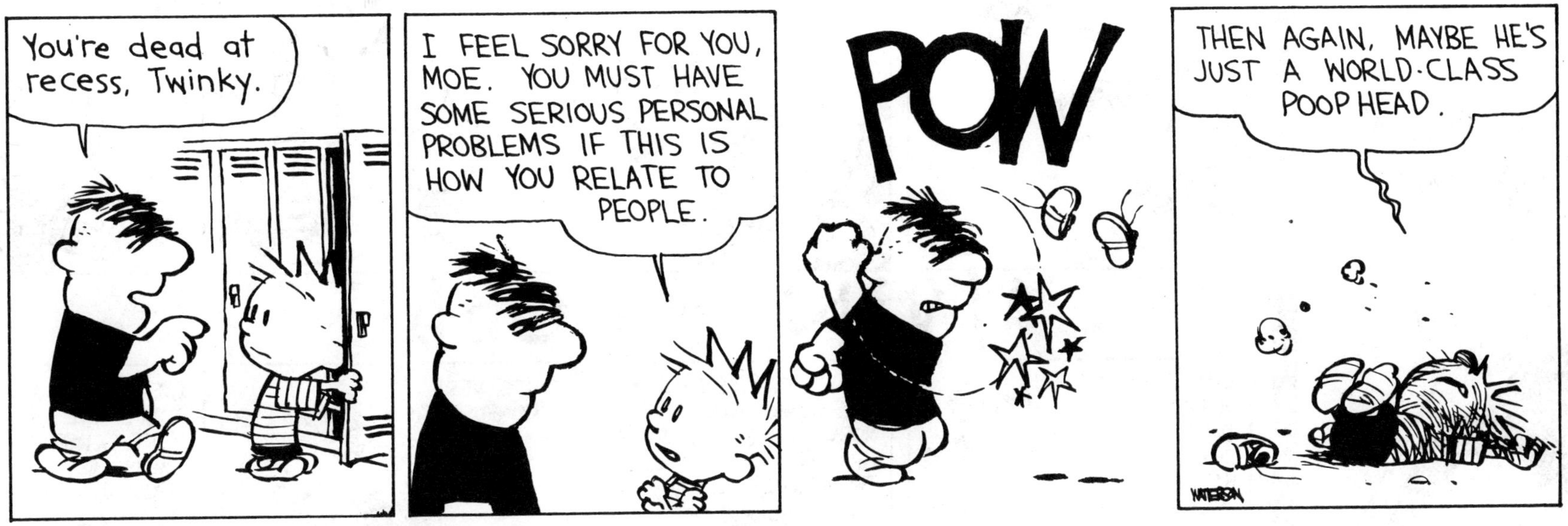
You're dead at recess, Twinky.
I FEEL SORRY FOR YOU, MOE. YOU MUST HAVE SOME SERIOUS PERSONAL PROBLEMS IF THIS IS HOW YOU RELATE TO PEOPLE.
POW
THEN AGAIN, MAYBE HE'S JUST A WORLD-CLASS POOP HEAD.

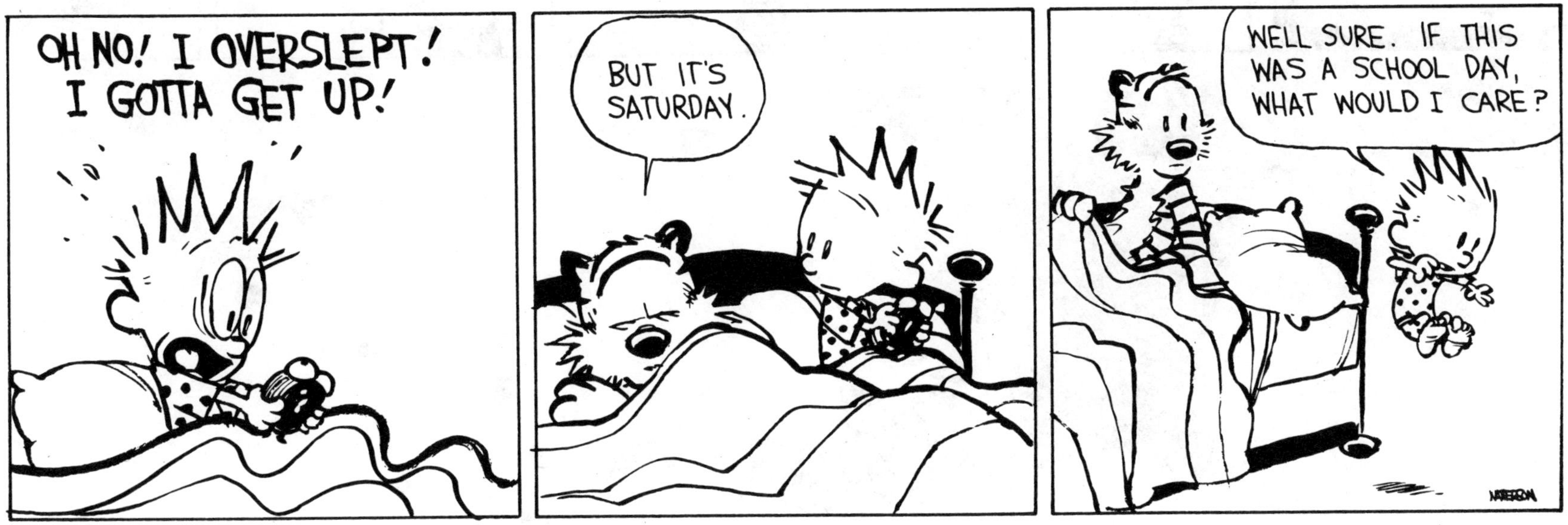
OH NO! I OVERSLEPT! I GOTTA GET UP!
BUT IT'S SATURDAY.
WELL SURE. IF THIS WAS A SCHOOL DAY, WHAT WOULD I CARE?

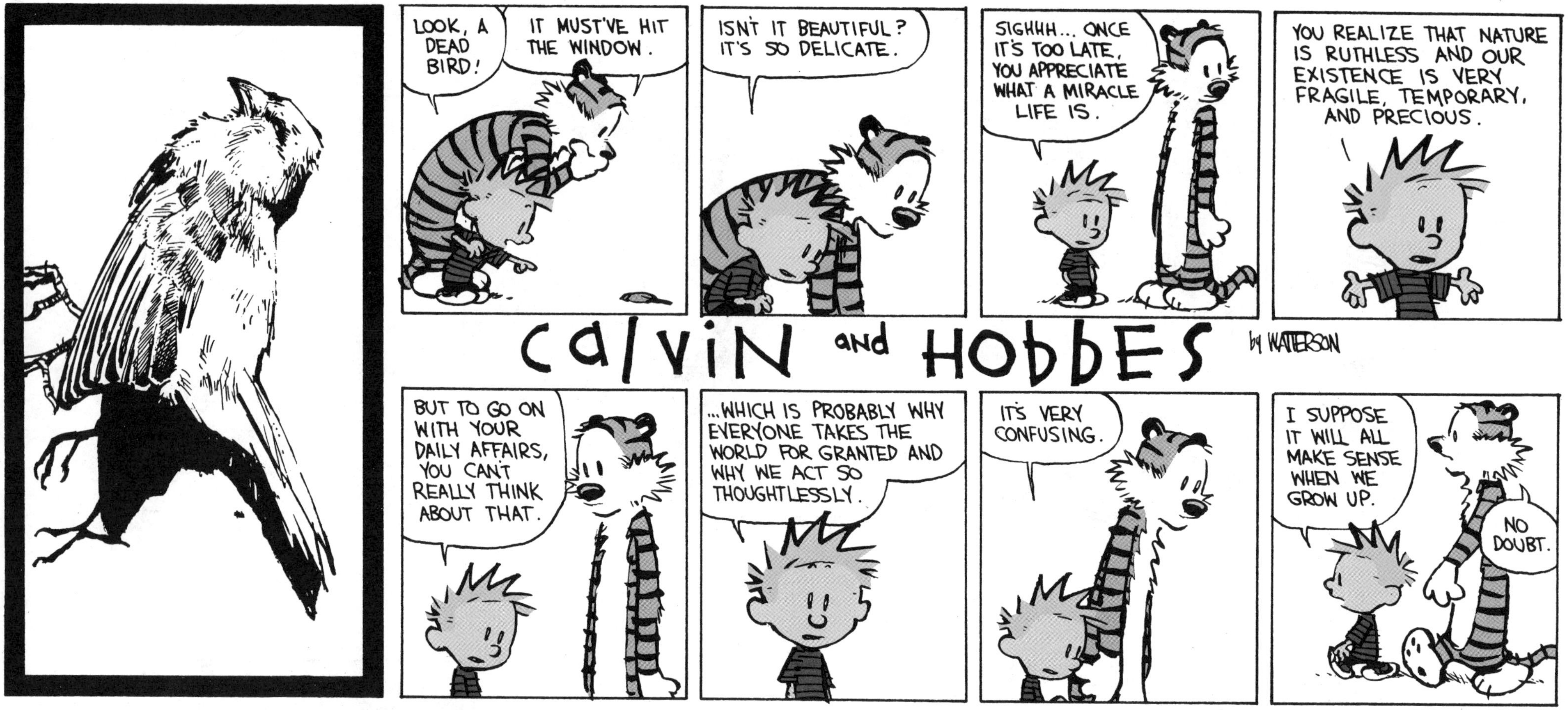
LOOK, A DEAD BIRD!
IT MUST'VE HIT THE WINDOW.
ISN'T IT BEAUTIFUL? IT'S SO DELICATE.
SIGHHH... ONCE IT'S TOO LATE, YOU APPRECIATE WHAT A MIRACLE LIFE IS.
YOU REALIZE THAT NATURE IS RUTHLESS AND OUR EXISTENCE IS VERY FRAGILE, TEMPORARY, AND PRECIOUS.
CALVIN and HOBBES
by WATTERSON
BUT TO GO ON WITH YOUR DAILY AFFAIRS, YOU CAN'T REALLY THINK ABOUT THAT.
...WHICH IS PROBABLY WHY EVERYONE TAKES THE WORLD FOR GRANTED AND WHY WE ACT SO THOUGHTLESSLY.
IT'S VERY CONFUSING.
I SUPPOSE IT WILL ALL MAKE SENSE WHEN WE GROW UP.
NO DOUBT.

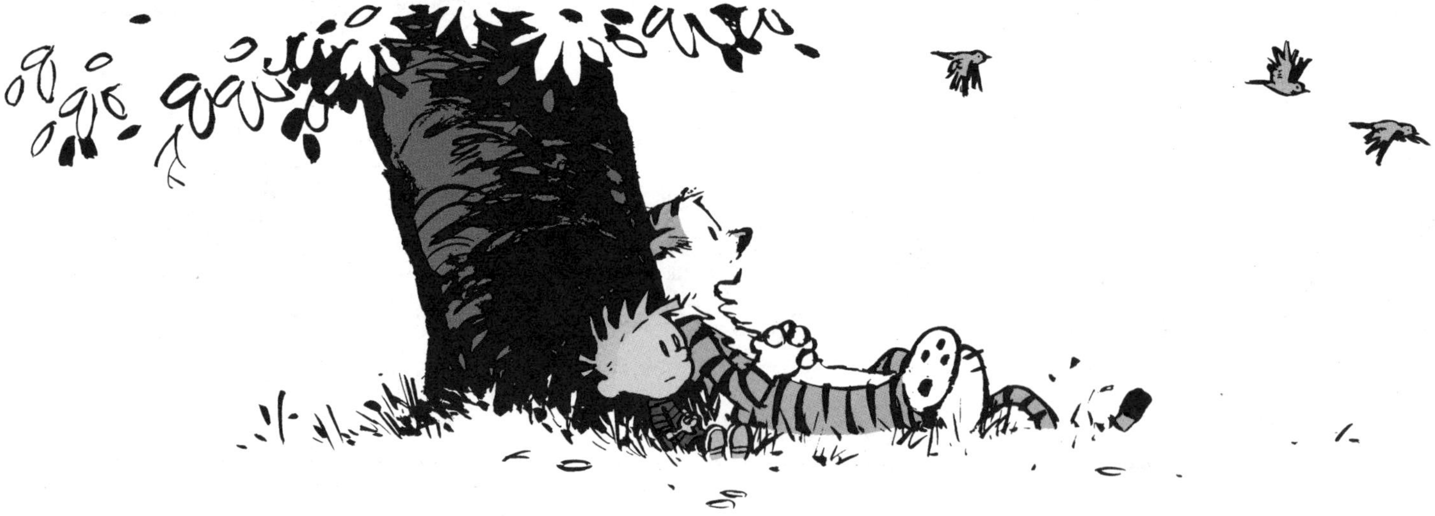

YOUR NEW POLLS ARE IN, DAD.
MM.
A VAST MAJORITY OF HOUSEHOLD SIX-YEAR-OLDS SAY YOU'RE NOT LIVING UP TO THEIR EXPECTATIONS OF FATHERHOOD.
WHAT WERE THEIR EXPECTATIONS?
THAT YOU'D BE MORE LIKE AN AUTOMATIC TELLER MACHINE.
WHERE DO YOU POLLSTERS FIND THESE RESPONDENTS?

THE MORE YOU KNOW, THE HARDER IT IS TO TAKE DECISIVE ACTION.
ONCE YOU BECOME INFORMED, YOU START SEEING COMPLEXITIES AND SHADES OF GRAY.
YOU REALIZE THAT NOTHING IS AS CLEAR AND SIMPLE AS IT FIRST APPEARS. ULTIMATELY, KNOWLEDGE IS PARALYZING.
BEING A MAN OF ACTION, I CAN'T AFFORD TO TAKE THAT RISK.
YOU'RE IGNORANT, BUT AT LEAST YOU ACT ON IT.

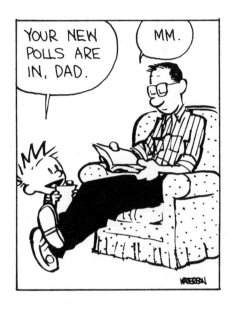

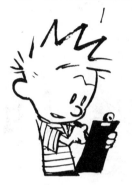

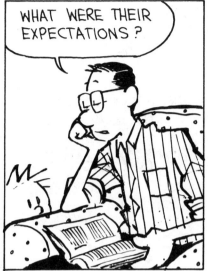

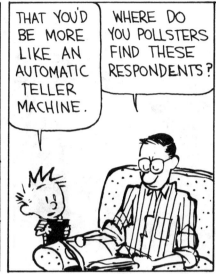

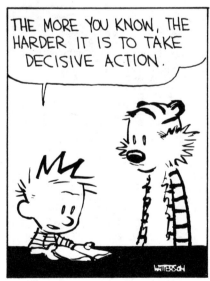

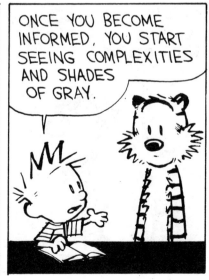

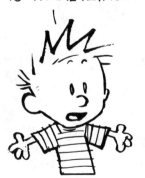

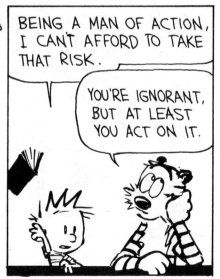

HAVE YOU BEEN READING ABOUT THE "ELECTRONIC SUPERHIGHWAY"?
PRETTY SOON, COMPUTERS, TELEPHONES AND TVs WILL ALL BE HOOKED TOGETHER TO BRING INSTANTANEOUS, INTERACTIVE COMMUNICATION RIGHT INTO OUR HOMES!
BUT DAD SAYS HE LIKED IT BETTER WHEN YOU HAD TO COMMUNICATE BY MAIL, AND YOU KNEW YOU WOULDN'T HEAR BACK FROM ANYBODY FOR AT LEAST A WEEK.
OF COURSE, YOUR DAD THINKS TRANSPORTATION SHOULD'VE STOPPED WITH THE BICYCLE.
I'M A 21ST-CENTURY KID TRAPPED IN A 19TH-CENTURY FAMILY.

WAIT! DON'T HIT ME! THERE'S SOMETHING ON YOUR BACK!
I'm sure.
I'M SERIOUS! IT'S A NOTE! YOUR MOM MUST'VE PINNED IT ON YOUR SHIRT.
What's it say?
IT SAYS, "SOMEBODY RUN THIS BOY OVER WITH A TRUCK."
IF I'M GOING TO GET CLOBBERED, I LIKE TO DESERVE IT.

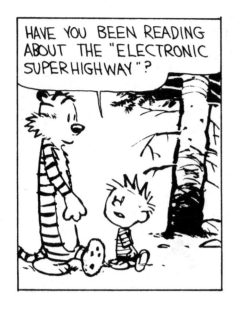

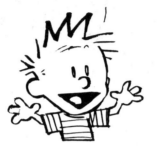

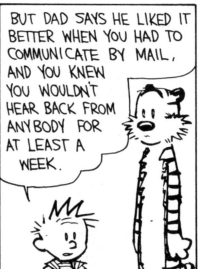

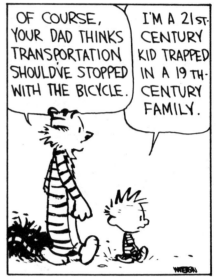

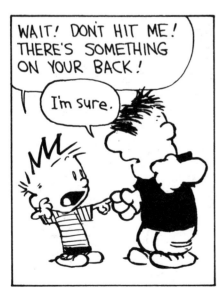

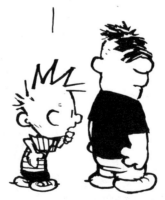

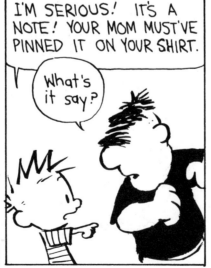

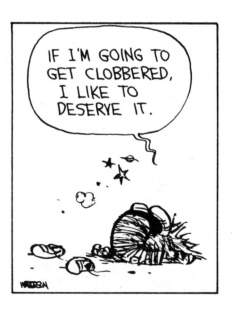

MY WATCH TELLS THE TIME, THE DAY, AND THE DATE.
IT DOESN'T TELL WHAT MONTH IT IS, THOUGH. I NEED A WATCH THAT TELLS THE MONTH.
I SUPPOSE THEY FIGURE IF YOU DON'T KNOW WHAT MONTH IT IS, YOU'RE NOT THE TYPE WHO'D WEAR A WATCH.

MOM WANTS TO KNOW IF WE'D LIKE TO GO TO THE ZOO TODAY.
CAN WE TOUR A PRISON AFTERWARD?
NO THANKS.

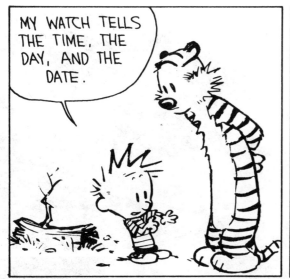

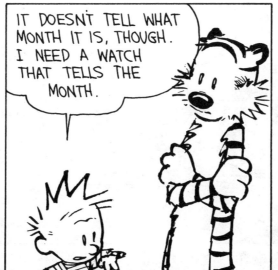

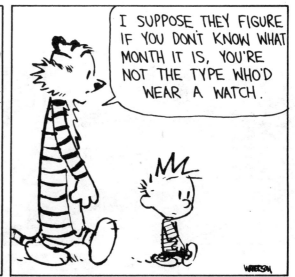

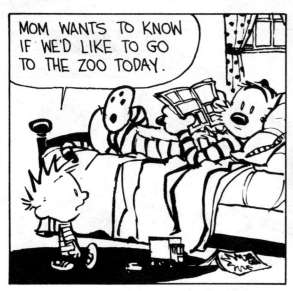

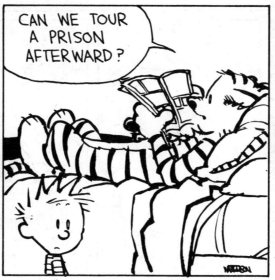

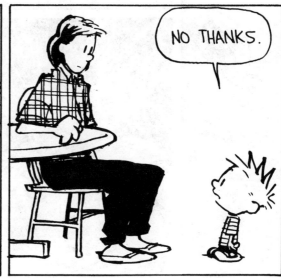

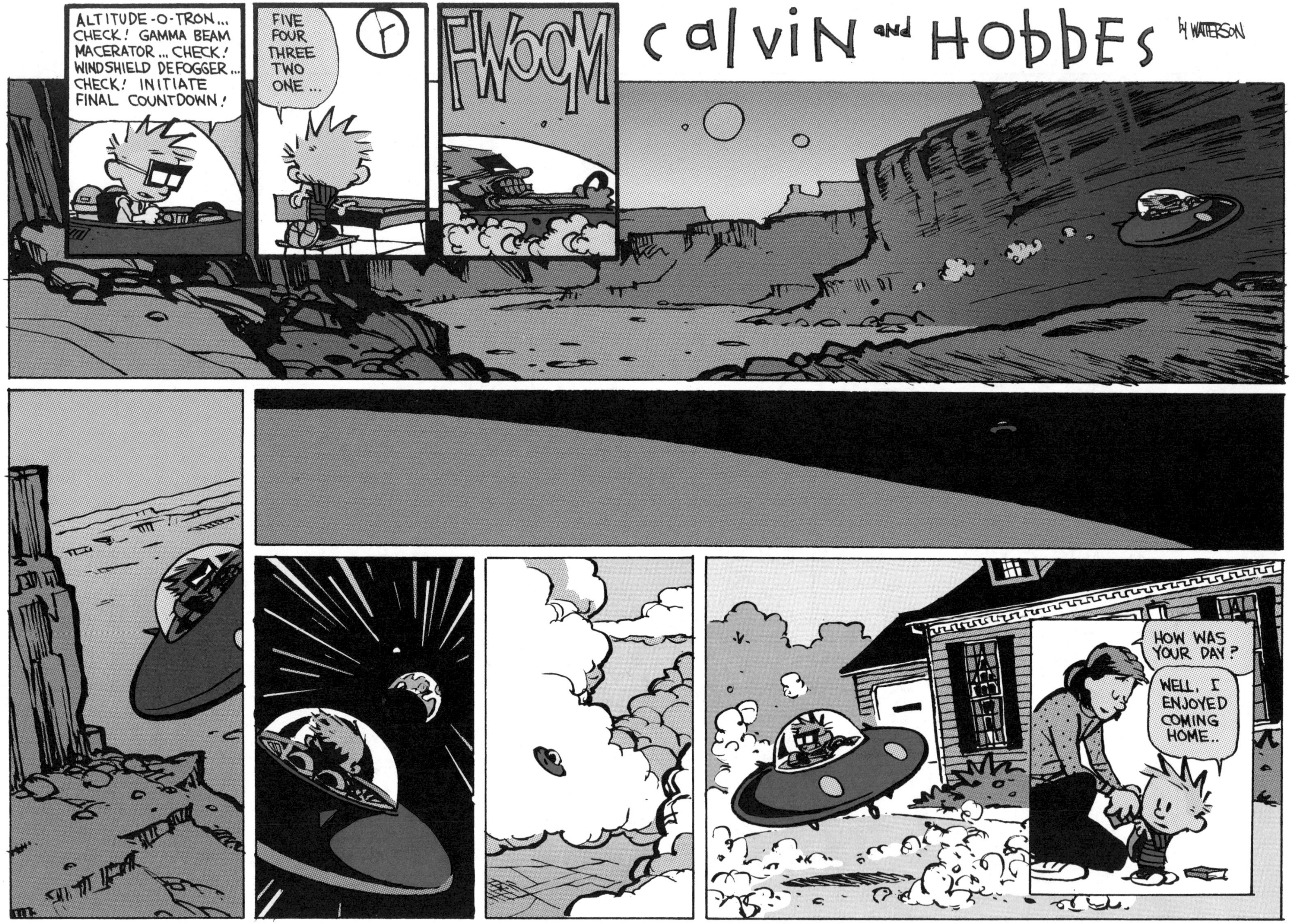
calvin and HOBBES
by WATTERSON
ALTITUDE-O-TRON... CHECK! GAMMA BEAM MACERATOR... CHECK! WINDSHIELD DEFOGGER... CHECK! INITIATE FINAL COUNTDOWN!
FIVE FOUR THREE TWO ONE...
FWOOM
HOW WAS YOUR DAY?
WELL, I ENJOYED COMING HOME..

PSST, SUSIE! WHAT'S THE ANSWER TO QUESTION TWO?
"ELI WHITNEY AND THE COTTON GIN."
BUT THIS IS A MATH PROBLEM.
IT'S A TRICK QUESTION.
HOW COME **YOU** WROTE SOMETHING DIFFERENT?
I'M GOING TO GET THIS QUESTION WRONG, SO IT WON'T LOOK LIKE YOU COPIED.
WOW, THANKS!
OH, I OWE IT TO YOU.

OK, THAT'S HOW WE'LL DO KICK OFFS.
GO WITH WHAT WORKS, I GUESS.

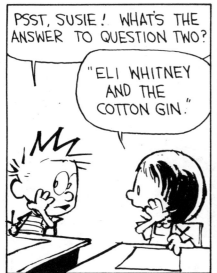

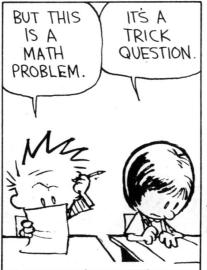

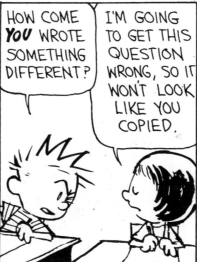

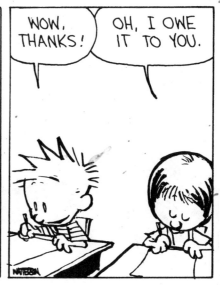

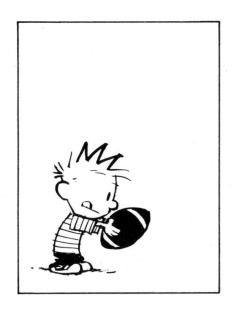

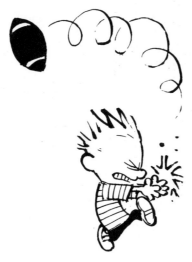

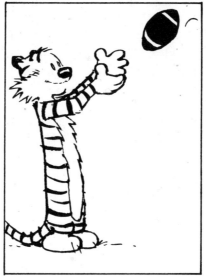

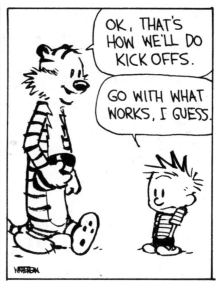

OOH, WOOK AT DA BIG, STWIPEY PUTTY! IS OO A FUZZY, FWIENDWY PUTTY??
TIGERS DON'T LIKE TO BE CALLED "PUTTIES."
WATTERSON

IF HEAVEN IS GOOD, AND IF I LIKE TO BE BAD, HOW AM I SUPPOSED TO BE HAPPY THERE?
HOW WILL YOU GET TO HEAVEN IF YOU LIKE TO BE BAD?
LET'S SAY I DIDN'T **DO** WHAT I **WANTED** TO DO.
SUPPOSE I LED A BLAMELESS LIFE! SUPPOSE I DENIED MY TRUE DARK NATURE!
WATTERSON
I'M NOT SURE I HAVE THAT MUCH IMAGINATION.
MAYBE HEAVEN IS A PLACE WHERE YOU'RE **ALLOWED** TO BE BAD!

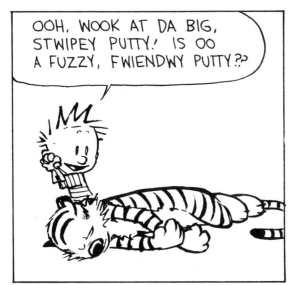

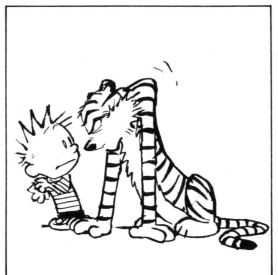

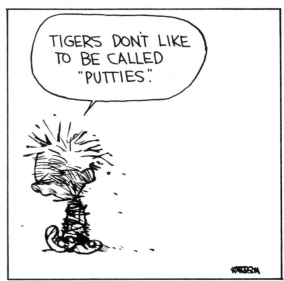

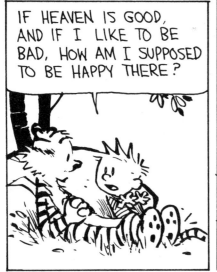

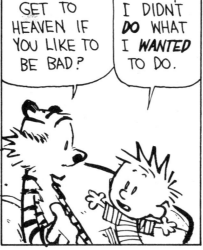

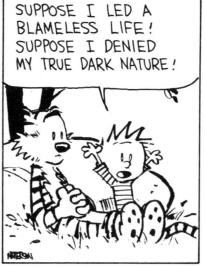

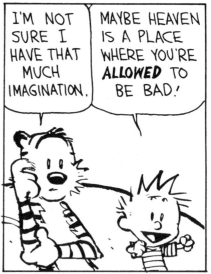

CALVIN, YOUR TEST WAS AN ABSOLUTE DISGRACE! IT'S OBVIOUS YOU HAVEN'T READ ANY OF THE MATERIAL.

OUR FIRST PRESIDENT WAS *NOT* CHEF BOY-AR-DEE AND YOU OUGHT TO BE ASHAMED TO HAVE TURNED IN SUCH PREPOSTEROUS ANSWERS!

I JUST DON'T TEST WELL.

LOOK, HOBBES! IF YOU DRY YOUR TEETH, YOU CAN CURL YOUR UPPER LIP AND IT WILL STICK!

SEE? THEN YOU TAKE A PIECE OF TAPE...

.. AND USE IT TO PULL YOUR NOSTRILS UP! COOL, HUH?

WOW! I'LL BET IF YOU SHOWED YOUR DAD, HE'D GO TO WORK LIKE THAT!

YEAH!

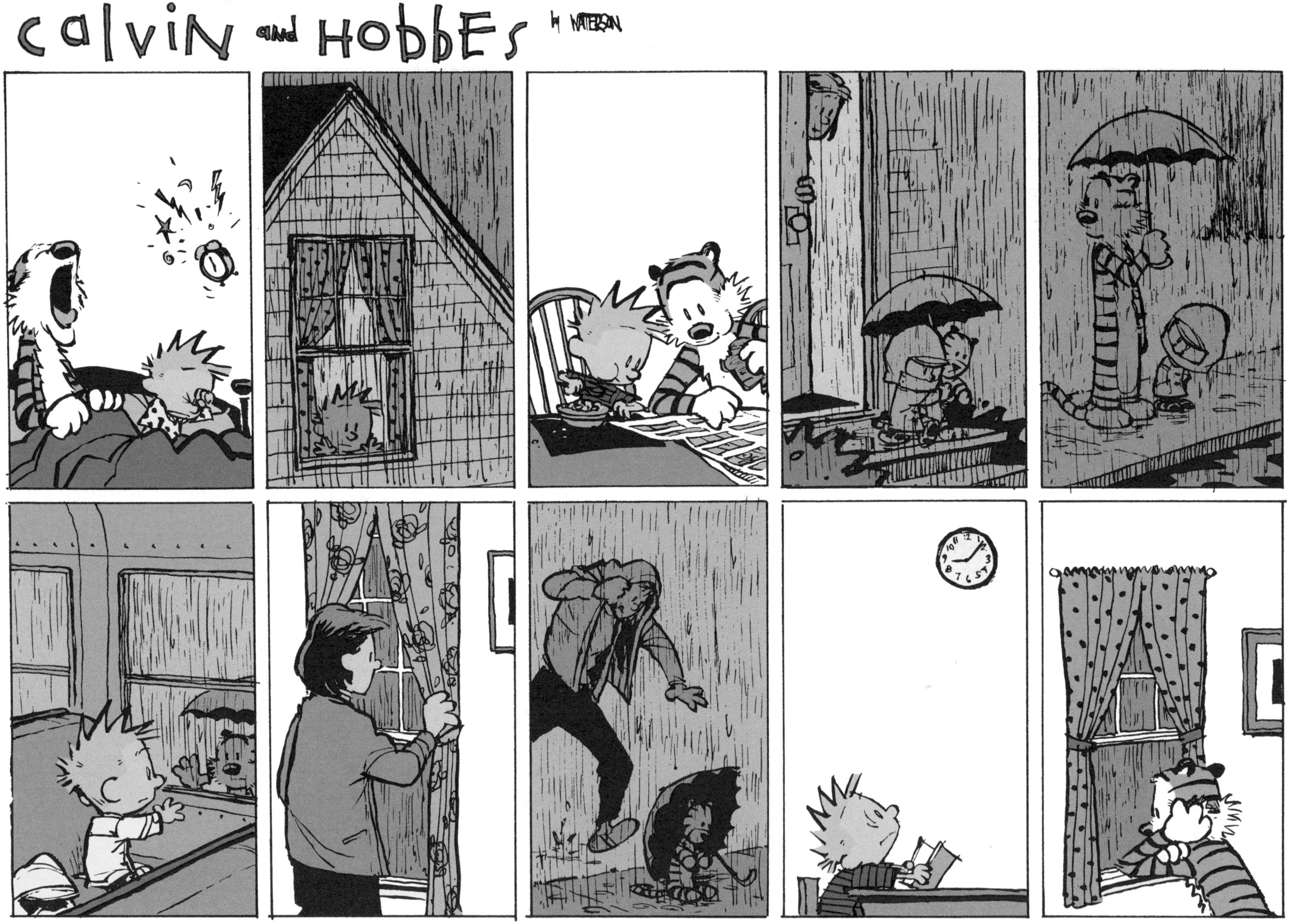
calvin and HOBBES
by WATTERSON

I LOVE MY SCHOOL BOOKS. JUST THINK! PRETTY SOON WE'LL HAVE READ **ALL** OF THIS!

I LIKE TO READ AHEAD AND SEE WHAT WE'RE GOING TO LEARN NEXT. IT'S SO EXCITING TO KNOW STUFF.

HAVING A BOOK IS LIKE HAVING A GOOD FRIEND WITH YOU.

IF YOU FLIP THE PAGES OF **MY** BOOK, AN ANIMATED T. REX DRIVES THE BATMOBILE AND EXPLODES!

SOMETIMES I THINK BOOKS ARE THE ONLY FRIENDS WORTH HAVING.

I DON'T NEED TO STUDY! I DON'T NEED TO LEARN!

I CAN ALWAYS GET BY ON MY GOOD LOOKS AND CHARM!

I DON'T HEAR YOU CONCURRING, HAIRBALL BREATH.

TELL ME, IS IT STATIC ELECTRICITY THAT MAKES YOUR HAIR DO THAT?

I GOT A SMILEY FACE STICKER ON MY QUIZ.
WHOOP-DE-DOO FOR YOU.
WHAT DID YOU GET?
NONE OF YOUR DARN BUSINESS!
YOU GOT A FROWNY FACE, DIDN'T YOU?
NO, AS A MATTER OF FACT, I DIDN'T!
I DIDN'T EVEN KNOW THEY MADE BARFING FACE STICKERS.
WATTERSON

MISS WORMWOOD, I'M NOT GOING TO LEARN THIS MATERIAL UNLESS YOU MAKE IT ENTHRALLING.
I SEE. AND WHAT WILL YOU DO IF THE REST OF YOUR LIFE DOESN'T ENTERTAIN YOU EVERY MINUTE?
8-2=
WHAT, ...YOU THINK I'LL LIVE SOMEPLACE THAT DOESN'T GET CABLE?!
WATTERSON

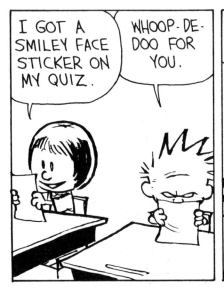

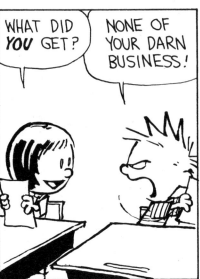

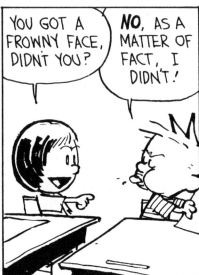

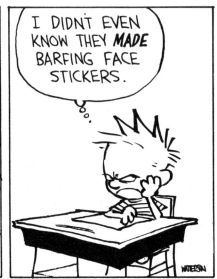

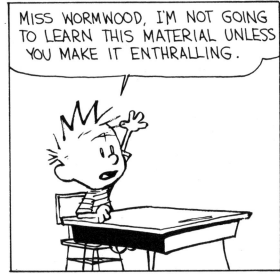

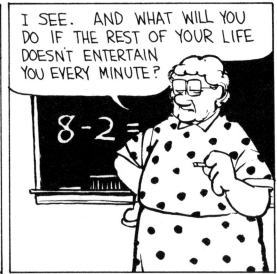

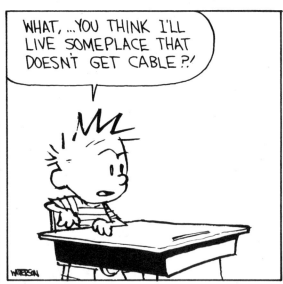

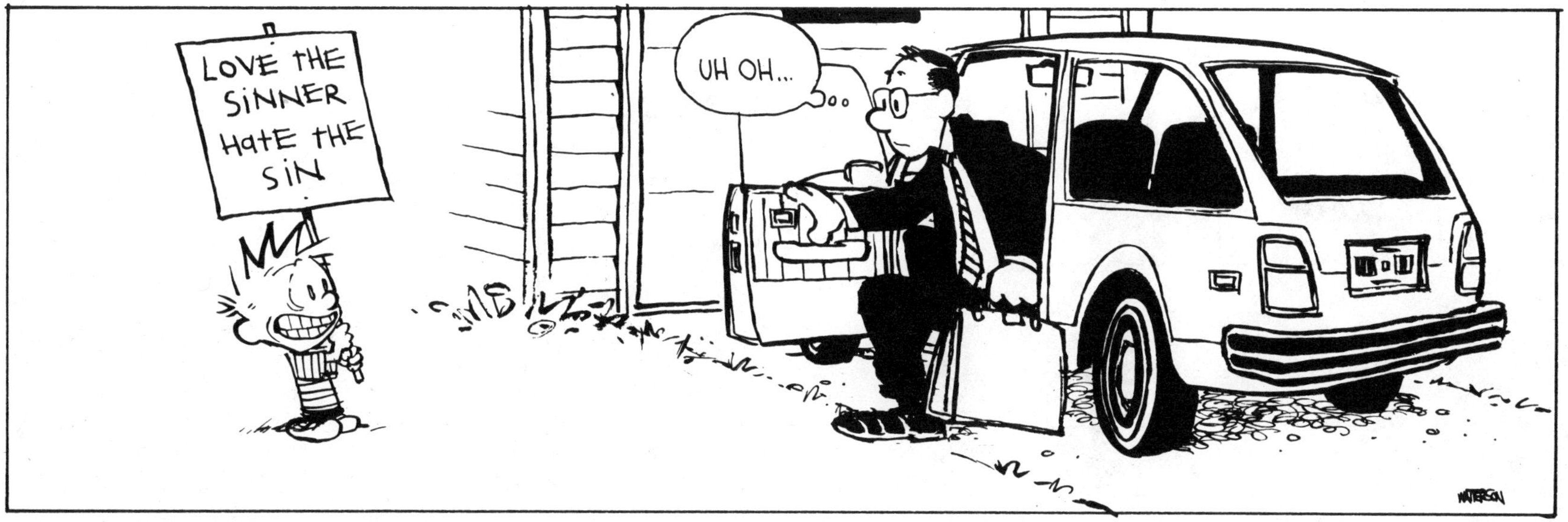
LOVE THE SINNER HATE THE SIN
UH OH...

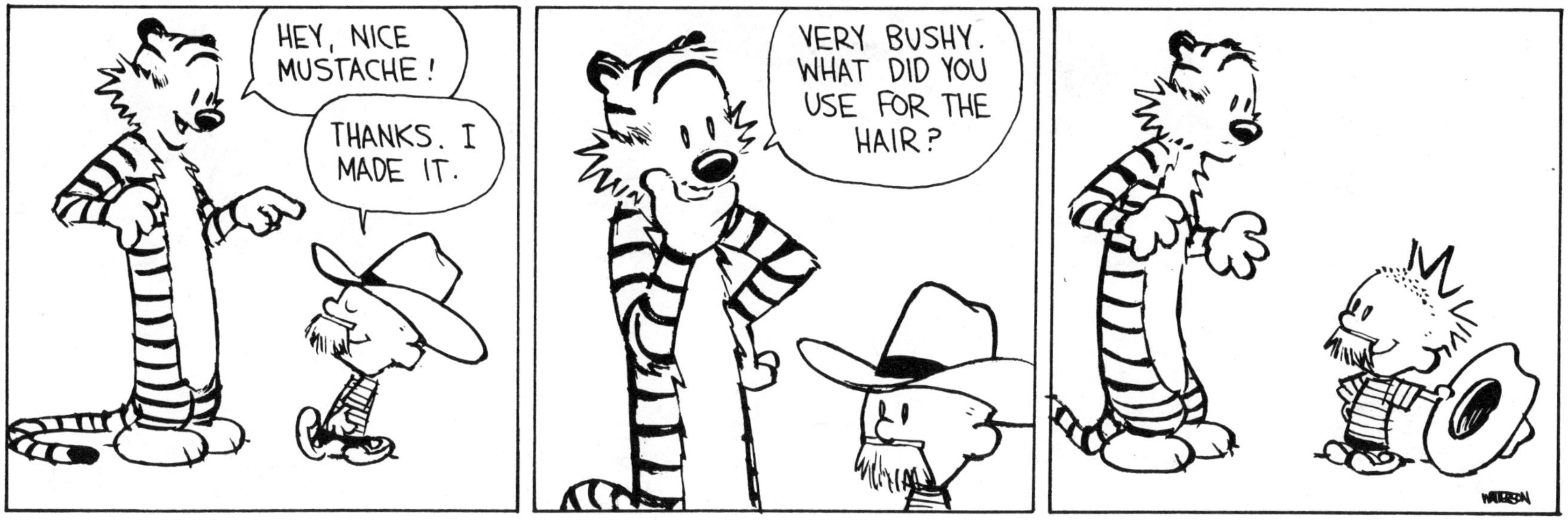
HEY, NICE MUSTACHE!
THANKS. I MADE IT.
VERY BUSHY. WHAT DID YOU USE FOR THE HAIR?

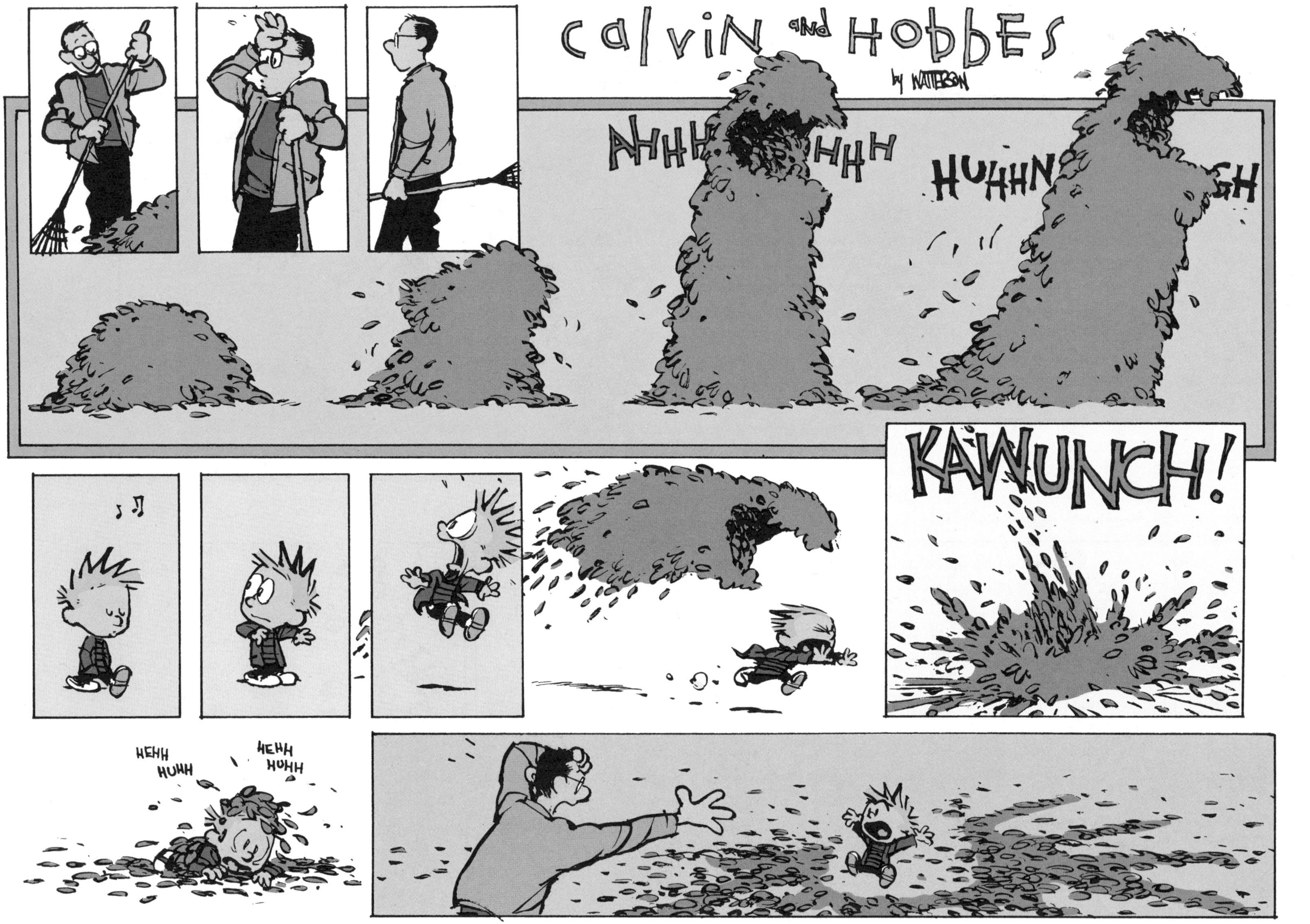
Calvin and Hobbes
by WATTERSON
AHHHHHHH
HUHHNGH
KAWUNCH!
HEHH HUHH
HEHH HUHH

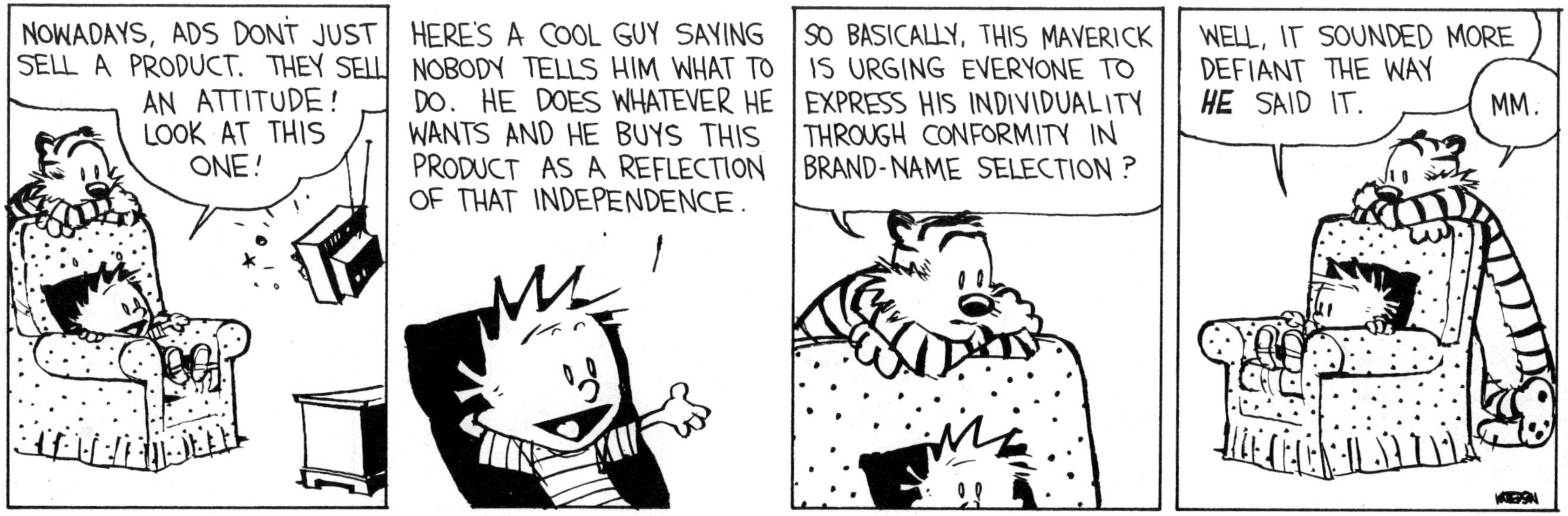
NOWADAYS, ADS DON'T JUST SELL A PRODUCT. THEY SELL AN ATTITUDE! LOOK AT THIS ONE!
HERE'S A COOL GUY SAYING NOBODY TELLS HIM WHAT TO DO. HE DOES WHATEVER HE WANTS AND HE BUYS THIS PRODUCT AS A REFLECTION OF THAT INDEPENDENCE.
SO BASICALLY, THIS MAVERICK IS URGING EVERYONE TO EXPRESS HIS INDIVIDUALITY THROUGH CONFORMITY IN BRAND-NAME SELECTION?
WELL, IT SOUNDED MORE DEFIANT THE WAY **HE** SAID IT.
MM.

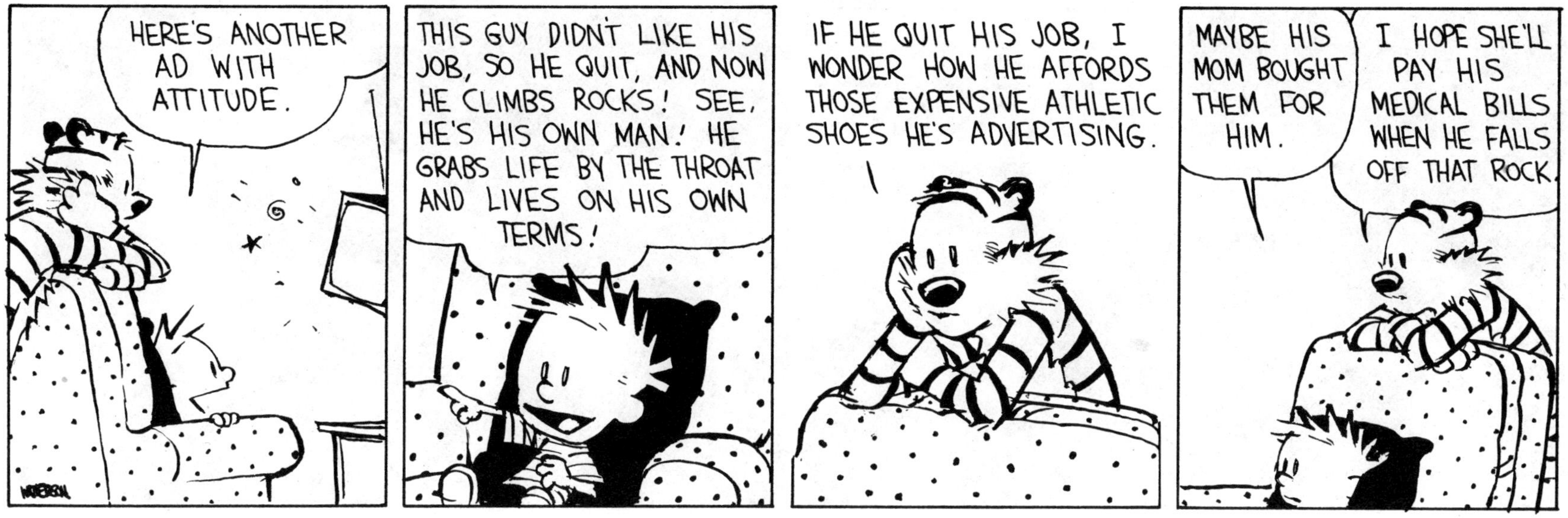
HERE'S ANOTHER AD WITH ATTITUDE.
THIS GUY DIDN'T LIKE HIS JOB, SO HE QUIT, AND NOW HE CLIMBS ROCKS! SEE, HE'S HIS OWN MAN! HE GRABS LIFE BY THE THROAT AND LIVES ON HIS OWN TERMS!
IF HE QUIT HIS JOB, I WONDER HOW HE AFFORDS THOSE EXPENSIVE ATHLETIC SHOES HE'S ADVERTISING.
MAYBE HIS MOM BOUGHT THEM FOR HIM.
I HOPE SHE'LL PAY HIS MEDICAL BILLS WHEN HE FALLS OFF THAT ROCK.

OW!!
MMF! NGGHH! RRRRGGG!
FWUPP
WATTERSON

I'M SIGNIFICANT!
SCREAMED THE DUST SPECK.
WATTERSON

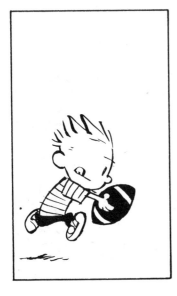

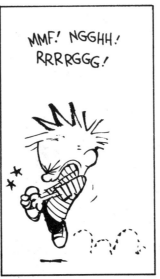

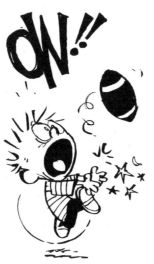

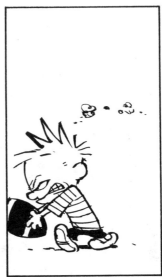

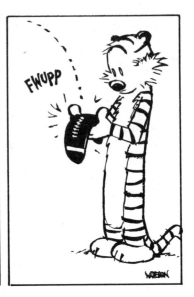

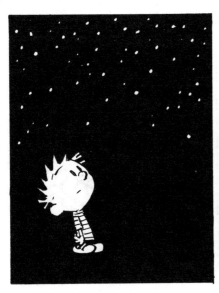

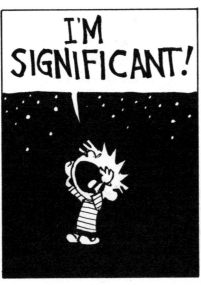

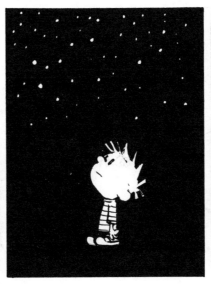

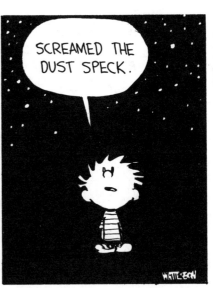

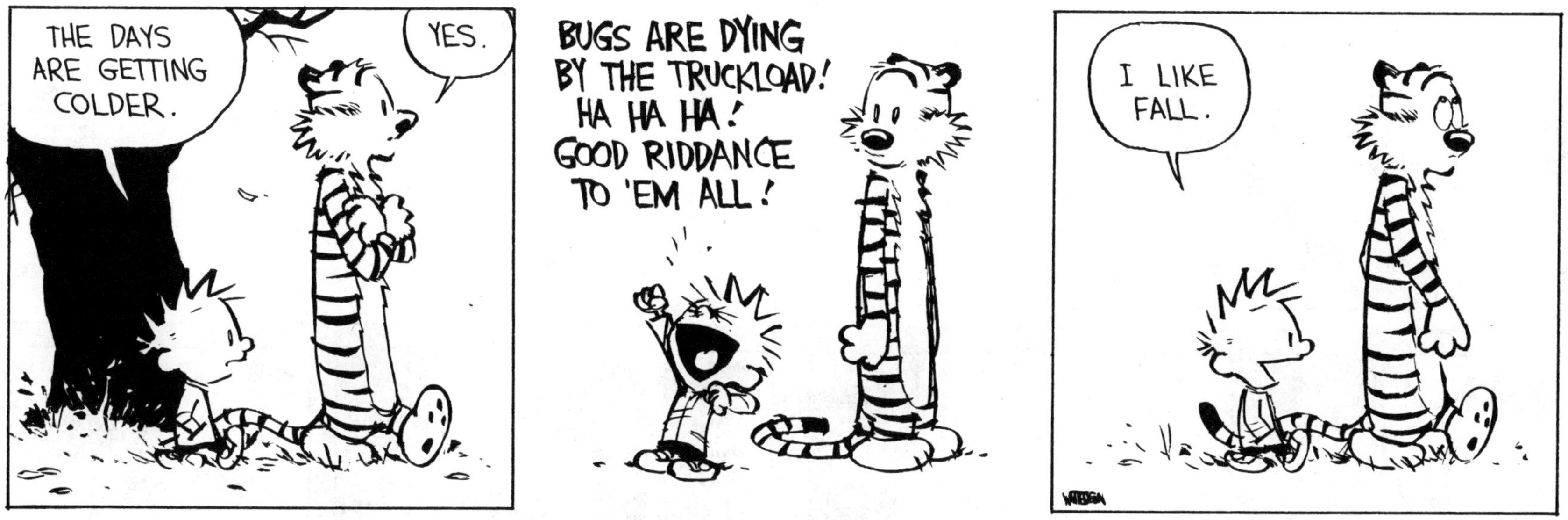
THE DAYS ARE GETTING COLDER.
YES.
BUGS ARE DYING BY THE TRUCKLOAD! HA HA HA! GOOD RIDDANCE TO 'EM ALL!
I LIKE FALL.

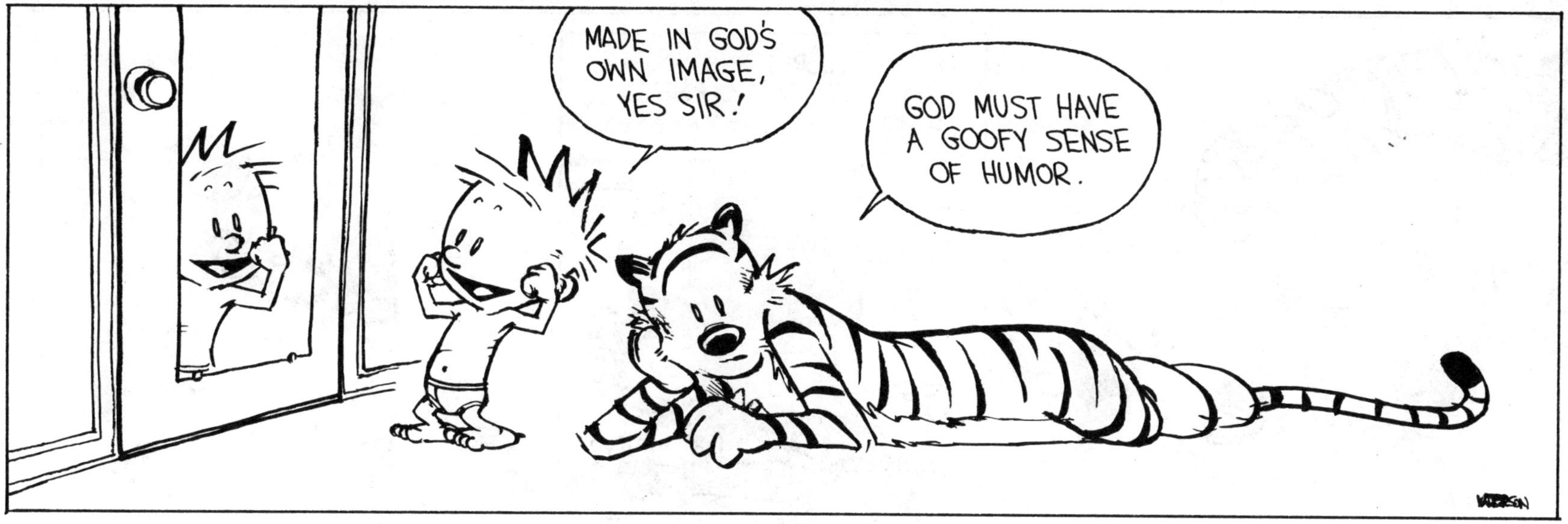
MADE IN GOD'S OWN IMAGE, YES SIR!
GOD MUST HAVE A GOOFY SENSE OF HUMOR.

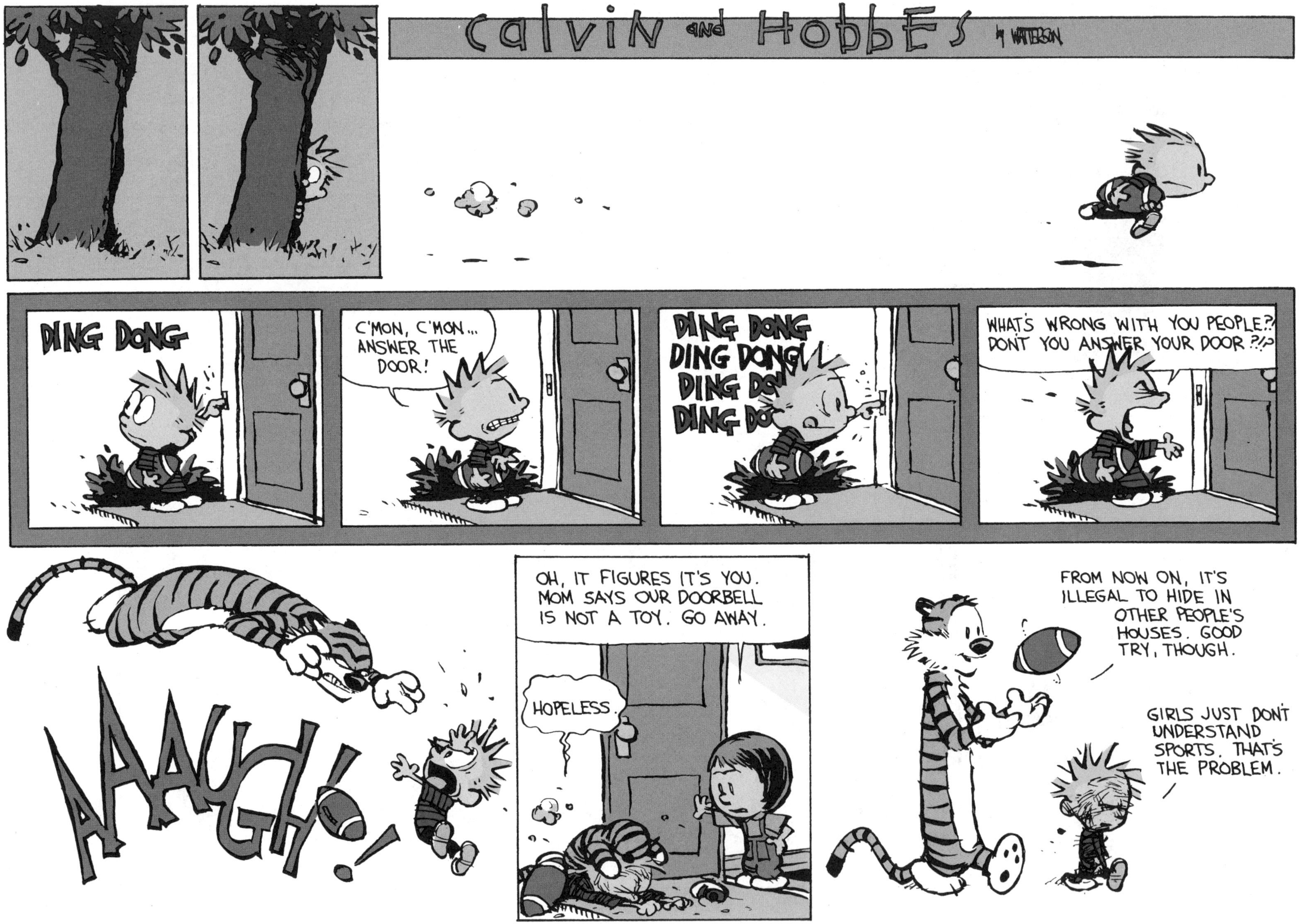
Calvin and Hobbes
by WATTERSON
DING DONG
C'MON, C'MON... ANSWER THE DOOR!
DING DONG
DING DONG
WHAT'S WRONG WITH YOU PEOPLE?! DON'T YOU ANSWER YOUR DOOR?!?
AAAUGH!!
OH, IT FIGURES IT'S YOU. MOM SAYS OUR DOORBELL IS NOT A TOY. GO AWAY.
HOPELESS.
FROM NOW ON, IT'S ILLEGAL TO HIDE IN OTHER PEOPLE'S HOUSES. GOOD TRY, THOUGH.
GIRLS JUST DON'T UNDERSTAND SPORTS. THAT'S THE PROBLEM.

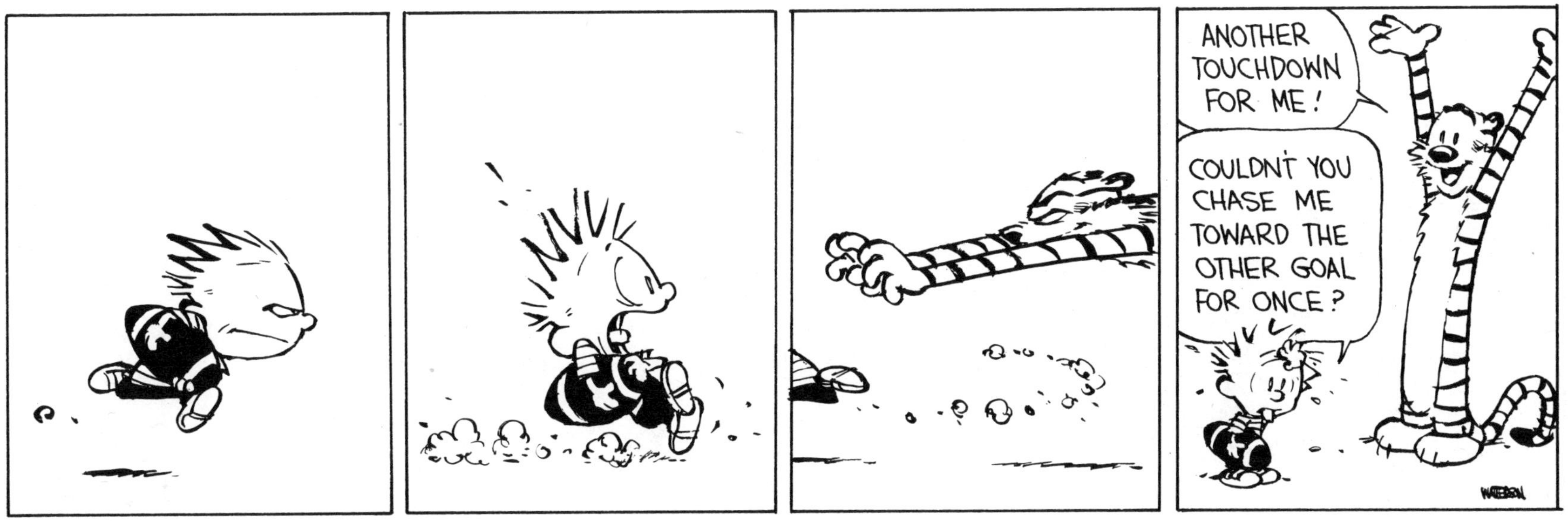
ANOTHER TOUCHDOWN FOR ME!
COULDN'T YOU CHASE ME TOWARD THE OTHER GOAL FOR ONCE?

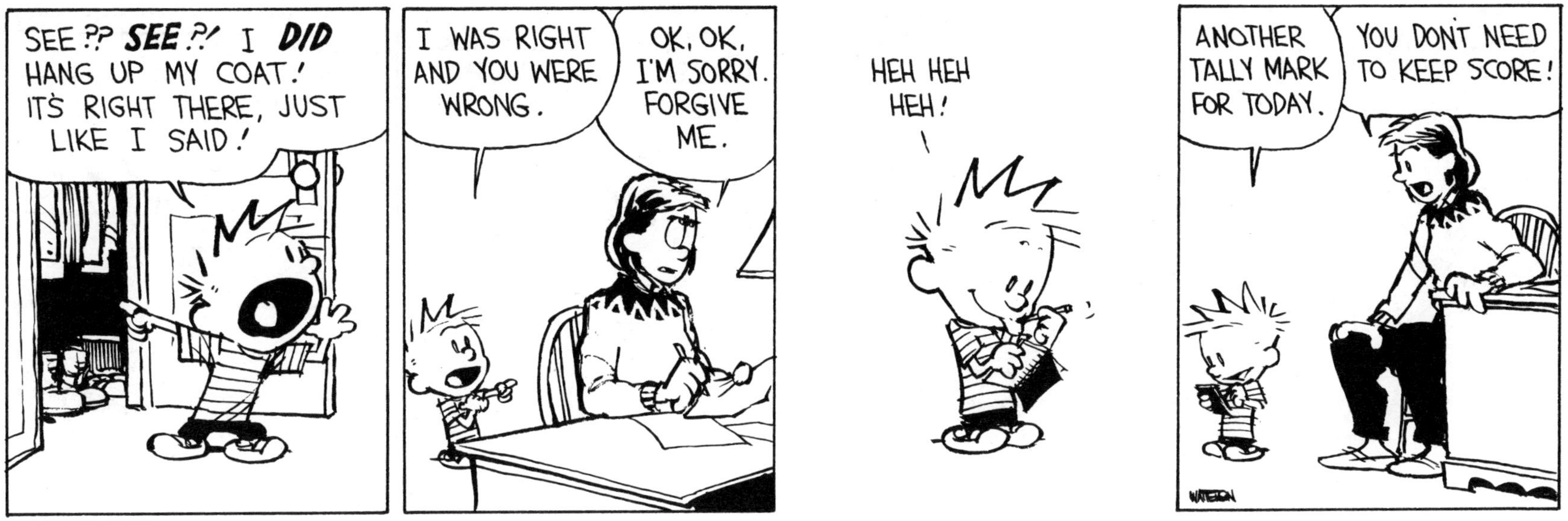
SEE?? SEE?! I DID HANG UP MY COAT! IT'S RIGHT THERE, JUST LIKE I SAID!
I WAS RIGHT AND YOU WERE WRONG.
OK, OK, I'M SORRY. FORGIVE ME.
HEH HEH HEH!
ANOTHER TALLY MARK FOR TODAY.
YOU DON'T NEED TO KEEP SCORE!

EVERYBODY SEEKS HAPPINESS! NOT **ME**, THOUGH! THAT'S THE DIFFERENCE BETWEEN ME AND THE REST OF THE WORLD!

HAPPINESS ISN'T GOOD ENOUGH FOR ME! I DEMAND EUPHORIA!

THE PROBLEM WITH YOU, HOBBES, IS YOU'RE ALWAYS AT A LOSS FOR WORDS.

I'VE FOUND THAT SAVES MANY A FRIENDSHIP.

HERE I AM, HAPPY AND CONTENT.

...BUT NOT EUPHORIC.

SO NOW I'M NO LONGER CONTENT. I'M UNHAPPY. MY DAY IS RUINED.

I NEED TO STOP THINKING WHILE I'M AHEAD.

IS HAMBURGER MEAT MADE OUT OF PEOPLE FROM HAMBURG?
OF COURSE NOT! IT'S GROUND BEEF.
I'M EATING A COW?
RIGHT.
I DON'T THINK I CAN FINISH THIS.

BONK
DID YOU SEE WHERE IT LANDED? LOOK FOR THE CRATER.
ARE WE A LITTLE SCARED OF THE BALL?

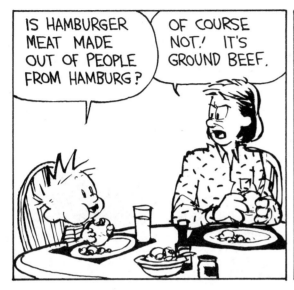

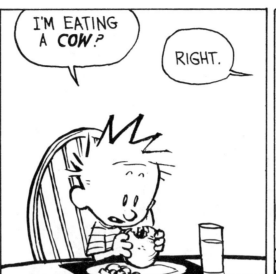

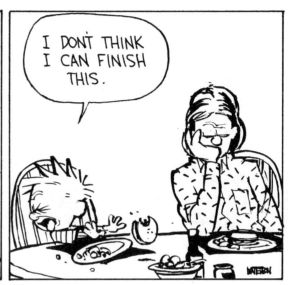

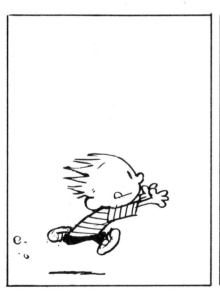

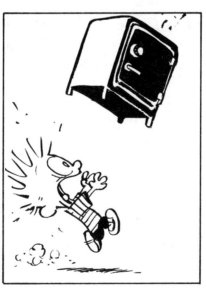

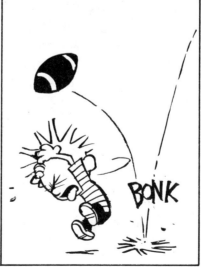

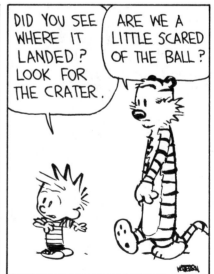

HOLD IT, MOE! BEFORE YOU WALLOP ME, I'M AFRAID YOU'LL HAVE TO SIGN THIS FORM.

What's this?

IT'S A STATEMENT ACKNOWLEDGING RESPONSIBILITY FOR YOUR BEHAVIOR.

YOU AGREE THAT HITTING ME ENTITLES ME TO UNLIMITED COMPENSATION FOR MEDICAL TREATMENT AS WELL AS REASONABLE DAMAGES FOR PAIN AND SUFFERING. YOU AFFIRM THAT YOU'RE INSURED FOR THESE COSTS AND...

NOBODY TAKES RESPONSIBILITY FOR HIS ACTIONS ANYMORE.

HERE, DAD. I'D LIKE YOU TO SIGN THIS FORM AND HAVE IT NOTARIZED.

"I, THE UNDERSIGNED DAD, ATTEST THAT I HAVE NEVER PARENTED BEFORE, AND INSOFAR AS I HAVE NO EXPERIENCE IN THE JOB,...

...I AM LIABLE FOR MY MISTAKES AND I AGREE TO PAY FOR ANY COUNSELING, IN PERPETUITY, CALVIN MAY REQUIRE AS A RESULT OF MY PARENTAL INEPTITUDE."

I DON'T SEE HOW YOU'RE ALLOWED TO HAVE A KID WITHOUT SIGNING ONE OF THOSE.

Panel 1: MISS WORMWOOD, I'D LIKE YOU TO SIGN THIS CONTRACT.

Panel 2: IT'S AN AGREEMENT THAT YOU'LL COMPENSATE ME FOR ANY LOSS OF JOB INCOME I MAY SUFFER AS AN ADULT BECAUSE OF A POOR FIRST-GRADE EDUCATION.

Panel 3: IF YOU GET A POOR FIRST-GRADE EDUCATION, IT WILL BE FROM *YOUR* LACK OF EFFORT, NOT MINE. GET BACK TO YOUR DESK.

Panel 4: BY GOLLY, *SOMEBODY* OUGHT TO PAY ME IF I DON'T LEARN ANYTHING.

Panel 5: HI SUSIE! WOULD YOU SIGN THIS LEGAL DOCUMENT?

WHAT IS IT?

Panel 6: IN ESSENCE, IT ANNULS OUR KNOWLEDGE OF EACH OTHER'S EXISTENCE AND IT PROHIBITS ANY FUTURE SOCIAL INTERACTION.

Panel 7: SPECIFICALLY, IT STATES THAT I'LL NEVER ASK YOU OUT ON A DATE, AND IT IMPOSES SEVERE PENALTIES ON ANY PARTY THAT ATTEMPTS TO ENGAGE THE OTHER IN CONVERSA...

Panel 8: IT'S ALMOST INSULTING HOW FAST SHE SIGNED THAT.

HERE, HOBBES. I'VE DRAWN UP A FRIENDSHIP CONTRACT FOR YOU TO SIGN.
A CONTRACT?
RIGHT. IT CODIFIES THE TERMS OF OUR FRIENDSHIP. YOU CAN RENEGOTIATE IN 20 YEARS.
PEOPLE ARE FRIENDS BECAUSE THEY WANT TO BE, NOT BECAUSE THEY HAVE TO BE!
THAT'S WHAT THIS FIXES.
IF YOUR FRIENDS ARE CONTRACTUAL, YOU DON'T HAVE ANY.

DAD, WHY DO MY EYES SHUT WHEN I SNEEZE?
IF YOUR LIDS WEREN'T CLOSED, THE FORCE OF THE EXPLOSION WOULD BLOW YOUR EYEBALLS OUT AND STRETCH THE OPTIC NERVE, SO YOUR EYES WOULD FLOP AROUND AND YOU'D HAVE TO POINT THEM WITH YOUR HANDS TO SEE ANYTHING.
GROSS.
HOW COME YOU KNOW SO MUCH?
IT'S ALL IN THE BOOK YOU GET WHEN YOU BECOME A FATHER.

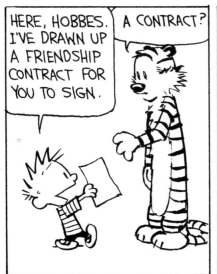

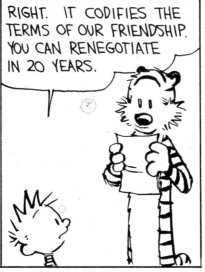

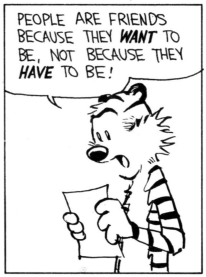

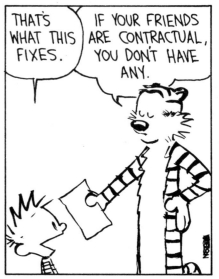

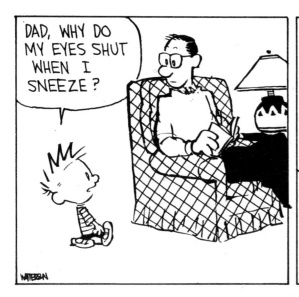

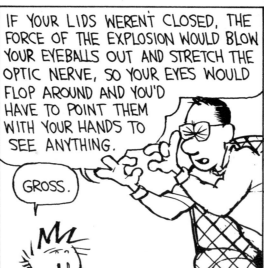

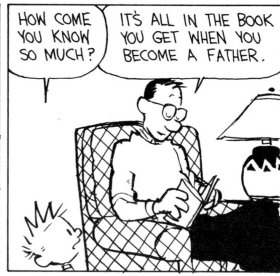

YOU SAY, WHEN YOU BECOME A FATHER, YOU GET A BOOK THAT EXPLAINS EVERYTHING IN THE WORLD?
RIGHT.
CAN I SEE IT?
NOPE, SORRY.
WHY NOT?
IT TELLS WHAT IT'S LIKE TO RAISE A KID.
SO?!
YOU'RE NOT ALLOWED TO KNOW THAT UNTIL IT'S TOO LATE NOT TO HAVE ONE.

AAAAAA!
A PERSON SHOULD BE SAFE FROM PREDATORS INSIDE HIS OWN HOUSE!
IF I HAD REFLEXES LIKE YOURS, I'D BE GLAD FOR THE OPPORTUNITY TO IMPROVE THEM.

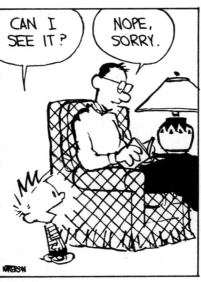

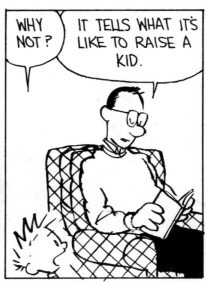

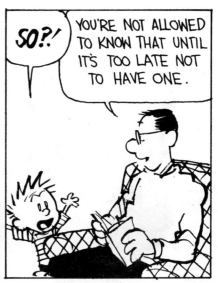

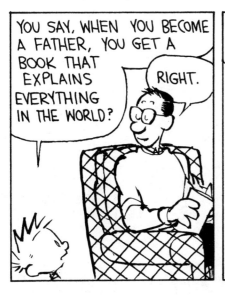

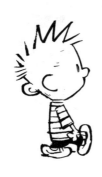

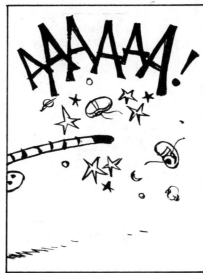

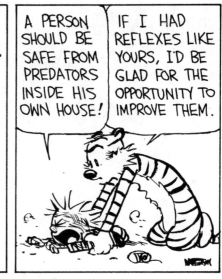

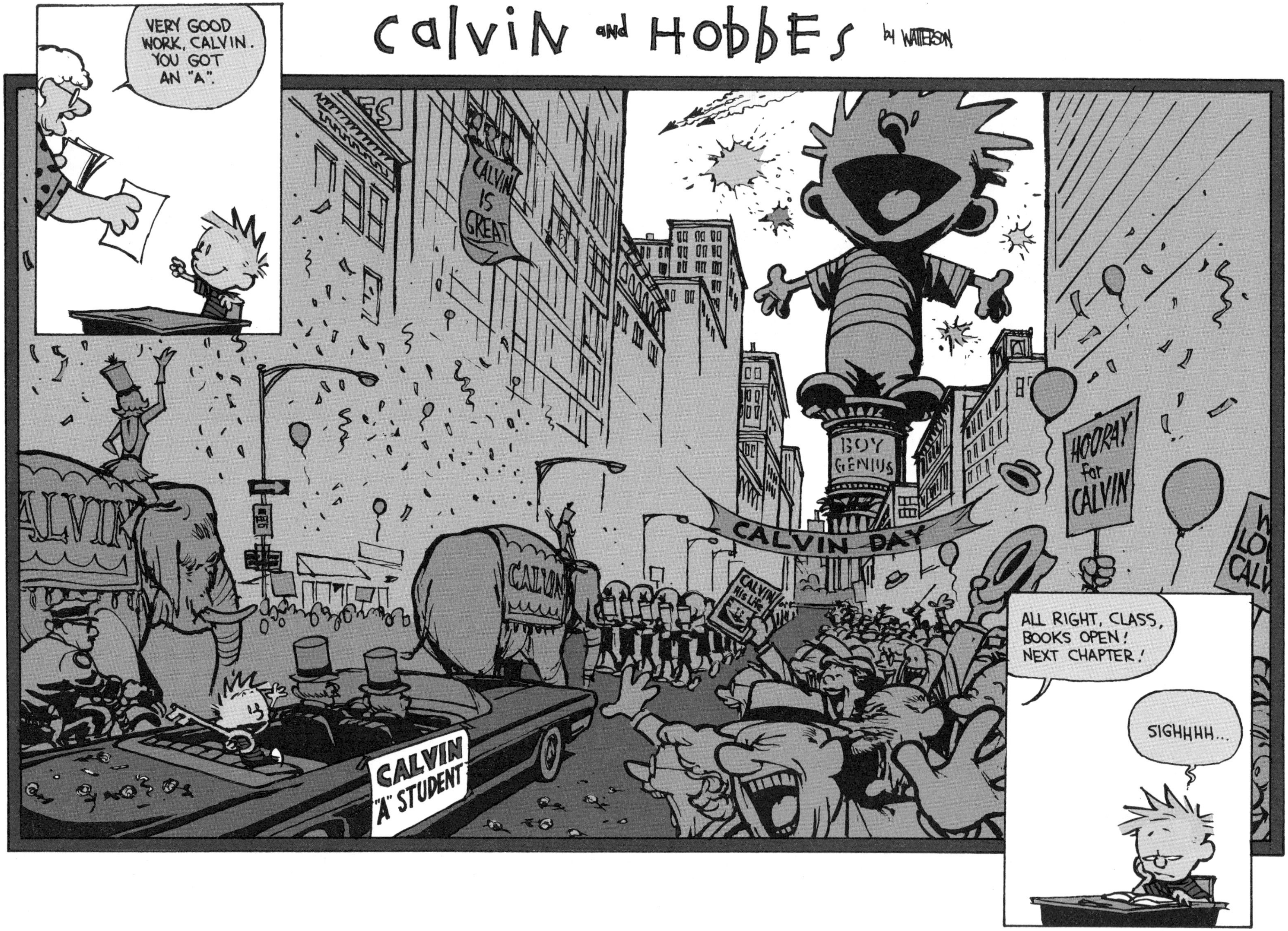
CALVIN and HOBBES by WATTERSON
VERY GOOD WORK, CALVIN. YOU GOT AN "A".
CALVIN IS GREAT
BOY GENIUS
CALVIN DAY
HOORAY for CALVIN
CALVIN His Life
CALVIN
CALVIN
CALVIN "A" STUDENT
ALL RIGHT, CLASS, BOOKS OPEN! NEXT CHAPTER!
SIGHHHH...

HEY, LOOK AT ME!

"NUDE DESCENDING A STAIRCASE"!

NOBODY UNDERSTANDS ART.

..SIGHH... THEY SAY NOBODY LIES ON HIS DEATHBED WISHING HE'D SPENT MORE TIME AT THE OFFICE.

WELL, I'D BETTER GET TO THE OFFICE.

THAT WAS OBVIOUSLY SOME SORT OF COMMENTARY.

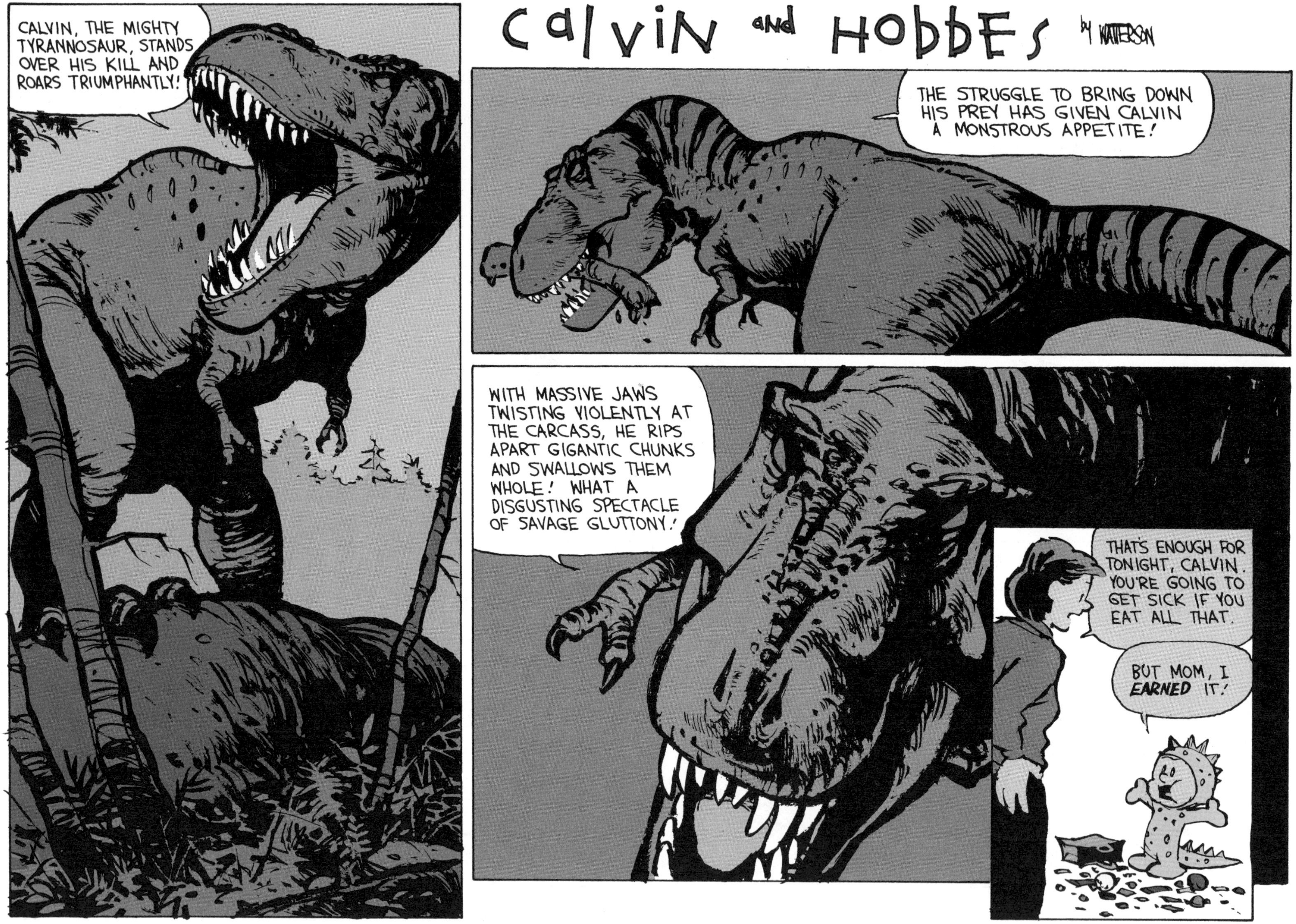
Calvin and Hobbes
by WATTERSON
CALVIN, THE MIGHTY TYRANNOSAUR, STANDS OVER HIS KILL AND ROARS TRIUMPHANTLY!
THE STRUGGLE TO BRING DOWN HIS PREY HAS GIVEN CALVIN A MONSTROUS APPETITE!
WITH MASSIVE JAWS TWISTING VIOLENTLY AT THE CARCASS, HE RIPS APART GIGANTIC CHUNKS AND SWALLOWS THEM WHOLE! WHAT A DISGUSTING SPECTACLE OF SAVAGE GLUTTONY!
THAT'S ENOUGH FOR TONIGHT, CALVIN. YOU'RE GOING TO GET SICK IF YOU EAT ALL THAT.
BUT MOM, I *EARNED* IT!

DOGGONE IT, HE'S GOT ALL THE COVERS AGAIN.
ZZ
ZZ... HMM? OH YES, I'M **VERY** FOND OF CALVIN. ...PASS THE GRAVY, PLEASE. ZZZ.
BRRR..
ZZ

WHY SHOULD I TAKE A BATH? I'M JUST GOING TO GET DIRTY AGAIN.
WHY SHOULD I BRUSH MY TEETH? I'M JUST GOING TO EAT AGAIN.
WHY SHOULD I COMB MY HAIR? IT'S JUST GOING TO GET MESSED UP AGAIN.
I'D RATHER BE EFFICIENT THAN HYGIENIC.

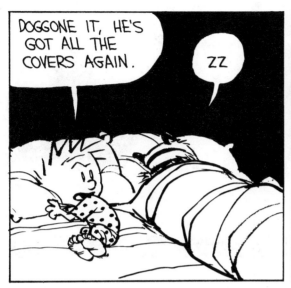

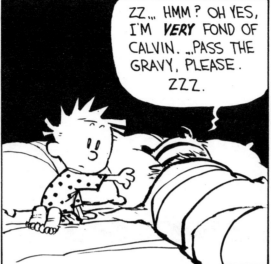

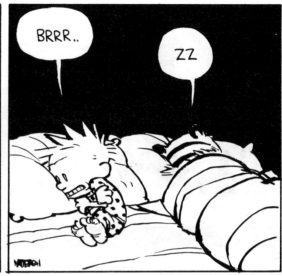

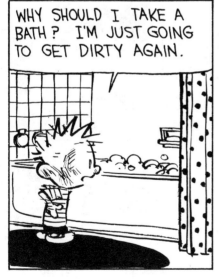

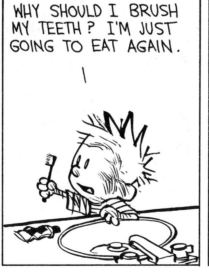

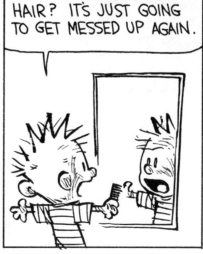

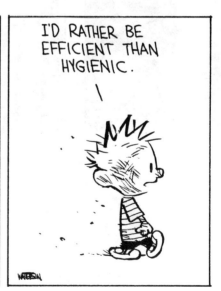

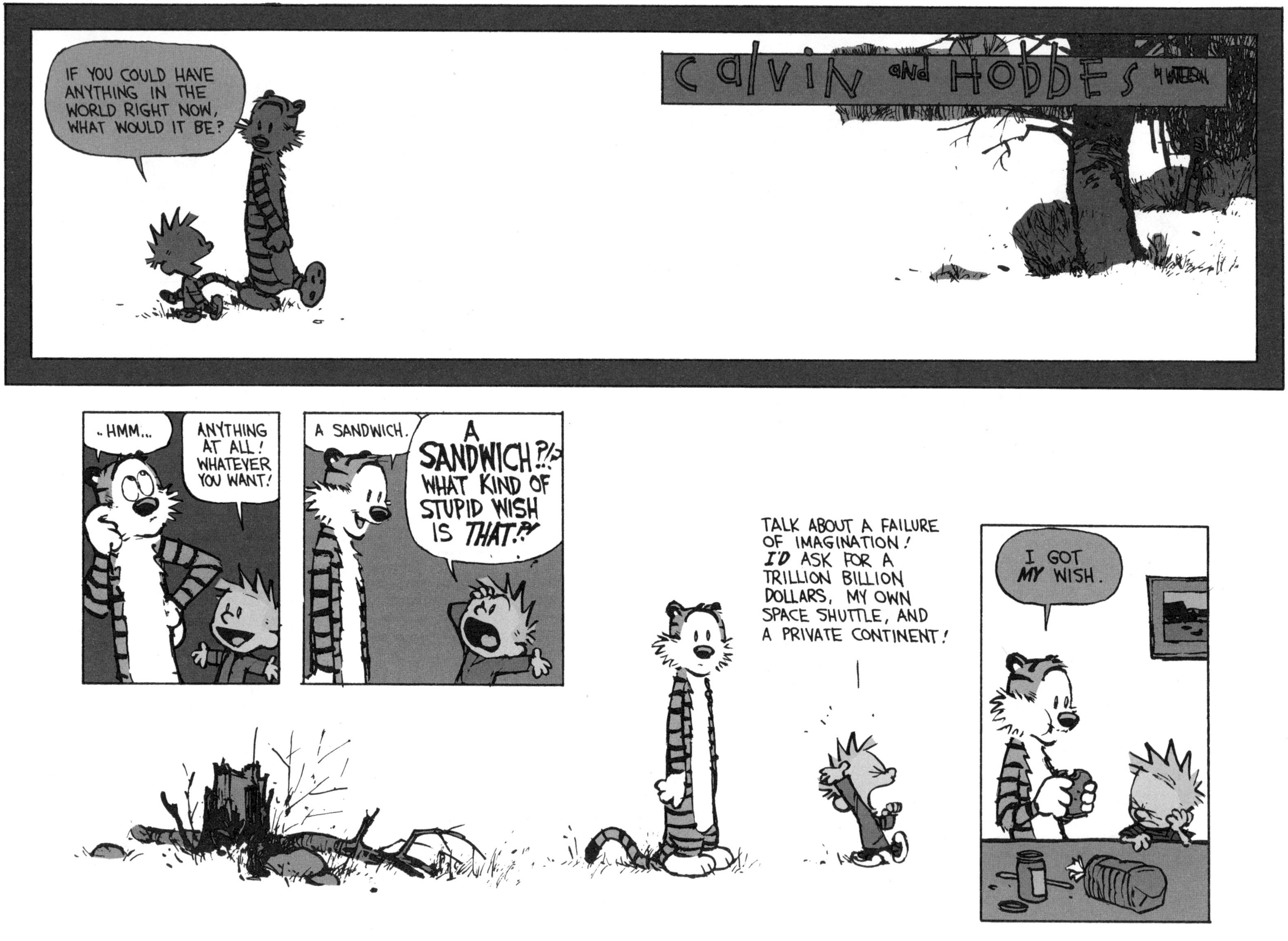
Calvin and HOBBES by WATTERSON
IF YOU COULD HAVE ANYTHING IN THE WORLD RIGHT NOW, WHAT WOULD IT BE?
.. HMM...
ANYTHING AT ALL! WHATEVER YOU WANT!
A SANDWICH.
A SANDWICH?!? WHAT KIND OF STUPID WISH IS THAT?!
TALK ABOUT A FAILURE OF IMAGINATION! I'D ASK FOR A TRILLION BILLION DOLLARS, MY OWN SPACE SHUTTLE, AND A PRIVATE CONTINENT!
I GOT MY WISH.

HI, IT'S ME, YOUR BIG ACCOMPLISHMENT IN LIFE!
I'M DEPRESSED.

DID YOU CHECK THE POCKETS OF MY PANTS BEFORE YOU WASHED THEM?
YES..
DID YOU FIND ANYTHING... UM... SURPRISING?
LIKE WHAT?
LET'S JUST SAY WE NEED SOME BIG GLOVES AND A HEAVY STICK... FAST..
DO YOU MEAN YOU DON'T KNOW WHERE THIS THING IS ?!

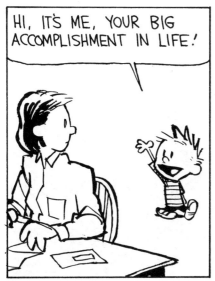

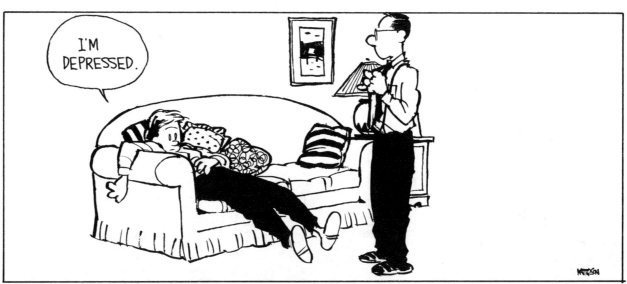

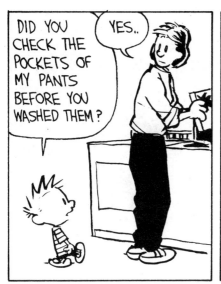

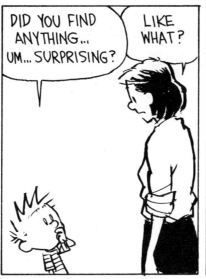

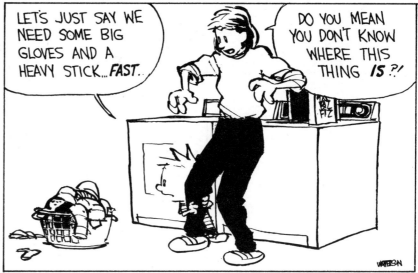

OH NO! MOM PACKED A PIECE OF PIE IN MY LUNCH! SHE HATES ME! I REFUSE TO EAT IT!
YOU DON'T LIKE PIE?
NOT THIS KIND.
WHAT KIND IS IT?
COW PIE.
MISS WORMWOOD!
WANT IT? IT'S FRESH.

I WISH I HAD A HEAVIER COAT.
THEATRICS NOTWITHSTANDING, THE THERMOSTAT STAYS WHERE IT IS.

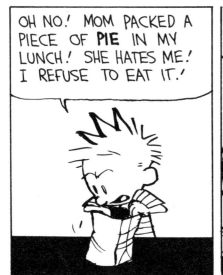

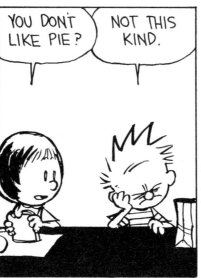

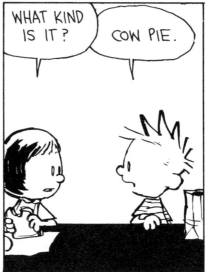

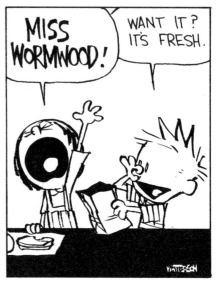

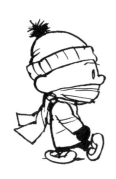

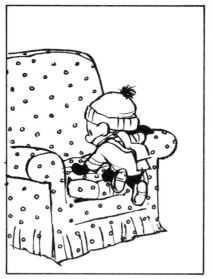

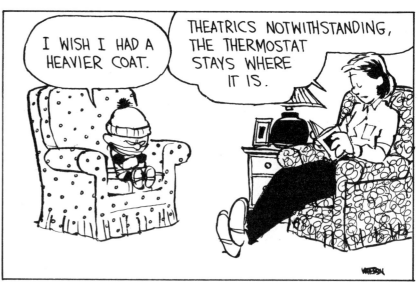

BBRRBBRBRBB
BEEP BEEP

BRRMMBB BRBBRB

GAAAAA!
OOMP

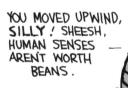
YOU MOVED UPWIND, SILLY! SHEESH, HUMAN SENSES AREN'T WORTH BEANS.

GET OFF ME, YOU PSYCHOTIC SAVAGE!

Calvin and Hobbes by WATTERSON

YOUR NATURE PROGRAM IS ON. DON'T YOU WANT TO WATCH IT?

NO!

..AND SO, IN 1654...

HKGHHKKGHH

MYSTERIOUS PLANET ZARTOK-3 APPEARS FROM...

KHGHHKGGH

PAY ATTENTION!

WHEN YOU CHANGE THE CHANNEL, I DON'T THINK THE ORIGINAL PROGRAM SHOULD BE ABLE TO CHANGE IT BACK.

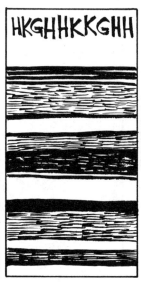

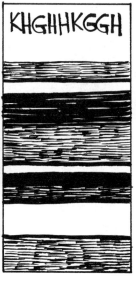

MOM, WHAT WAS I LIKE AS A BABY?

STINKY.

STINKY??

STINKY.

IT'S ALWAYS SHOCKING TO SEE ONE'S EXISTENCE REDUCED TO A BLURB.

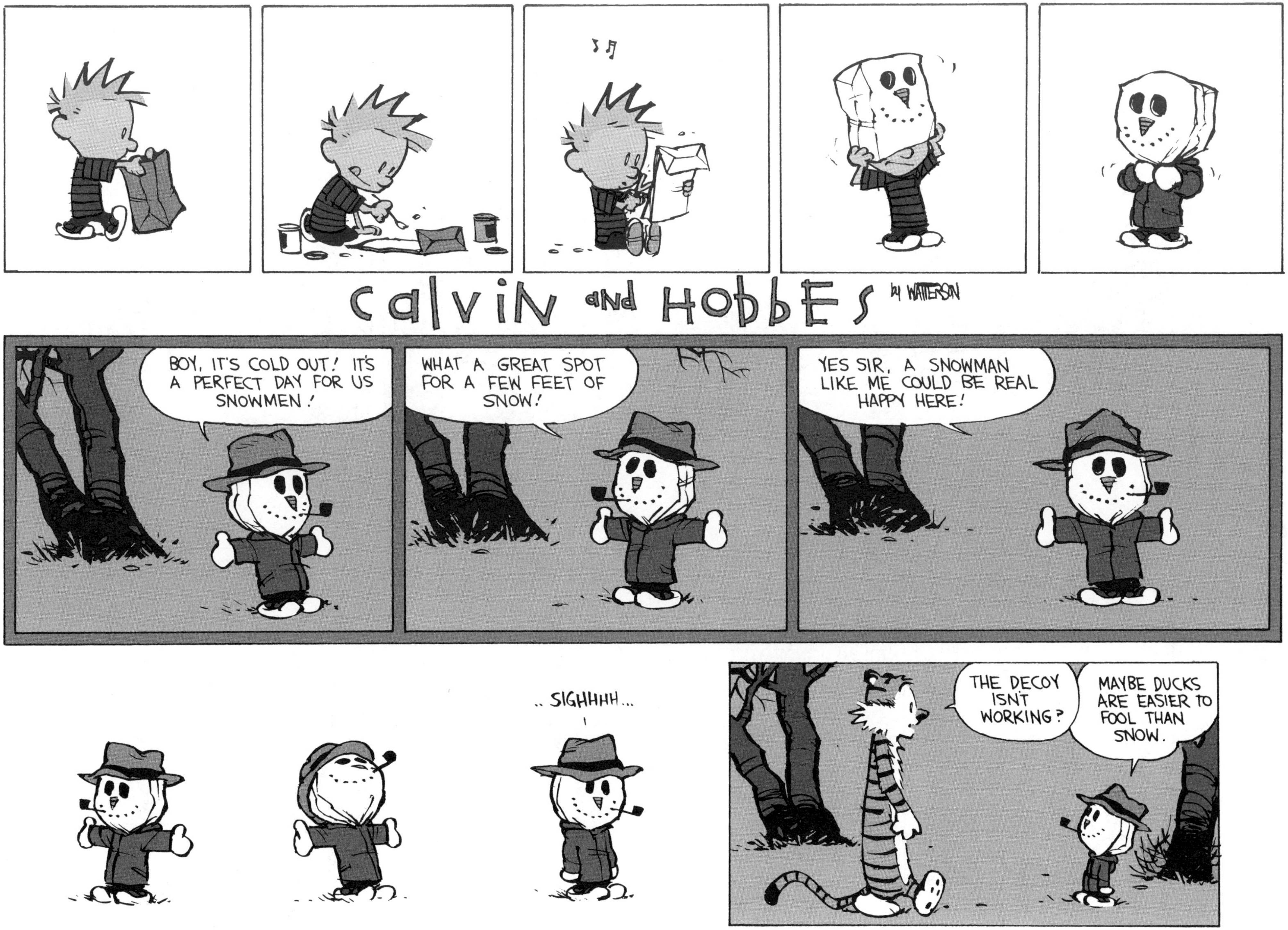

Calvin and Hobbes by WATTERSON
BOY, IT'S COLD OUT! IT'S A PERFECT DAY FOR US SNOWMEN!
WHAT A GREAT SPOT FOR A FEW FEET OF SNOW!
YES SIR, A SNOWMAN LIKE ME COULD BE REAL HAPPY HERE!
.. SIGHHHH...
THE DECOY ISN'T WORKING?
MAYBE DUCKS ARE EASIER TO FOOL THAN SNOW.

I NEED SOME HELP WITH MY HOMEWORK, HOBBES.
WHAT'S THE ASSIGNMENT?
I'M SUPPOSED TO WRITE A PAPER THAT PRESENTS BOTH SIDES OF AN ISSUE AND THEN DEFENDS ONE OF THE ARGUMENTS.
WHAT'S YOUR ISSUE?
THAT'S THE PROBLEM. I CAN'T THINK OF ANYTHING TO ARGUE.
THAT'S HARD TO BELIEVE.
I'M ALWAYS RIGHT AND EVERYBODY ELSE IS ALWAYS WRONG! WHAT'S TO ARGUE ABOUT?!

HELP ME THINK OF AN ISSUE TO DEBATE FOR THIS DUMB PAPER.
WELL, WHAT ISSUES DO YOU CARE ABOUT?
I DON'T CARE ABOUT ISSUES! I'VE GOT BETTER THINGS TO DO THAN ARGUE WITH EVERY WRONG-HEADED CRACKPOT WITH AN IGNORANT OPINION! I'M A BUSY MAN!
I SAY, EITHER AGREE WITH ME OR TAKE A HIKE! I'M RIGHT, PERIOD! END OF DISCUSSION!
UM.... RIGHT.
THERE, SEE? EVERYBODY'S HAPPY.

SO WHAT AM I GOING TO WRITE ABOUT?
HMM... WE'LL NEED TO PUT ON OUR THINKING CAPS.
HEY! THINKING CAPS! THAT'S WHAT WE NEED! C'MON!
THIS IS A GREAT IDEA! BOY, WHERE WOULD I BE WITHOUT YOU?
CONCEIVABLY, YOU MIGHT BE WORKING ON YOUR ASSIGNMENT.

WE'LL USE THIS COLANDER FOR THE THINKING CAP! ITS METAL SURFACE CAN CONDUCT ELECTRICAL BRAIN IMPULSES AND REFLECT BRAIN WAVES!
NEXT WE'LL NEED TO ATTACH THOSE INPUT AND OUTPUT STRINGS AND A GROUNDING STRING.
WHY A GROUNDING STRING?
IT'S LIKE A LIGHTNING ROD FOR BRAINSTORMS ...I WANT TO KEEP MY IDEAS GROUNDED IN REALITY.
I THINK YOU'RE TOO LATE.
WE'LL ALSO NEED TO BUILD A TRANSFORMER FOR THE ATOMIC CEREBRAL ENHANCE-O-TRON.

THE THINKING CAP IS ALL SET! LET'S TURN IT ON!
CEREBRAL ENHANCE-O-TRON
CLICK.
BRZAP.
DID IT WORK?
I THINK SO.
I FEEL SMARTER ALREADY.

WHAT HAPPENED TO YOUR HEAD?!?
EVIDENTLY, AN UNANTICIPATED PHYSIOLOGICAL CONSEQUENCE OF CEREBRAL AUGMENTATION. MY BRAIN SWELLED.
IF YOUR HATS DON'T FIT, WILL YOU GIVE THEM TO ME?
MY POWERFUL BRAIN IS UNRAVELING THE MYSTERIES OF THE UNIVERSE.
IT'S AMAZING! ALL NATURAL LAWS CAN BE REDUCED TO ONE SIMPLE, UNIFYING EQUATION!
REALLY? WHAT IS IT?
ALREADY MY POWERFUL BRAIN IS BORED WITH SUCH SIMPLE PROBLEMS AND IS NOW WORKING ON WHY GIRLS ARE SO OBNOXIOUS.

NOW THAT THE THINKING CAP HAS ENLARGED YOUR BRAIN, YOU CAN WRITE YOUR HOMEWORK PAPER.

I CONCUR.

CALVIN, DINNERTIME.

UH OH. WAIT UNTIL YOUR PARENTS SEE YOUR HEAD!

I AM APPLYING MY POWERFUL BRAIN TO THE DILEMMA.

I KNOW! WE'LL WRAP MY HEAD IN THIS BEDSHEET! *THAT* WILL ALLAY ANY SUSPICION!

YOUR POWERFUL BRAIN MUST KNOW SOMETHING I DON'T.

CALVIN, COME DOWN FOR DINNER! I'M NOT CALLING YOU AGAIN!

HURRY UP WITH THE TURBAN!

THERE.

SORRY I'M LATE. I WAS UNAVOIDABLY DETAINED.

CALVIN, WE DON'T EAT AT THE TABLE LOOKING LIKE THAT. TAKE OFF THE SHEET.

UH... HEH HEH.. ..UM..

THANK YOU.

I DON'T KNOW WHY I WORRY. THEY NEVER NOTICE ANYTHING.

I BROUGHT YOU SOME FISH FROM DINNER. OBVIOUSLY I DON'T NEED TO EAT BRAIN FOOD NOW.
OH BOY.
OK, LET'S GET DOWN TO BUSINESS. I'LL APPLY MY POWERFUL BRAIN TO THE PROBLEM OF MY HOMEWORK.
...HMMMMMM...
HOW'S IT GOING?
GOOD! I JUST REMEMBERED WHAT THE ASSIGNMENT WAS.
WATTERSON

MY POWERFUL BRAIN HAS COME UP WITH A TOPIC FOR MY PAPER.
GREAT.
I'LL WRITE ABOUT THE DEBATE OVER TYRANNOSAURS. WERE THEY FEARSOME PREDATORS OR DISGUSTING SCAVENGERS?
WHICH SIDE WILL YOU DEFEND?
OH, I BELIEVE THEY WERE FEARSOME PREDATORS, DEFINITELY.
HOW COME?
THEY'RE **SO** MUCH COOLER THAT WAY.
WATTERSON

LET'S SEE... TO ARGUE THAT TYRANNOSAURS WERE PREDATORS AND NOT SCAVENGERS, WE'LL NEED TO WRITE A BRIEF OVERVIEW OF CARNOSAUR EVOLUTION.

THEN WE'LL DELVE INTO SKELETAL STRUCTURE, SKULL DESIGN, ARM STRENGTH, POTENTIAL RUNNING SPEED, AND ENVIRONMENTAL FACTORS.

...BUT FIRST, WE'LL DRAW SOME PICTURES OF A T. REX EATING PEOPLE IN THE NATURAL HISTORY MUSEUM.

I NOTICE YOUR HEAD IS SHRINKING BACK TO NORMAL SIZE.

YOUR FOREHEAD IS BACK TO NORMAL.

THE BRAIN ENHANCEMENT MUST HAVE WORN OFF.

BUT YOU HAVEN'T WRITTEN YOUR PAPER YET.

OH, THAT'S THE EASY PART. THE *HARD* PART WAS GETTING A TOPIC AND MAKING THESE FUNNY DRAWINGS.

NOW ALL I HAVE TO DO IS WRITE EVERYTHING I KNOW ABOUT TYRANNOSAURS. IT'LL BE A BREEZE.

FOR ONCE I'M *GUARANTEED* A GOOD GRADE!

CALVIN, TIME FOR BED.

TIME FOR BED ??
THAT'S WHAT I SAID.
BUT I HAVEN'T FINISHED MY PAPER FOR SCHOOL YET! I NEED MORE TIME!
HOW MUCH MORE DO YOU HAVE TO DO?
I JUST HAVE TO WRITE IT.

YOU MEAN IT'S BEDTIME AND YOU HAVEN'T EVEN STARTED WRITING YOUR PAPER FOR SCHOOL ?! WHAT HAVE YOU BEEN DOING ALL EVENING ??
WELL FIRST, HOBBES AND I INVENTED AND CONSTRUCTED A THINKING CAP THAT AUGMENTED MY BRAIN SO I COULD THINK UP A GOOD TOPIC, AND THEN WE DREW ILLUSTRATIONS OF...
THAT DOESN'T SOUND LIKE A VERY GOOD TIME BUDGET TO ME.
I WASN'T EXPECTING TO GET AUDITED SO SOON.

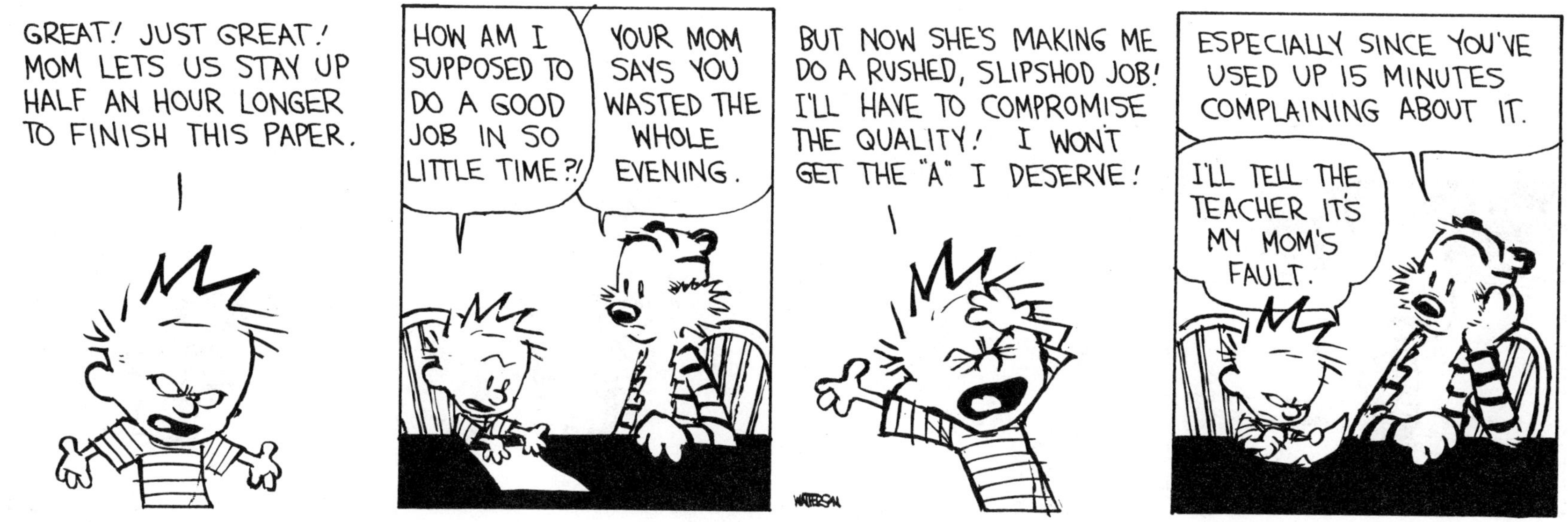
GREAT! JUST GREAT! MOM LETS US STAY UP HALF AN HOUR LONGER TO FINISH THIS PAPER.
HOW AM I SUPPOSED TO DO A GOOD JOB IN SO LITTLE TIME?!
YOUR MOM SAYS YOU WASTED THE WHOLE EVENING.
BUT NOW SHE'S MAKING ME DO A RUSHED, SLIPSHOD JOB! I'LL HAVE TO COMPROMISE THE QUALITY! I WON'T GET THE "A" I DESERVE!
ESPECIALLY SINCE YOU'VE USED UP 15 MINUTES COMPLAINING ABOUT IT.
I'LL TELL THE TEACHER IT'S MY MOM'S FAULT.

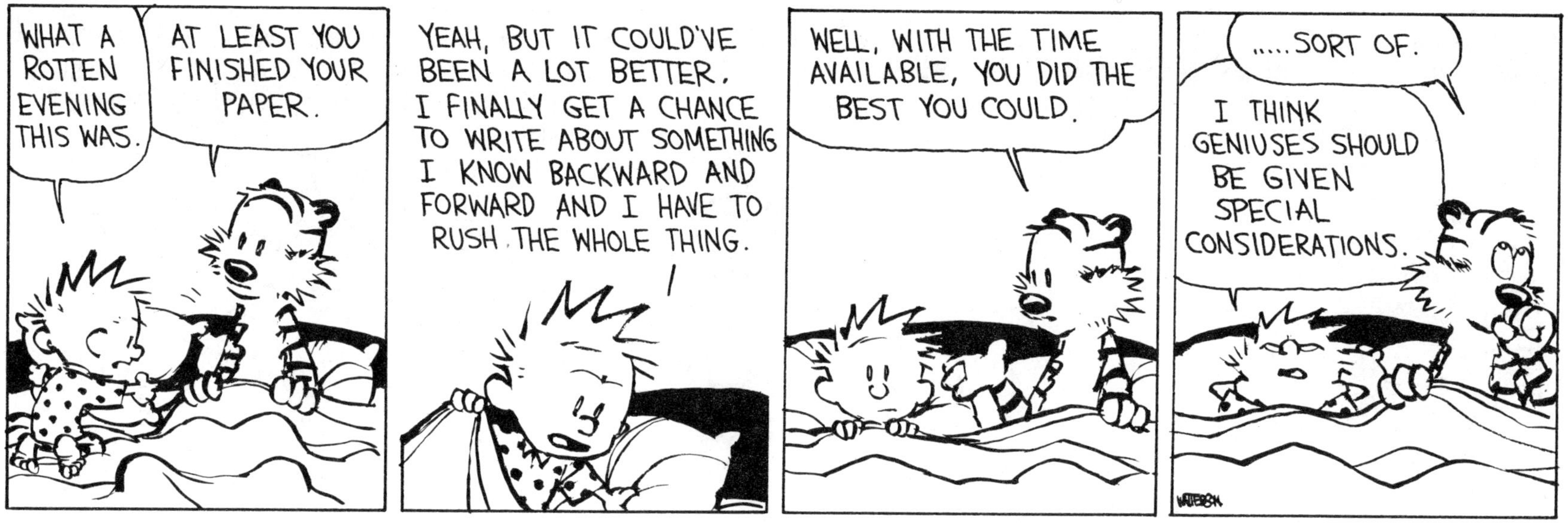
WHAT A ROTTEN EVENING THIS WAS.
AT LEAST YOU FINISHED YOUR PAPER.
YEAH, BUT IT COULD'VE BEEN A LOT BETTER. I FINALLY GET A CHANCE TO WRITE ABOUT SOMETHING I KNOW BACKWARD AND FORWARD AND I HAVE TO RUSH THE WHOLE THING.
WELL, WITH THE TIME AVAILABLE, YOU DID THE BEST YOU COULD.
I THINK GENIUSES SHOULD BE GIVEN SPECIAL CONSIDERATIONS.
.....SORT OF.

MY PAPER IS ENTITLED, "TYRANNOSAURUS REX: FEARSOME PREDATOR OR LOATHSOME SCAVENGER?"

AHEM..." I SAY TYRANNOSAURS WERE PREDATORS, BECAUSE IT WOULD BE SO BOGUS IF THEY JUST ATE THINGS THAT WERE ALREADY DEAD. THE END."

I'M A CONCISE WRITER, OK ?!?

MISS WORMWOOD WAS GOING TO GIVE ME A "D-" ON MY PAPER, BUT I TALKED TO HER AFTER CLASS AND TOLD HER HOW I RAN OUT OF TIME AND COULDN'T WRITE ALL I KNEW ABOUT TYRANNOSAURS.

SHE SAID I'D HAD PLENTY OF TIME TO DO THE ASSIGNMENT, BUT SHE ADMITTED THAT MAYBE I'D PICKED TOO COMPLEX A SUBJECT.

SO SHE RAISED MY GRADE TO A "D" AND TOLD ME I SHOULD TRY TO PICK REALISTIC GOALS AND PLAN MY TIME BETTER.

I GUESS WE LEARNED A LESSON, HUH?

I'LL SAY. SMOOTH-TALKING THE TEACHER REALLY PAYS OFF!

HELLO, CALVIN. I AM DOCTOR 5-40.
Y-YOU'RE A ROBOT ?!?
HA HA. AFFIRMATIVE. WE WOULDN'T TRUST A DELICATE OPERATION LIKE THIS TO CLUMSY HUMAN HANDS, NOW WOULD WE?
UM... I GUESS NOT...
HOW'S THE ANESTHETIC? FEEL ANYTHING?
...NO..
GOOD. THIS WILL JUST TAKE A MOMENT.
HOLD THIS JAR, WOULD YOU? TA DE TUM TUM... A LITTLE GRAY MATTER HERE, A DAB THERE... AH, THAT SHOULD DO IT.
BRAINS
WOW, THAT WAS EASY!
HOW DO YOU FEEL?
SMART!
THIS KNOWLEDGE IMPLANT SHOULD PROVIDE ALL THE WISDOM YOU'LL EVER NEED.
GREAT! NO MORE SCHOOL! THANKS, DOCTOR!
GO HOME AND HAVE 12 YEARS OF FUN.
Calvin and Hobbes
by WATTERSON
ELEMENTARY SCHO
5
SIGHHH

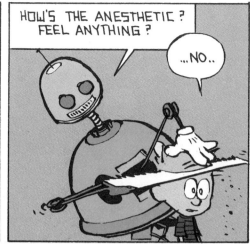

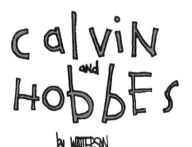

14... 52...
POW
WAAUGH
YOU'RE SUPPOSED TO WAIT UNTIL I HIKE THE BALL!!
OOPS. SORRY.
DARN TIGERS. YOU CAN EXPLAIN THE RULES TO 'EM, BUT YOU CAN'T SUPPRESS THEIR SURPRISE POUNCE INSTINCT.

YESTERDAY DAD WENT OUT TO BUY A HARDCOVER NOVEL.
HE SAID HE WANTED TO READ SOMETHING LONG, RICH, AND THOUGHT-PROVOKING FOR A CHANGE, AND HE WANTED A CLOTH BINDING SO HIS BOOK COULD BE CARRIED AROUND AND REREAD LATER.
THEN HE SAID HE WAS GOING TO BUY THE BOOK WITH CASH, SO NOBODY COULD TRACE THE PURCHASE TO HIM AND EXPLOIT HIS INTERESTS FOR COMMERCIAL PURPOSES.
YOUR DAD'S GOING INTO THE FUTURE KICKING AND SCREAMING, ISN'T HE?
WHAT IF HE'S TURNING INTO SOME KIND OF SUBVERSIVE?

MOM, CAN I GET A BIG TATTOO? I WANT A WINGED SERPENT COILING AROUND ONE ARM, CLUTCHING A SHIP ON MY CHEST, WITH...

..UM... I MEAN... ... WELL...

..SIGHHHH..

DID YOU KNOW MOM CAN COMMUNICATE TELEPATHICALLY?

I'm gonna pound you at recess, Twinky.

YOU'D BETTER BE NICE TO ME, MOE.

Haw! Why?

BECAUSE SOMEDAY MY TAX DOLLARS WILL BE PAYING FOR YOUR PRISON CELL.

POW!!

MY WHOLE PROBLEM IS MY LIPS MOVE WHEN I THINK.

YOU KNOW, EVERYTHING I AM ... MY UNIQUE SPIRIT AND PERSONALITY ... EVERY-THING THAT MAKES ME **ME** ...
... IS DEPENDENT ON THE PROPER FUNCTIONING OF THIS COMPLEX, FRAGILE AND MIRACULOUS CHUNK OF MEAT THAT IS MY BODY.
INTERESTING OBSERVATION.
WELL, IT JUST OCCURRED TO ME.
WAHOOOOOOOO

THEY SAY THE WORLD IS A STAGE.
BUT OBVIOUSLY THE PLAY IS UNREHEARSED AND EVERYBODY IS AD-LIBBING HIS LINES.
MAYBE THAT'S WHY IT'S HARD TO TELL IF WE'RE IN A TRAGEDY OR A FARCE.
WE NEED MORE SPECIAL EFFECTS AND DANCE NUMBERS.

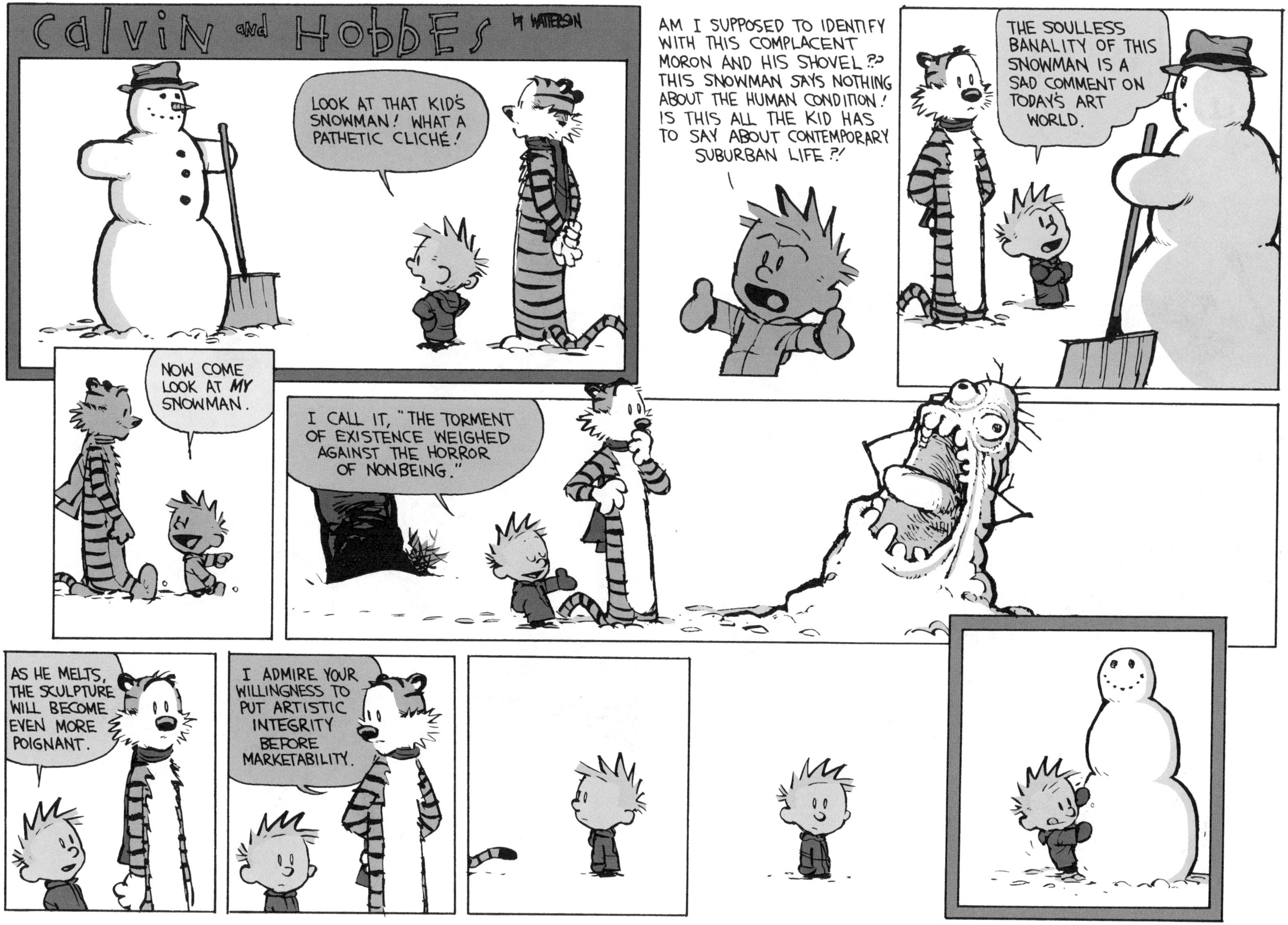
Calvin and Hobbes
by WATTERSON
LOOK AT THAT KID'S SNOWMAN! WHAT A PATHETIC CLICHÉ!
AM I SUPPOSED TO IDENTIFY WITH THIS COMPLACENT MORON AND HIS SHOVEL?? THIS SNOWMAN SAYS NOTHING ABOUT THE HUMAN CONDITION! IS THIS ALL THE KID HAS TO SAY ABOUT CONTEMPORARY SUBURBAN LIFE?!
THE SOULLESS BANALITY OF THIS SNOWMAN IS A SAD COMMENT ON TODAY'S ART WORLD.
NOW COME LOOK AT MY SNOWMAN.
I CALL IT, "THE TORMENT OF EXISTENCE WEIGHED AGAINST THE HORROR OF NONBEING."
AS HE MELTS, THE SCULPTURE WILL BECOME EVEN MORE POIGNANT.
I ADMIRE YOUR WILLINGNESS TO PUT ARTISTIC INTEGRITY BEFORE MARKETABILITY.

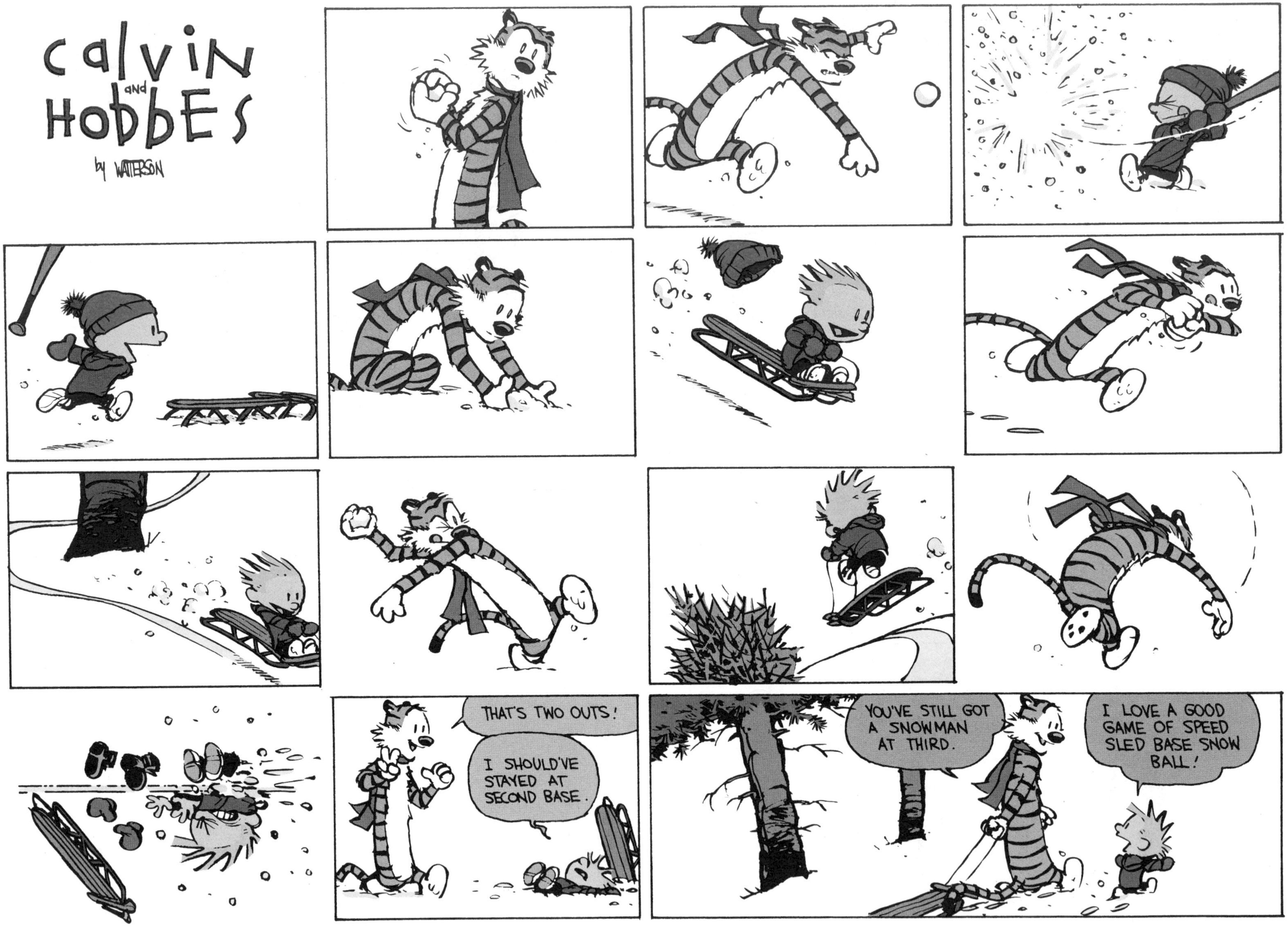
calvin and HOBBES
by WATTERSON
THAT'S TWO OUTS!
I SHOULD'VE STAYED AT SECOND BASE.
YOU'VE STILL GOT A SNOWMAN AT THIRD.
I LOVE A GOOD GAME OF SPEED SLED BASE SNOW BALL!

YEP, CHRISTMAS IS JUST AROUND THE CORNER.

AND WHAT BETTER WAY TO CELEBRATE A RELIGIOUS HOLIDAY THAN WITH A MONTH OF FRENZIED CONSUMERISM!

I'M SURPRISED OTHER RELIGIONS HAVEN'T PICKED UP ON THAT.

GETTING LOADS OF LOOT IS A VERY SPIRITUAL EXPERIENCE FOR ME.

DEAR Santa,
EVERY YEAR at THIS TIME I SEND YOU a LIST of WHat I WaNT FOR CHRISTMAS.

AND EVERY YEAR YOU CALLOUSLY IGNORE it aND BRING ME Practical THINGS I doN't WaNT at aLL. WHat's THE DEAL?!

ARE YOU INSANE?? HaVE YOU GONE SENILE?? CaN't YOU REaD?? OR aRE YOU JUST a ViNDictive, TWISTED ELF BENT ON DESTROYING LITTLE KiDS' DREaMS?!?!

YOU MIGHT WANT TO SLEEP ON THIS ONE.

I KNOW, BUT IT FELT GOOD TO WRITE IT.

Dear Santa,

Last year I did not receive the 15,000 items I requested for Christmas.

I can only conclude that your secretarial staff must be a bunch of underpaid and woefully unprepared temps, and my letter was misfiled.

To avoid a similar disaster this year, just write me a check for five million dollars, and I'll buy the stuff myself.

SEE, **THIS** YEAR I WON'T BE DISAPPOINTED.

I'D LEAVE OUT THE PART ABOUT THE TEMPS.

Dear Santa,

Hello, I am Calvin's new baby brother, Melville.

Enclosed is a list of what I want for Christmas. Please don't confuse MY list with Calvin's. There are TWO kids at this house now.

MAN, IF SANTA FALLS FOR THIS, I'LL ADD A NEW BROTHER EVERY YEAR!

"MELVILLE"?

66

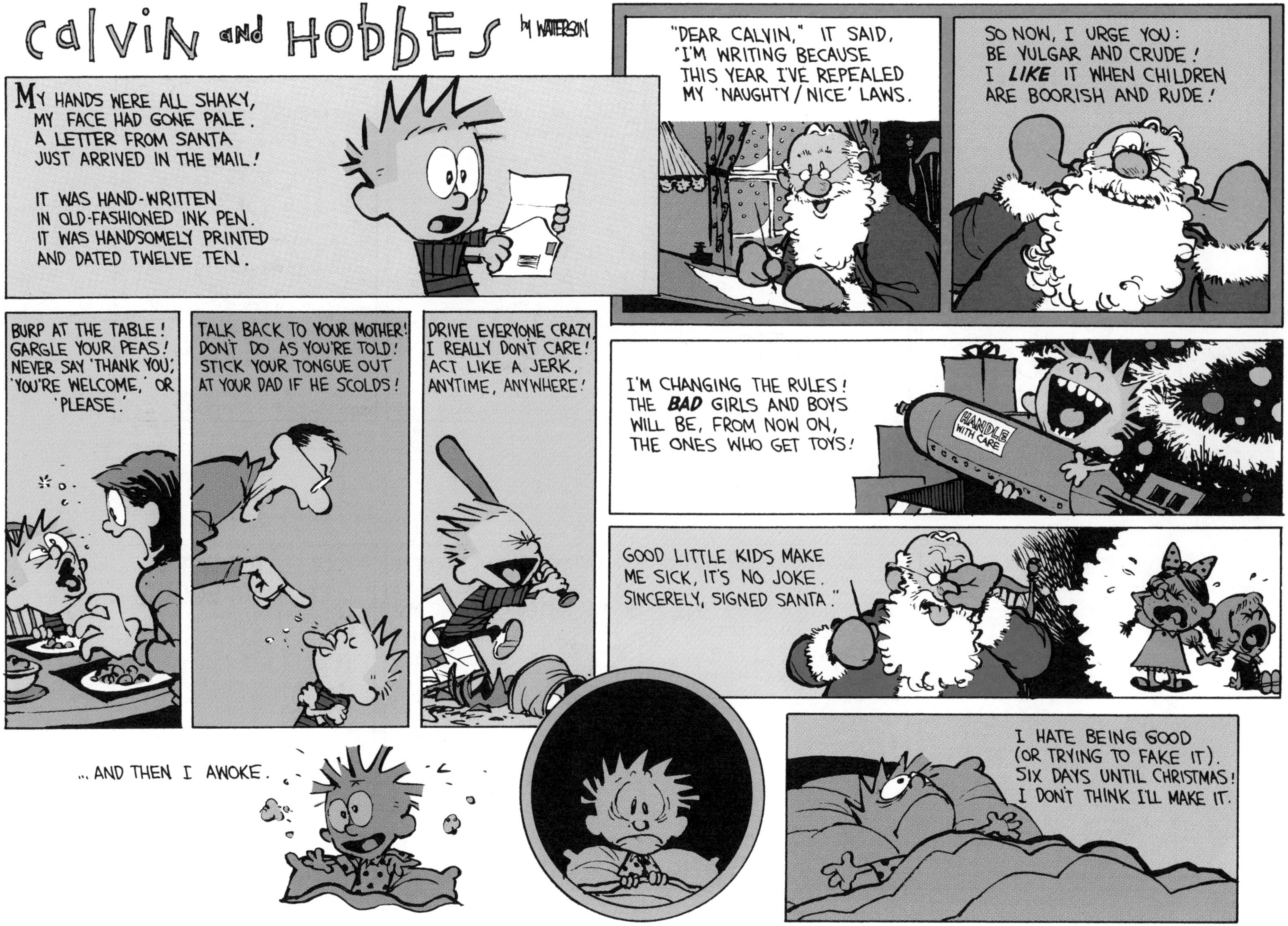
Calvin and HOBBES by WATTERSON
MY HANDS WERE ALL SHAKY, MY FACE HAD GONE PALE. A LETTER FROM SANTA JUST ARRIVED IN THE MAIL!
IT WAS HAND-WRITTEN IN OLD-FASHIONED INK PEN. IT WAS HANDSOMELY PRINTED AND DATED TWELVE TEN.
"DEAR CALVIN," IT SAID, "I'M WRITING BECAUSE THIS YEAR I'VE REPEALED MY 'NAUGHTY / NICE' LAWS.
SO NOW, I URGE YOU: BE VULGAR AND CRUDE! I **LIKE** IT WHEN CHILDREN ARE BOORISH AND RUDE!
BURP AT THE TABLE! GARGLE YOUR PEAS! NEVER SAY 'THANK YOU,' 'YOU'RE WELCOME,' OR 'PLEASE.'
TALK BACK TO YOUR MOTHER! DON'T DO AS YOU'RE TOLD! STICK YOUR TONGUE OUT AT YOUR DAD IF HE SCOLDS!
DRIVE EVERYONE CRAZY, I REALLY DON'T CARE! ACT LIKE A JERK, ANYTIME, ANYWHERE!
I'M CHANGING THE RULES! THE **BAD** GIRLS AND BOYS WILL BE, FROM NOW ON, THE ONES WHO GET TOYS!
HANDLE WITH CARE
GOOD LITTLE KIDS MAKE ME SICK, IT'S NO JOKE. SINCERELY, SIGNED SANTA."
... AND THEN I AWOKE.
I HATE BEING GOOD (OR TRYING TO FAKE IT). SIX DAYS UNTIL CHRISTMAS! I DON'T THINK I'LL MAKE IT.

NO SNOW.
...WHICH MEANS I CAN'T PASTE ANYONE WITH A SNOWBALL... WHICH MEANS I'M GOOD... WHICH MEANS I'LL GET LOTS OF CHRISTMAS PRESENTS! HA!
NOTHING IN LIFE IS EVER EASY.
WATTERSON

LOOK AT ALL THIS SNOW!
I'M BEING TESTED.
WE GOT THIS SNOW SO I'D BE TEMPTED TO SMACK SUSIE WITH A SLUSHBALL AND FORFEIT ALL MY CHRISTMAS PRESENTS.
TO EVALUATE MY CHARACTER, MY IMMEDIATE PLEASURE IS BEING PITTED AGAINST MY FUTURE GREED!
POOR SUSIE.
IT'S NOT A FOREGONE CONCLUSION!
WATTERSON

THE DAY AFTER CHRISTMAS IS GOING TO BE EPIC.

THROWING THESE SNOWBALLS WOULD GIVE ME IMMEDIATE AND CERTAIN PLEASURE.

REFRAINING FROM THROWING THESE SNOWBALLS IN THE HOPE OF BEING REWARDED AT CHRISTMAS IS DELAYED AND *UN*CERTAIN PLEASURE.

AS USUAL, GOODNESS HARDLY PUTS UP A FIGHT.

WHAT IF THERE IS NO SANTA CLAUS?
YOU KNOW, A LOT OF THIS SANTA STUFF IS HARD TO BELIEVE. THE FLYING REINDEER, GOING AROUND THE WORLD IN ONE NIGHT, THE WHOLE CHIMNEY BIT...
WHAT IF IT'S ALL SOME CRUEL HOAX AND I'M BEING GOOD FOR *NOTHING*?
YOU'VE **ALWAYS** BEEN GOOD FOR NOTHING!
IF HE EXISTS, SANTA WILL FORGIVE THIS ONE.

I'M NOT BAD. I'M JUST... UM...
...EXUBERANT! THERE'S NOTHING WRONG WITH BEING EXUBERANT!
HEADS UP!
POW!
GO ON, EXPLAIN THE SEMANTICS TO YOUR MOM.
YIKES, SHE GOT HER WIND BACK AND SHE'S GAINING!

PIFF
SANTA'S GONNA SKIP YOUR HOUSE FOR THAT, CALVIN!
I FIGURE THIS DOESN'T REALLY COUNT AGAINST ME, SINCE SHE'S SO SANCTIMONIOUS AND I KEEP MISSING.

HA HA! ACQUITTAL ON ALL CHARGES! COMPLETE EXONERATION! HA HA HA!
MERRY CHRISTMAS TO YOU TOO, DEAR.
PHEW, WHAT'S THAT SMELL? HAS SOMEONE BEEN EATING TUNA FISH AT THIS HORRIBLE HOUR?!

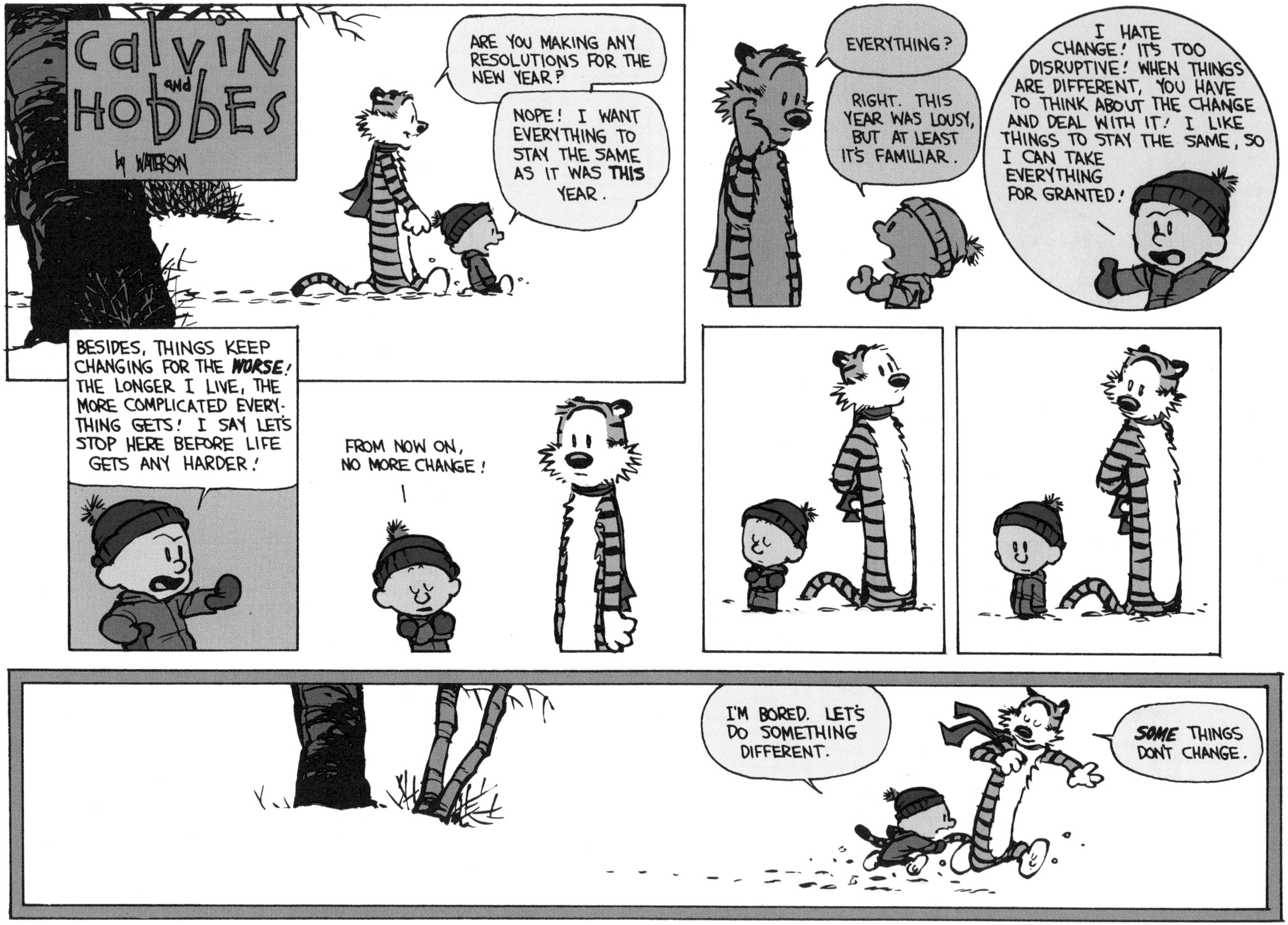
Calvin and Hobbes
by WATTERSON
ARE YOU MAKING ANY RESOLUTIONS FOR THE NEW YEAR?
NOPE! I WANT EVERYTHING TO STAY THE SAME AS IT WAS **THIS** YEAR.
EVERYTHING?
RIGHT. THIS YEAR WAS LOUSY, BUT AT LEAST IT'S FAMILIAR.
I HATE CHANGE! IT'S TOO DISRUPTIVE! WHEN THINGS ARE DIFFERENT, YOU HAVE TO THINK ABOUT THE CHANGE AND DEAL WITH IT! I LIKE THINGS TO STAY THE SAME, SO I CAN TAKE EVERYTHING FOR GRANTED!
BESIDES, THINGS KEEP CHANGING FOR THE ***WORSE***! THE LONGER I LIVE, THE MORE COMPLICATED EVERYTHING GETS! I SAY LET'S STOP HERE BEFORE LIFE GETS ANY HARDER!
FROM NOW ON, NO MORE CHANGE!
I'M BORED. LET'S DO SOMETHING DIFFERENT.
SOME THINGS DON'T CHANGE.

Y-YAWNN

THERE'S NO SEDATIVE LIKE SEEING A TIGER LYING IN THE SUN.

HEY DAD, WHY DON'T YOU CUT DOWN ALL THE TREES ON OUR HILL AND PUT IN A SKI LIFT?

BECAUSE A SKI LIFT WOULD BE UGLY, NOISY, AND COMPLETELY UNNECESSARY.

THE PROBLEM WITH DAD IS HE DOESN'T KNOW PROGRESS WHEN HE HEARS IT.

AAUGHH
I MEANT TO DO THAT.
THEN IT WORKED VERY WELL.

I'VE LOST MY MARBLES.
EVERYONE SUSPECTED AS MUCH.
WELL, I HOPE SOMEBODY FINDS THEM THEN.
HEY!!

I NEED A NEW TOBOGGAN.
WHAT FOR?
MINE IS OUTDATED. I'M SURE THE '94 MODELS HAVE ALL SORTS OF NEW FEATURES, COLORS AND OPTIONS.
TOBOGGANS DON'T COME IN MODEL YEARS.
THEY DON'T??
I TELL YOU, HOBBES, THERE'S A FORTUNE TO BE MADE!

WHAT THE...??
I'M NOT PLAYING WITH A FULL DECK!
THAT'S WHAT PEOPLE SAY.
REALLY? THEN WHY DIDN'T SOMEBODY GO BUY SOME NEW CARDS?!
HEY!!

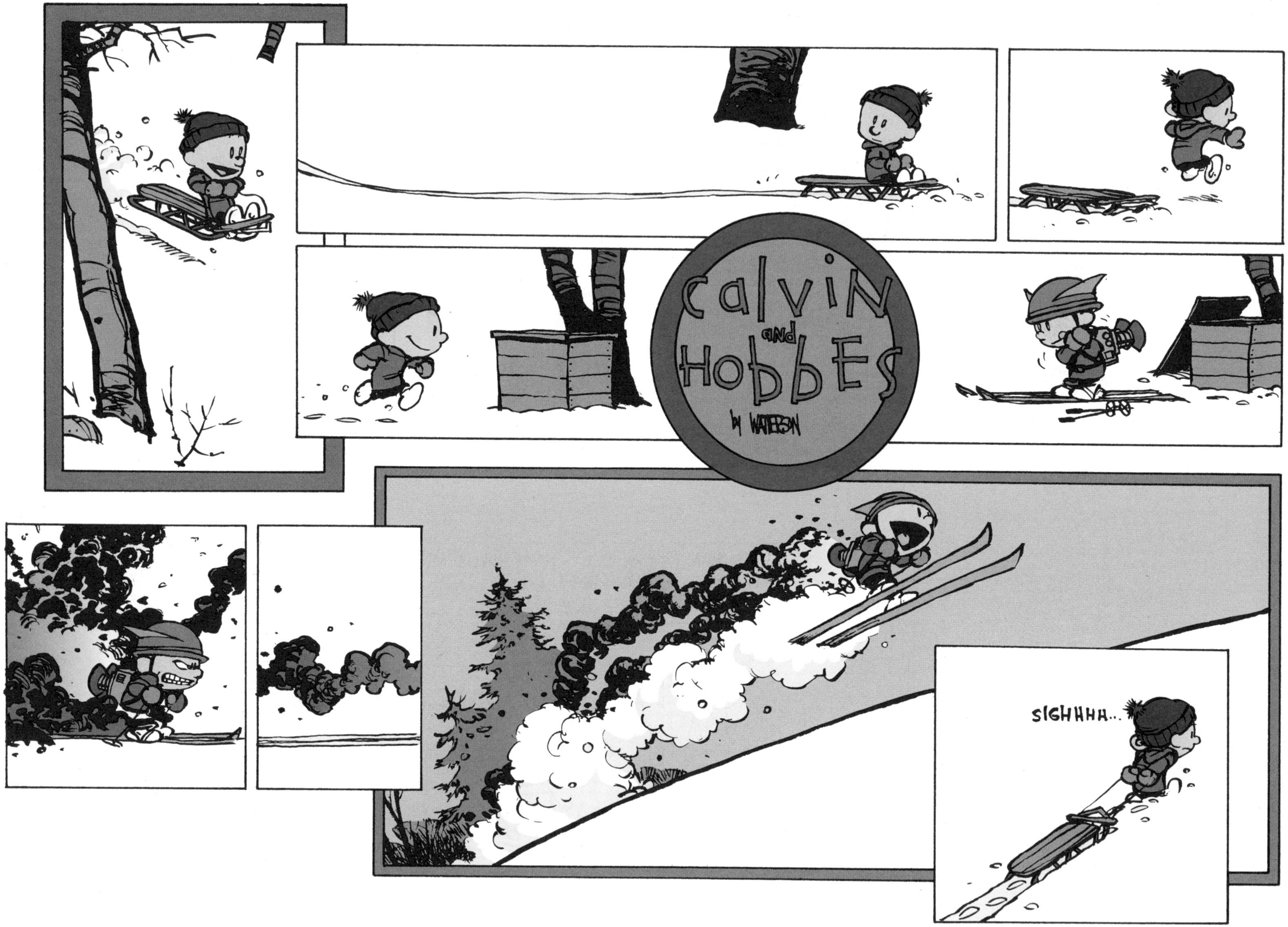
Calvin and Hobbes
by WATTERSON
SIGHHHH...

I RESENT THE QUALITY OF NETWORK PROGRAMMING! IT'S ALL FLUFF, VIOLENCE, SENSATIONALISM AND SLEAZE!
I HUNGER FOR SERIOUS, TASTEFUL ENTERTAINMENT THAT RESPECTS MY INTELLIGENCE!
SO TURN OFF THE STUPID TV AND READ A BOOK.
ALL RIGHT, I LIED. SUE ME.

WHY DOES HE HAVE A HOT WATER BOTTLE ON HIS HEAD?
HE'S COMMITTING SUICIDE.

I'LL TAKE ONE CARD.
OK.
I FOLD.
ARE YOU CHEATING?!

INCREDIBLY, PEOPLE NEVER EXPECT TO GET HIT WITH A SNOWBALL IN THE HOUSE.
I'LL SEE YOU IN YOUR ROOM MOMENTARILY.

IF ANYONE HITS ME WITH A SNOWBALL, I'LL HIT **HIM** WITH 250 SNOWBALLS!
WHAT IF SOMEBODY HITS **YOU** WITH 250 SNOWBALLS?
..SIGHHH..

THIS WILL BE MY STRONGEST FORT EVER!
WITH THESE MASSIVE WALLS, I'LL BE SAFE FROM ANY ATTACK!
HELLLP!!

WE GOT SOME NEW SNOW LAST NIGHT! LET'S LOOK FOR ANIMAL TRACKS!
HERE ARE SOME BIRD TRACKS. LOOK, YOU CAN SEE WING IMPRESSIONS WHERE THEY TOOK OFF!
AND THESE ARE RABBIT TRACKS. LOOKS LIKE THEY WERE GOING PRETTY FAST.
NO WONDER! LOOK AT *THESE* TRACKS! SOMETHING WAS CHASING THEM ALL OVER THE PLACE!
calvin and HOBBES by WATTERSON
HMM... BIG PADS... COULD BE A WOLF, BUT THERE ARE NO CLAW IMPRESSIONS. IT'S MORE LIKE A BOBCAT, OR A MOUNTAIN LION, OR...
..OR....
THIS EXPLAINS THE COLD WET FEET IN MY BED THIS MORNING.
THE SNOW WAS FALLING AND I THOUGHT, "THE BIRDS AND RABBITS AROUND HERE NEED SOME EXERCISE."

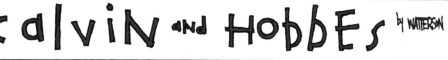

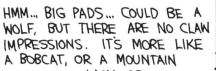

I DON'T THINK THE SCHOOLS ASSIGN ENOUGH HOMEWORK.

SOME KIDS AT SCHOOL GOT FILTHY RICH TODAY.
REALLY? HOW?
THEY GRABBED HIM BY THE DRINKING FOUNTAIN.

HERE, YOU'LL PROBABLY WANT THIS PILLOW.
WHAT FOR?
IT'S LIKE AN AIR BAG. HOLD IT IN FRONT OF YOUR HEAD LIKE THIS AS WE GO DOWN.
DON'T YOU FEEL SAFER NOW?
I CERTAINLY DO.
WATTERSON

YES!
POW
WASN'T THAT A GREAT SHOT?? WHAT CONTROL! WHAT FORM! DID YOU NOTICE THE TOP SPIN? DID YOU NOTICE HOW I PACKED THE SNOW SO THAT...
A **REAL** FRIEND WOULD'VE BEEN HAPPY FOR ME!
WATTERSON

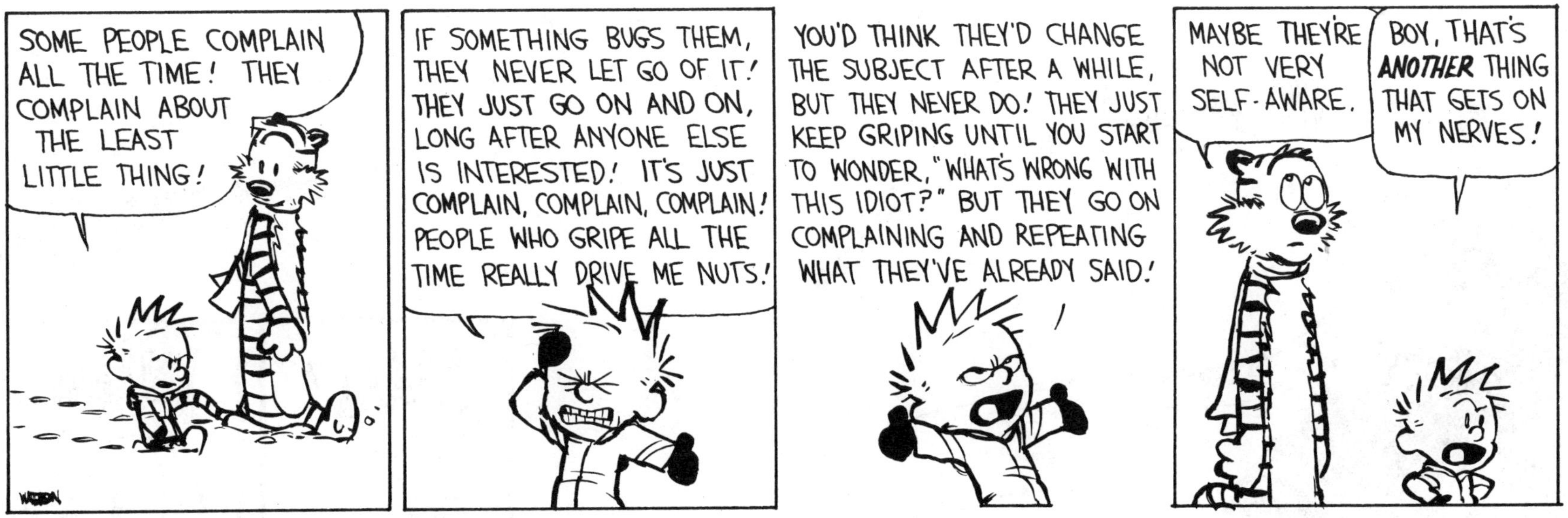
SOME PEOPLE COMPLAIN ALL THE TIME! THEY COMPLAIN ABOUT THE LEAST LITTLE THING!
IF SOMETHING BUGS THEM, THEY NEVER LET GO OF IT! THEY JUST GO ON AND ON, LONG AFTER ANYONE ELSE IS INTERESTED! IT'S JUST COMPLAIN, COMPLAIN, COMPLAIN! PEOPLE WHO GRIPE ALL THE TIME REALLY DRIVE ME NUTS!
YOU'D THINK THEY'D CHANGE THE SUBJECT AFTER A WHILE, BUT THEY NEVER DO! THEY JUST KEEP GRIPING UNTIL YOU START TO WONDER, "WHAT'S WRONG WITH THIS IDIOT?" BUT THEY GO ON COMPLAINING AND REPEATING WHAT THEY'VE ALREADY SAID!
MAYBE THEY'RE NOT VERY SELF-AWARE.
BOY, THAT'S **ANOTHER** THING THAT GETS ON MY NERVES!

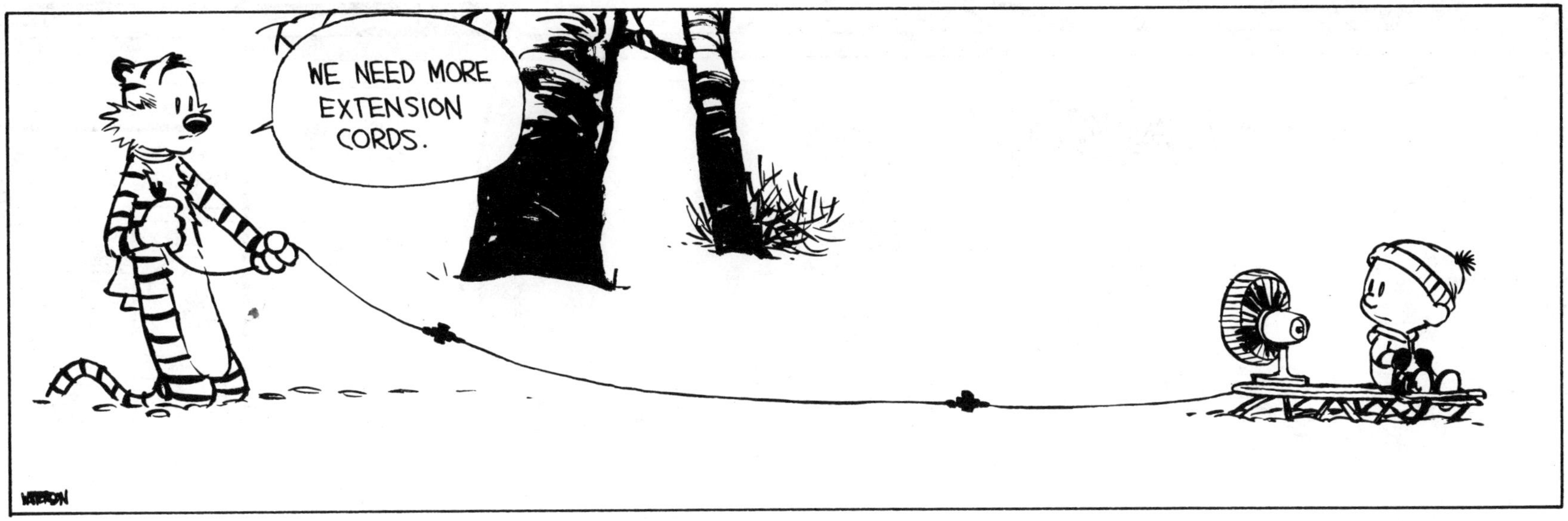
WE NEED MORE EXTENSION CORDS.

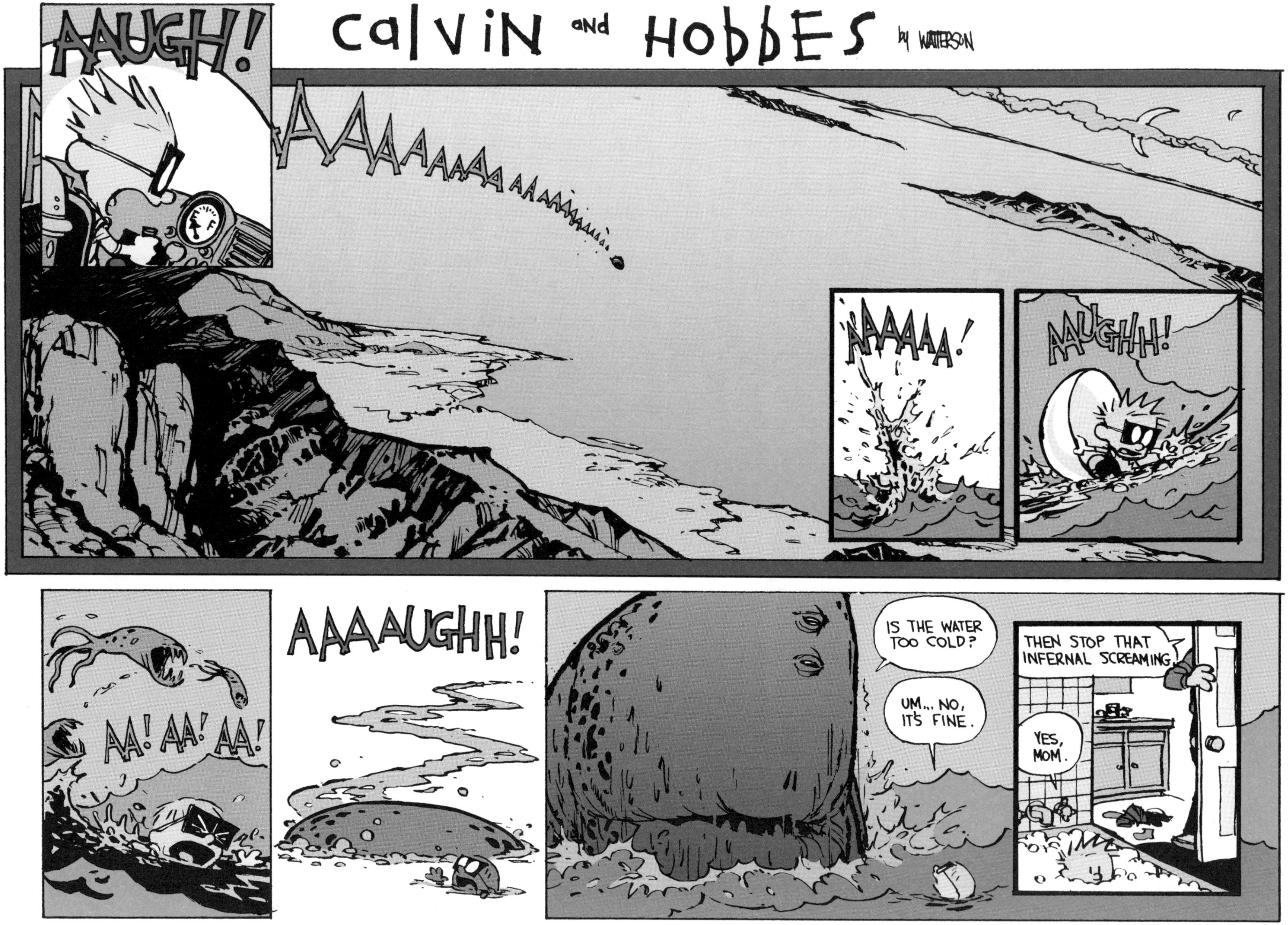
Calvin and Hobbes
by WATTERSON
AAUGH!
AAAAAAAAAAAAAAA
AAAAAA!
AAUGHHH!
AA! AA! AA!
AAAAUGHH!
IS THE WATER TOO COLD?
UM... NO, IT'S FINE.
THEN STOP THAT INFERNAL SCREAMING.
YES, MOM.

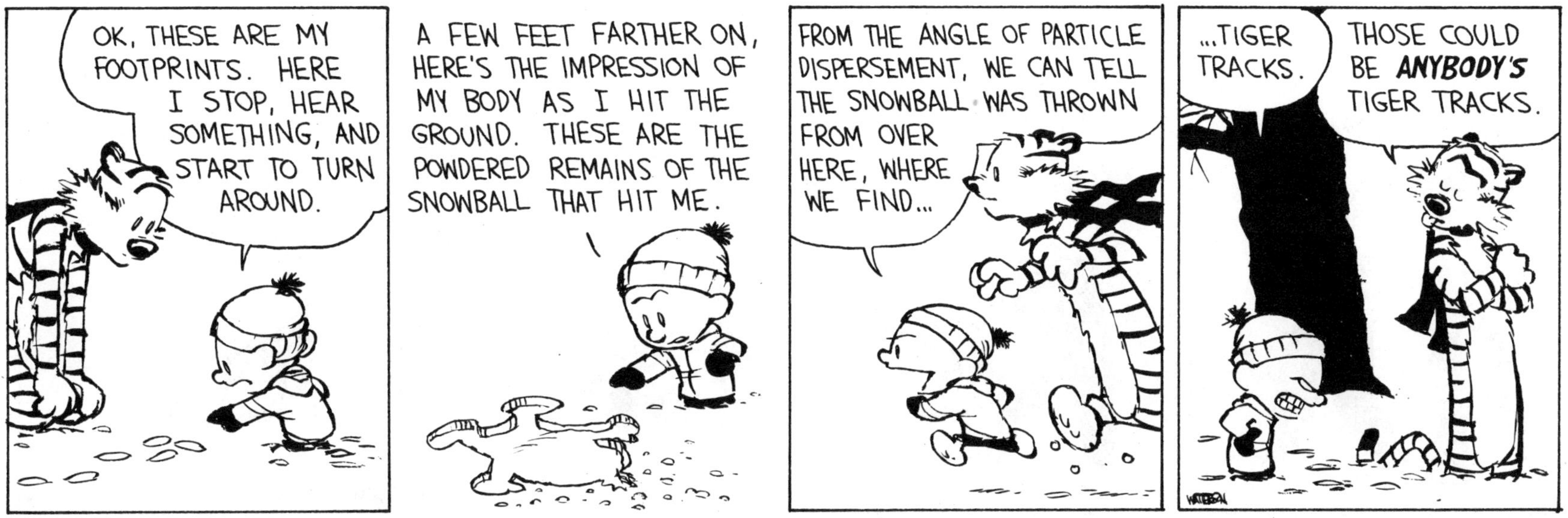
OK, THESE ARE MY FOOTPRINTS. HERE I STOP, HEAR SOMETHING, AND START TO TURN AROUND.
A FEW FEET FARTHER ON, HERE'S THE IMPRESSION OF MY BODY AS I HIT THE GROUND. THESE ARE THE POWDERED REMAINS OF THE SNOWBALL THAT HIT ME.
FROM THE ANGLE OF PARTICLE DISPERSEMENT, WE CAN TELL THE SNOWBALL WAS THROWN FROM OVER HERE, WHERE WE FIND...
...TIGER TRACKS.
THOSE COULD BE **ANYBODY'S** TIGER TRACKS.

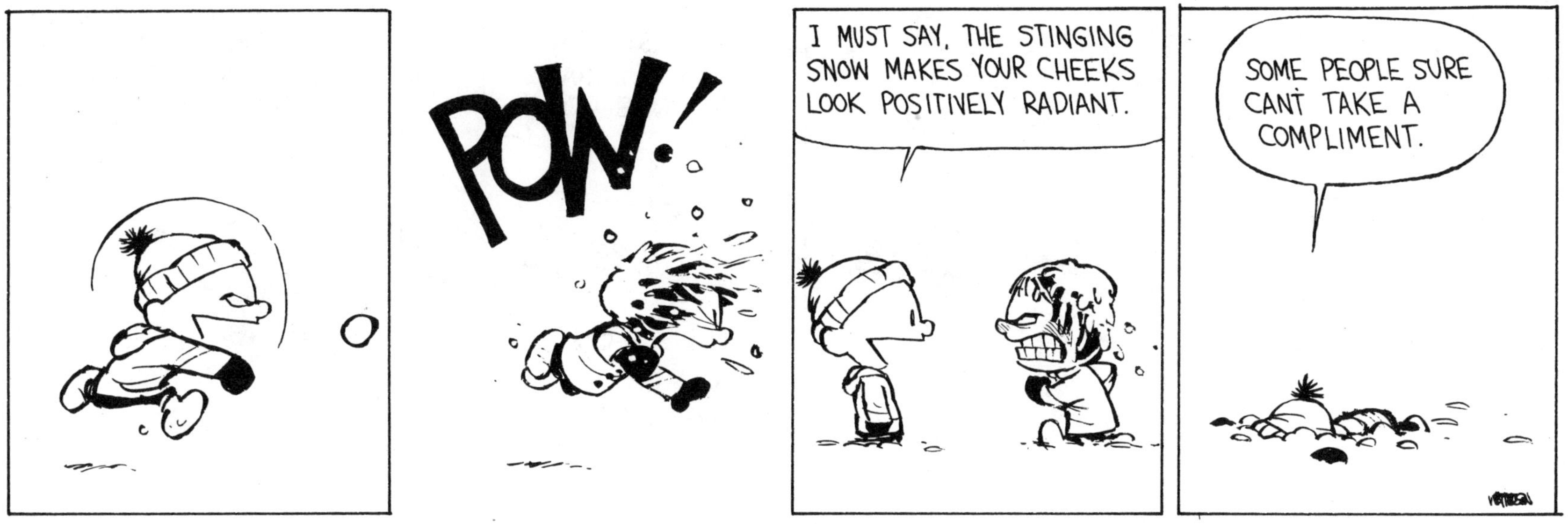
POW!
I MUST SAY, THE STINGING SNOW MAKES YOUR CHEEKS LOOK POSITIVELY RADIANT.
SOME PEOPLE SURE CAN'T TAKE A COMPLIMENT.

SHRIMP.

CIRCUMSTANTIAL EVIDENCE, THAT'S ALL YOU'VE GOT!
YOU CAN'T GET A FAIR TRIAL IN THIS TOWN.

I COULDN'T STAND BEING A GIRL.
I CAN'T STAND YOU EITHER WAY.
WHEN GUYS GROW UP, THEY GET TO PLAY WITH CARS, SPORTS EQUIPMENT, CAMERAS, STEREOS, ELECTRIC TOOLS... YOU NAME IT.
BUT GIRLS DON'T GET ANY TOYS WHEN THEY GROW UP. WOMEN JUST BUY CLOTHES AND SHOES. HOW BORING. HOW SAD.
I GUESS GIRLS ACTUALLY MATURE AS THEY GET OLDER.
I CAN'T WAIT UNTIL I'M OLD ENOUGH TO "PUTTER AROUND."

ON THE OTHER HAND, THE NEIGHBORS KEEP PLANTING NICE BIG TREES NEXT TO US.

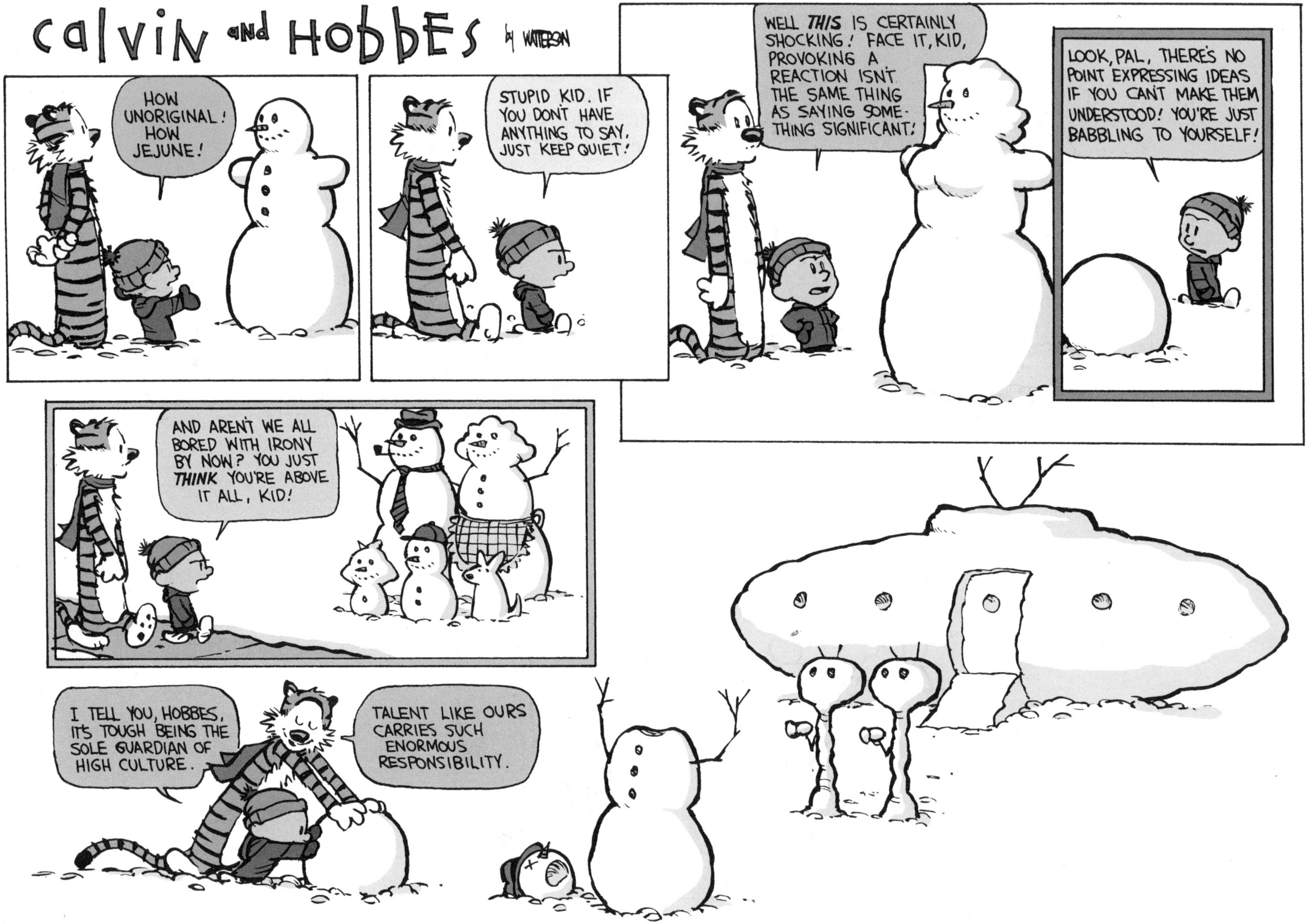
Calvin and Hobbes
by Watterson
HOW UNORIGINAL! HOW JEJUNE!
STUPID KID. IF YOU DON'T HAVE ANYTHING TO SAY, JUST KEEP QUIET!
WELL THIS IS CERTAINLY SHOCKING! FACE IT, KID, PROVOKING A REACTION ISN'T THE SAME THING AS SAYING SOMETHING SIGNIFICANT!
LOOK, PAL, THERE'S NO POINT EXPRESSING IDEAS IF YOU CAN'T MAKE THEM UNDERSTOOD! YOU'RE JUST BABBLING TO YOURSELF!
AND AREN'T WE ALL BORED WITH IRONY BY NOW? YOU JUST THINK YOU'RE ABOVE IT ALL, KID!
I TELL YOU, HOBBES, IT'S TOUGH BEING THE SOLE GUARDIAN OF HIGH CULTURE.
TALENT LIKE OURS CARRIES SUCH ENORMOUS RESPONSIBILITY.

OUR LIVES ARE FILLED WITH MACHINES DESIGNED TO REDUCE WORK AND INCREASE LEISURE. WE HAVE MORE LEISURE THAN MAN HAS EVER HAD.

AND WHAT DO WE DO WITH THIS LEISURE? EDUCATE OURSELVES? TAKE UP NEW INTERESTS? EXPLORE? INVENT? CREATE?

DAD, I CAN'T HEAR THIS COMMERCIAL.

IF IT WERE UP TO DAD, LEISURE WOULD BE AS BAD AS WORK.

I *KNOW* I HAVE HAT HAIR, SO YOU DON'T NEED TO TELL ME.

ACTUALLY, IT'S NOT THAT DIFFERENT.

SEE? IF YOU JUMP RIGHT, I DON'T NEED TO WASTE TIME SHOVELING THE ENTIRE WALK.

Test:
1. When did the Pilgrims land at Plymouth Rock?
1620.
AS YOU CAN SEE, I'VE MEMORIZED THIS UTTERLY USELESS FACT LONG ENOUGH TO PASS A TEST QUESTION. I NOW INTEND TO FORGET IT FOREVER. YOU'VE TAUGHT ME NOTHING EXCEPT HOW TO CYNICALLY MANIPULATE THE SYSTEM. CONGRATULATIONS.
THEY SAY THE SATISFACTION OF TEACHING MAKES UP FOR THE LOUSY PAY.

2. Where is Plymouth Rock?

I am not presently at liberty to divulge that information, as it might compromise our agents in the field.

I UNDERSTAND MY TESTS ARE POPULAR READING IN THE TEACHERS' LOUNGE.

Gimme a quarter, Twinky.

YOUR SIMIAN COUNTENANCE SUGGESTS A HERITAGE UNUSUALLY RICH IN SPECIES DIVERSITY.

What?

HERE YOU GO.

THAT WAS WORTH 25 CENTS.

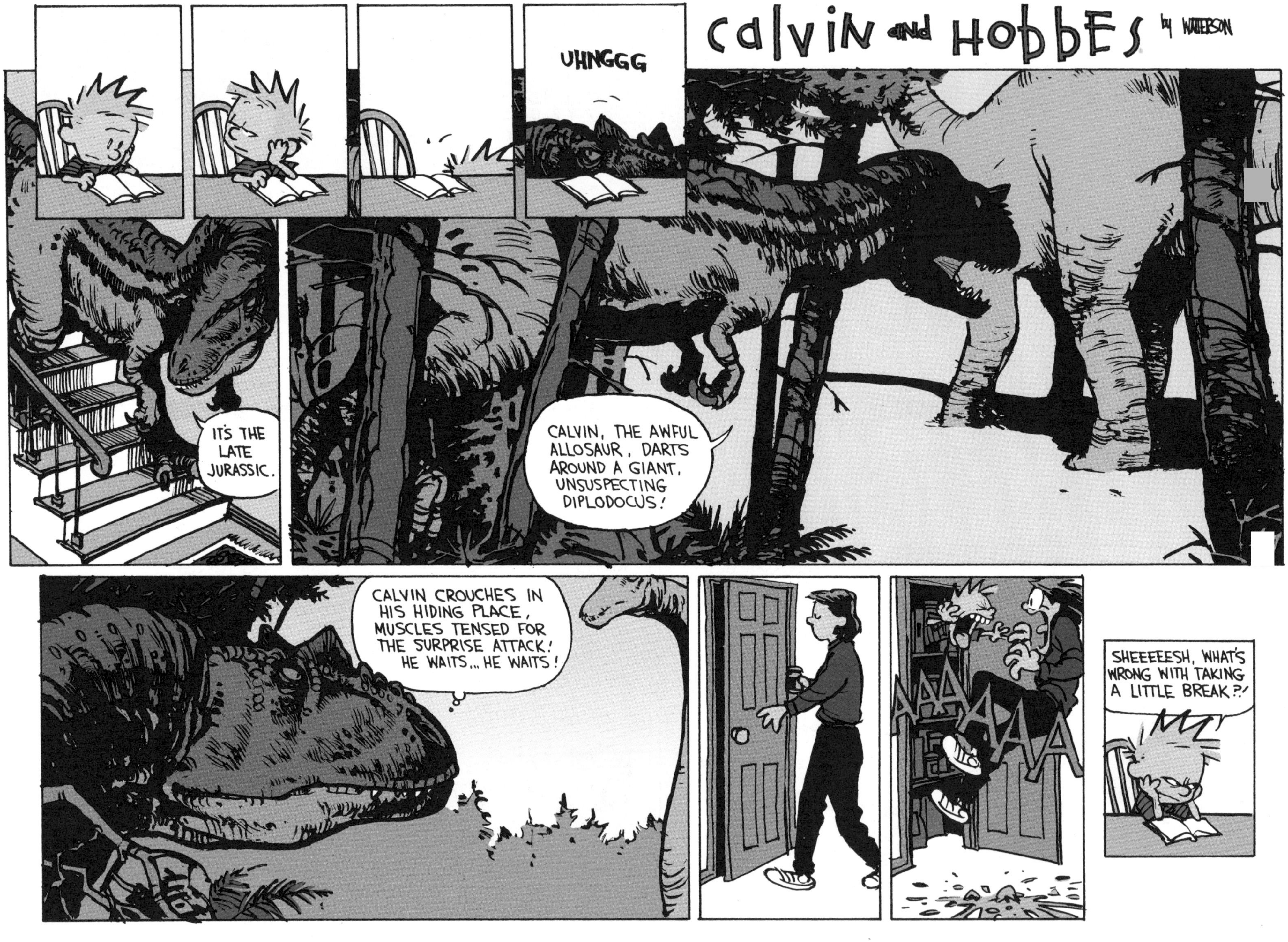
Calvin and Hobbes
by WATTERSON
UHNGGG
IT'S THE LATE JURASSIC.
CALVIN, THE AWFUL ALLOSAUR, DARTS AROUND A GIANT, UNSUSPECTING DIPLODOCUS!
CALVIN CROUCHES IN HIS HIDING PLACE, MUSCLES TENSED FOR THE SURPRISE ATTACK! HE WAITS... HE WAITS!
AAAAAAA
SHEEEEESH, WHAT'S WRONG WITH TAKING A LITTLE BREAK?!

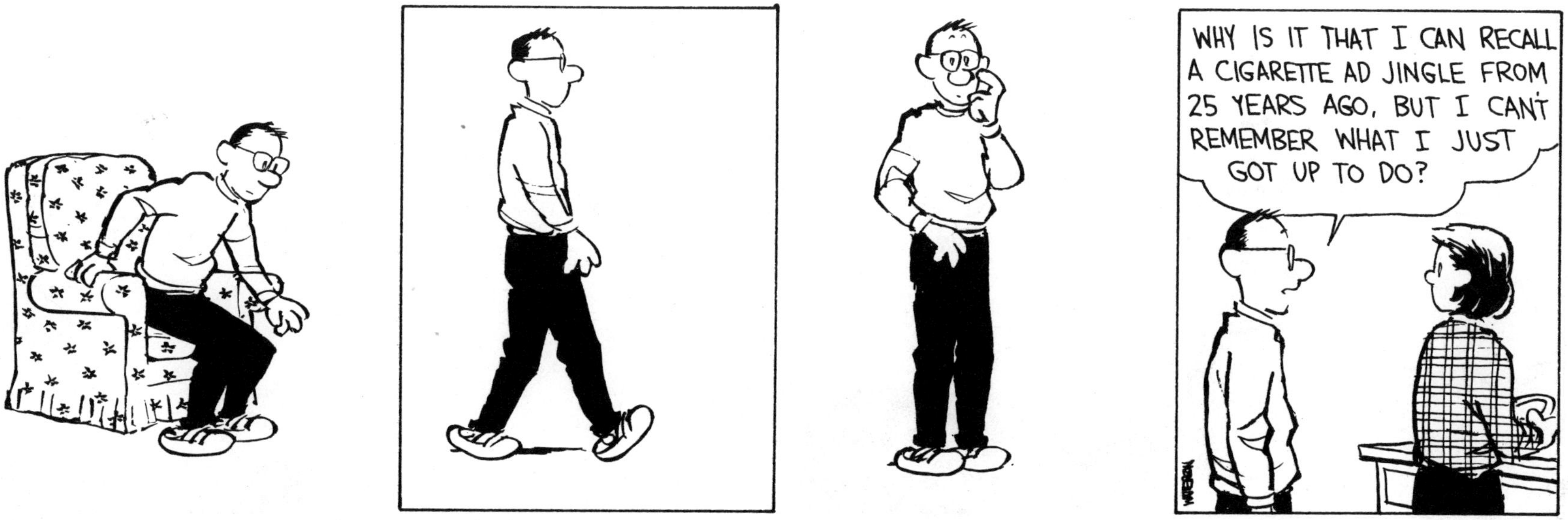
WHY IS IT THAT I CAN RECALL A CIGARETTE AD JINGLE FROM 25 YEARS AGO, BUT I CAN'T REMEMBER WHAT I JUST GOT UP TO DO?

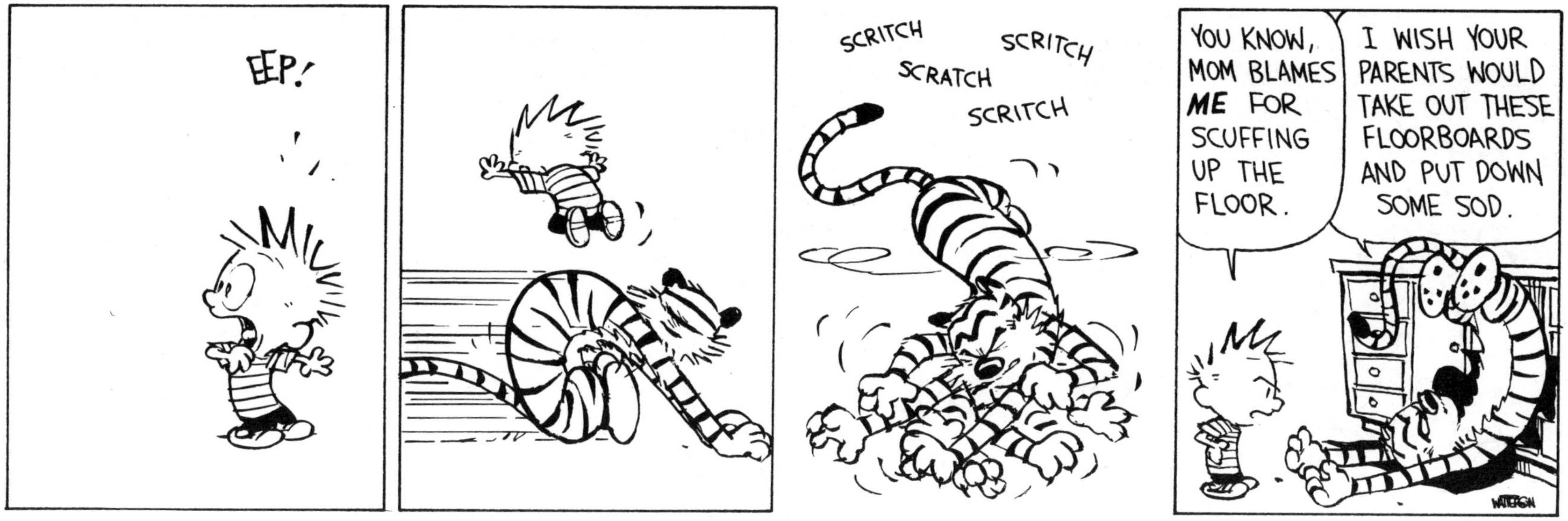
EEP!
SCRITCH
SCRATCH
SCRITCH
SCRITCH
YOU KNOW, MOM BLAMES ***ME*** FOR SCUFFING UP THE FLOOR.
I WISH YOUR PARENTS WOULD TAKE OUT THESE FLOORBOARDS AND PUT DOWN SOME SOD.

LOOK, MOM, I MADE YOU SOME SUBTITLES.

HMM?

WHEN YOU'RE TALKING TO ME, YOU CHOOSE THE APPROPRIATE CARD TO TRANSLATE WHAT YOU'RE SAYING, AND PROP IT AGAINST YOUR FEET FOR ME TO READ.

FOR EXAMPLE, IF YOU SAY "GO TO BED *NOW*," YOU CAN USE THIS CARD, WHICH SAYS, "YOU'VE GOT TEN MINUTES UNTIL I BLOW MY STACK." SEE? THEN I'LL KNOW WHAT YOU MEAN.

You've got ten minutes until I blow my stack.

I DON'T NEED TRANSLATION!

I'VE EVEN GOT SUBTITLES FOR PARENTISMS LIKE "YOU'RE GOING TO POKE SOMEBODY'S EYE OUT WITH THAT."

WHY ARE YOU FOLLOWING ME AROUND?

WHY ARE YOU FOLLOWING ME AROUND?

AND WHY ARE YOU REPEATING WHAT I SAY?

AND WHY ARE YOU REPEATING WHAT I SAY?

IF YOU'RE GOING TO KEEP DOING THAT, I JUST WON'T SAY ANYTHING.

IF YOU'RE GOING TO KEEP DOING THAT, I JUST WON'T SAY ANYTHING.

THE INCREDIBLY ANNOYING HUMAN ECHO STRIKES AGAIN!

STOP REPEATING EVERYTHING I SAY.
STOP REPEATING EVERYTHING I SAY.
QUIT IT.
QUIT IT.
I'M AN UGLY LITTLE MAGGOT WITH LUMPY GRAVY FOR BRAINS!
AT LEAST YOU HAVE THE COURAGE TO ADMIT IT.
SOONER OR LATER, EVERYONE FALLS FOR THAT.
WATTERSON

HOW MUCH LONGER ARE YOU GOING TO REPEAT WHATEVER I SAY?
HOW MUCH LONGER ARE YOU GOING TO REPEAT WHATEVER I SAY?
OK THEN, JUST KEEP AT IT, MR. ANNOYING HUMAN ECHO.
OK THEN, JUST KEEP AT IT, MR. ANNOYING HUMAN ECHO.
"WE CAN *A PRIORI* AND PRIOR TO ALL GIVEN OBJECTS HAVE A KNOWLEDGE OF THOSE CONDITIONS ON WHICH ALONE EXPERIENCE OF THEM IS POSSIBLE, BUT NEVER OF THE LAWS TO WHICH THINGS MAY IN THEMSELVES BE SUBJECT WITHOUT REFERENCE TO POSSIBLE EXPERIENCE."
WE CAN AH PEORIA AND.. UM.. SLOW DOWN WHAT? HOLD ON.
THBBPBPTT!
CHEATER.
WATTERSON

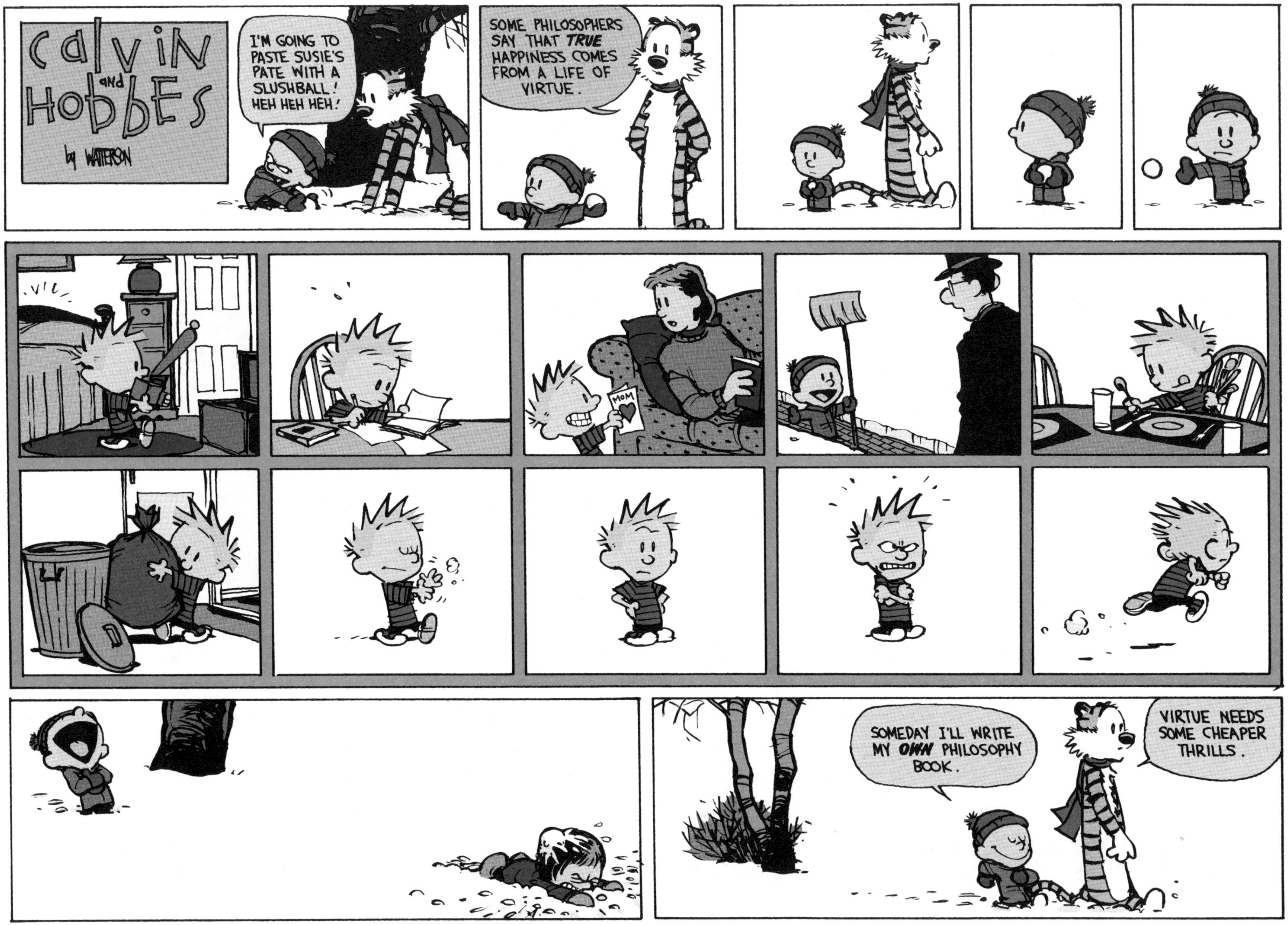
Calvin and Hobbes
by WATTERSON
I'M GOING TO PASTE SUSIE'S PATE WITH A SLUSHBALL! HEH HEH HEH!
SOME PHILOSOPHERS SAY THAT TRUE HAPPINESS COMES FROM A LIFE OF VIRTUE.
MOM
SOMEDAY I'LL WRITE MY OWN PHILOSOPHY BOOK.
VIRTUE NEEDS SOME CHEAPER THRILLS.

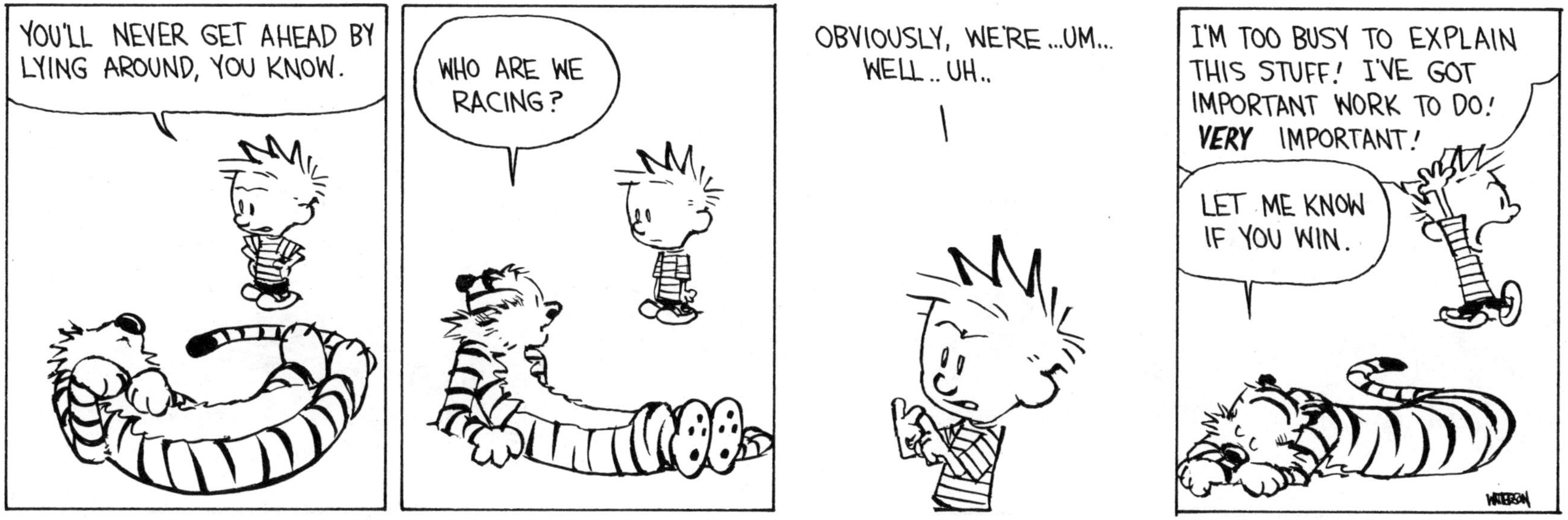
YOU'LL NEVER GET AHEAD BY LYING AROUND, YOU KNOW.
WHO ARE WE RACING?
OBVIOUSLY, WE'RE ...UM... WELL.. UH..
I'M TOO BUSY TO EXPLAIN THIS STUFF! I'VE GOT IMPORTANT WORK TO DO! **VERY** IMPORTANT!
LET ME KNOW IF YOU WIN.

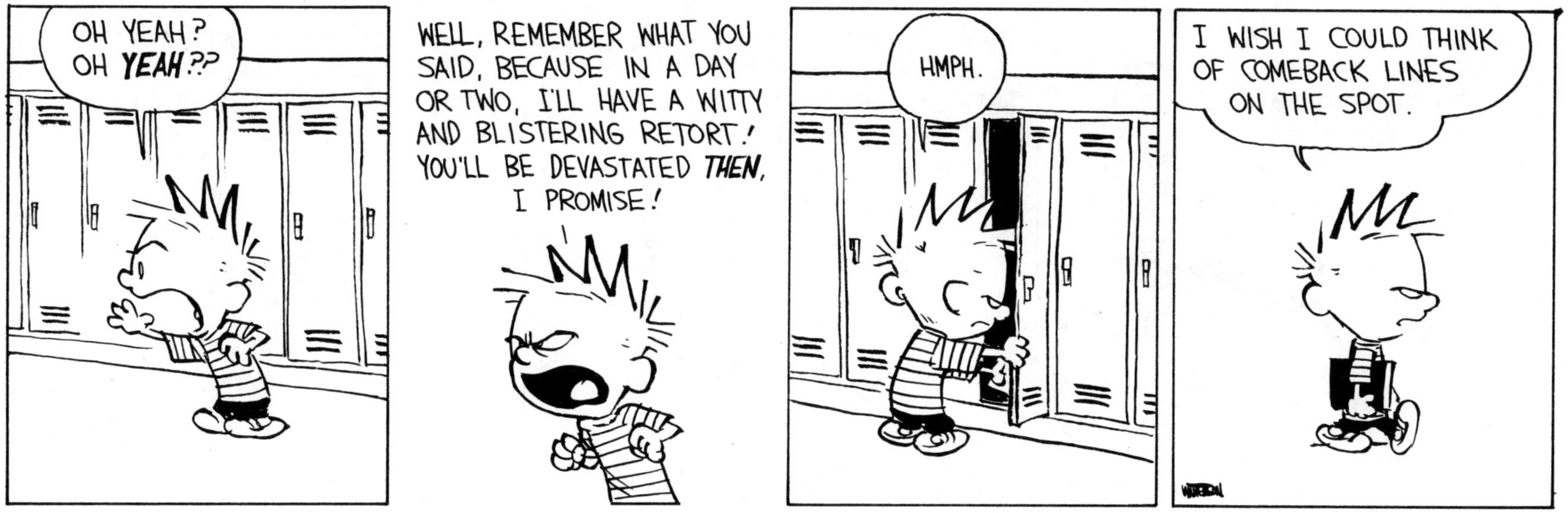
OH YEAH? OH **YEAH**??
WELL, REMEMBER WHAT YOU SAID, BECAUSE IN A DAY OR TWO, I'LL HAVE A WITTY AND BLISTERING RETORT! YOU'LL BE DEVASTATED **THEN**, I PROMISE!
HMPH.
I WISH I COULD THINK OF COMEBACK LINES ON THE SPOT.

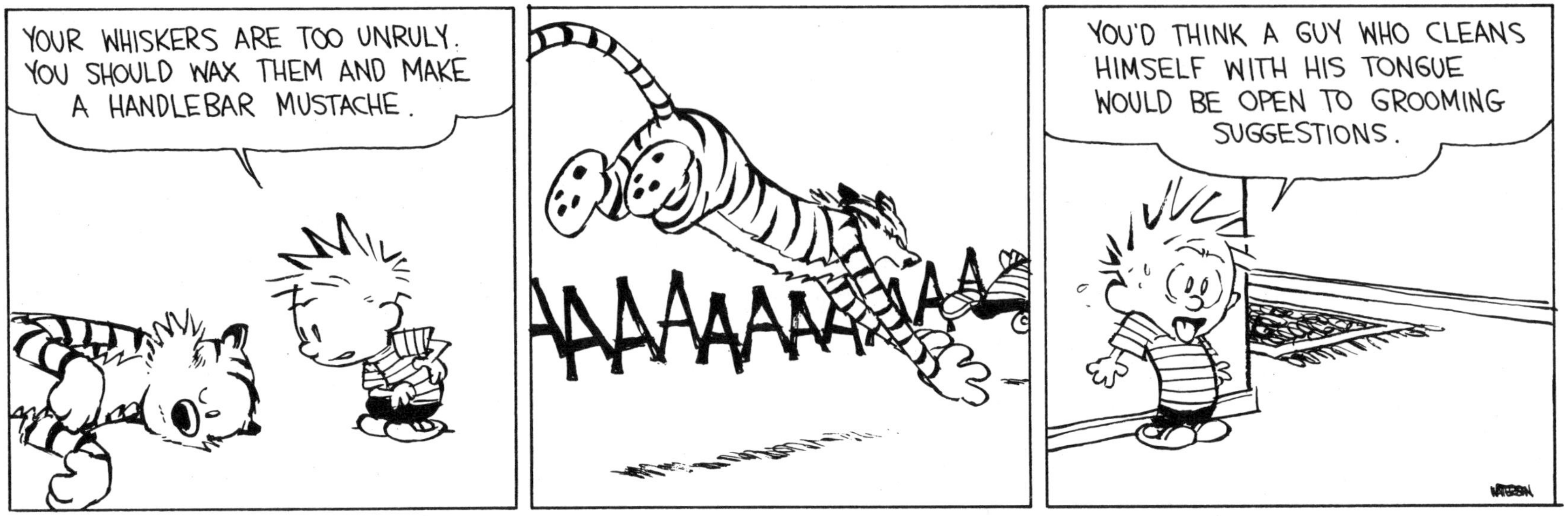
YOUR WHISKERS ARE TOO UNRULY. YOU SHOULD WAX THEM AND MAKE A HANDLEBAR MUSTACHE.
AAAAAAAAAAAAAA
YOU'D THINK A GUY WHO CLEANS HIMSELF WITH HIS TONGUE WOULD BE OPEN TO GROOMING SUGGESTIONS.

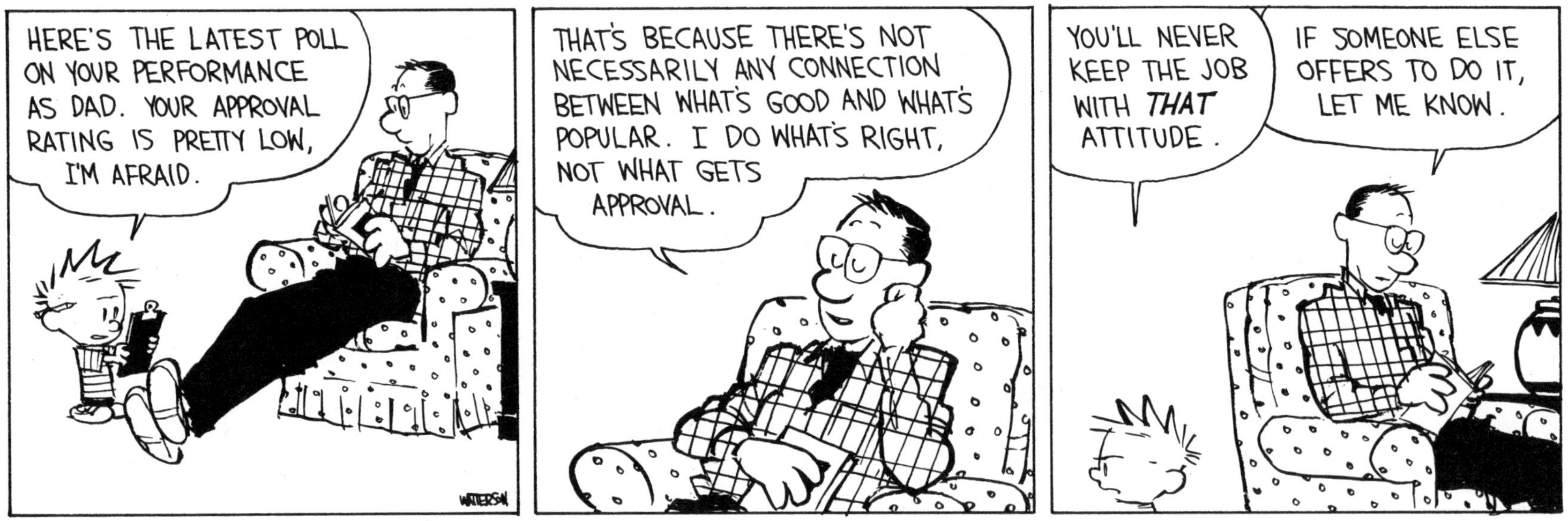
HERE'S THE LATEST POLL ON YOUR PERFORMANCE AS DAD. YOUR APPROVAL RATING IS PRETTY LOW, I'M AFRAID.
THAT'S BECAUSE THERE'S NOT NECESSARILY ANY CONNECTION BETWEEN WHAT'S GOOD AND WHAT'S POPULAR. I DO WHAT'S RIGHT, NOT WHAT GETS APPROVAL.
YOU'LL NEVER KEEP THE JOB WITH *THAT* ATTITUDE.
IF SOMEONE ELSE OFFERS TO DO IT, LET ME KNOW.

Test:
1. What important event took place on December 16, 1773?
I do NOT BELIEVE IN LINEAR TIME. THERE IS NO PAST AND FUTURE: ALL IS ONE, AND EXISTENCE IN THE TEMPORAL SENSE IS ILLUSORY. THIS QUESTION, THEREFORE, IS MEANINGLESS AND IMPOSSIBLE TO ANSWER.
WHEN IN DOUBT, DENY ALL TERMS AND DEFINITIONS.

YAAAAA
RRRRR RR R
OK, IT'S HARDER THAN IT LOOKS.
GOODNESS, HOW DID YOU GUYS EVER LIVE LONG ENOUGH TO INVENT TOOLS?

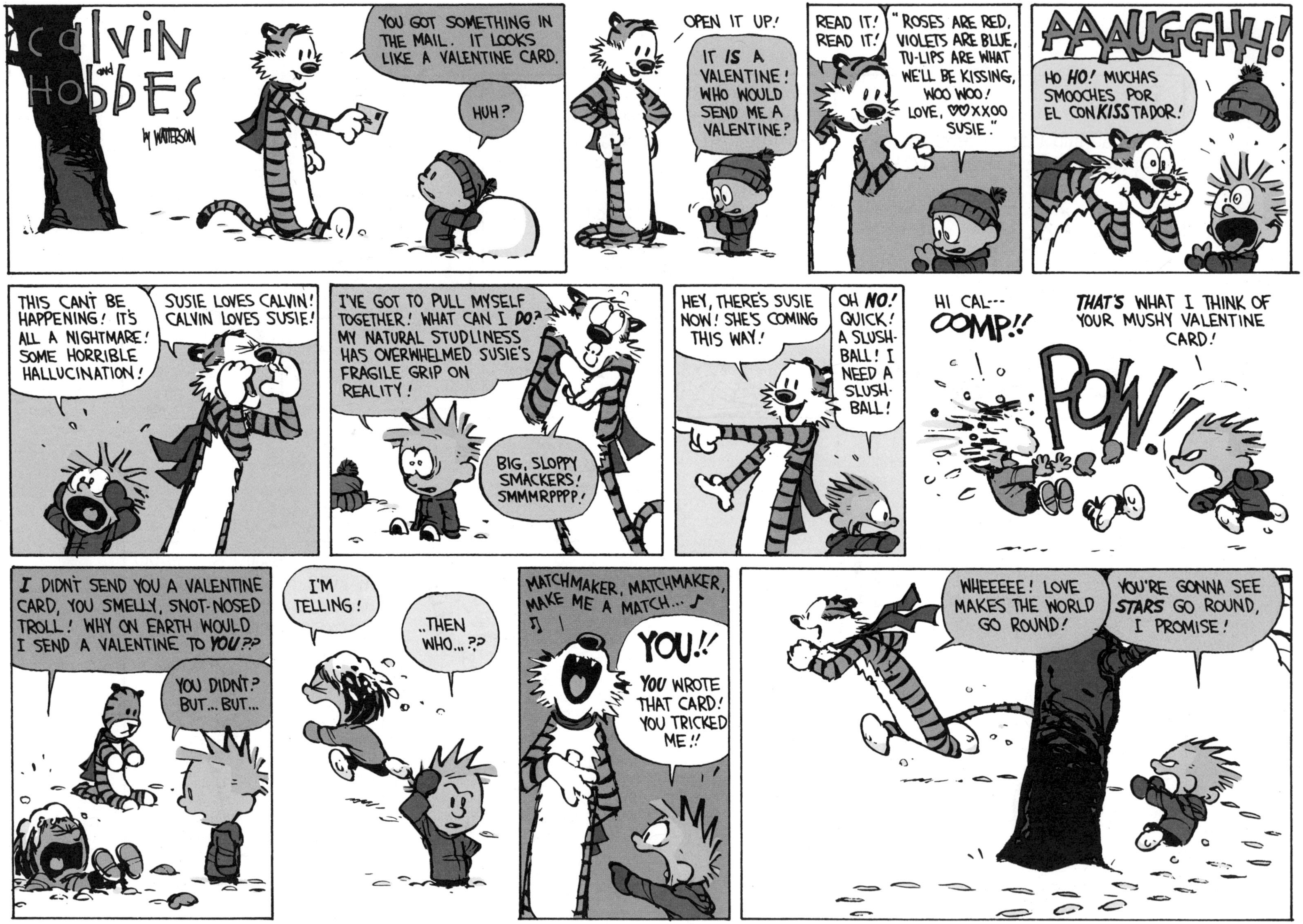
Calvin and Hobbes
by WATTERSON
YOU GOT SOMETHING IN THE MAIL. IT LOOKS LIKE A VALENTINE CARD.
HUH?
OPEN IT UP!
IT IS A VALENTINE! WHO WOULD SEND ME A VALENTINE?
READ IT! READ IT!
"ROSES ARE RED, VIOLETS ARE BLUE, TU-LIPS ARE WHAT WE'LL BE KISSING, WOO WOO! LOVE, ♡♡XXOO SUSIE."
AAAUGGHH!
HO HO! MUCHAS SMOOCHES POR EL CONKISSTADOR!
THIS CAN'T BE HAPPENING! IT'S ALL A NIGHTMARE! SOME HORRIBLE HALLUCINATION!
SUSIE LOVES CALVIN! CALVIN LOVES SUSIE!
I'VE GOT TO PULL MYSELF TOGETHER! WHAT CAN I DO? MY NATURAL STUDLINESS HAS OVERWHELMED SUSIE'S FRAGILE GRIP ON REALITY!
BIG, SLOPPY SMACKERS! SMMMRPPPP!
HEY, THERE'S SUSIE NOW! SHE'S COMING THIS WAY!
OH NO! QUICK! A SLUSH-BALL! I NEED A SLUSH-BALL!
HI CAL---
OOMP!!
THAT'S WHAT I THINK OF YOUR MUSHY VALENTINE CARD!
POW!!
I DIDN'T SEND YOU A VALENTINE CARD, YOU SMELLY, SNOT-NOSED TROLL! WHY ON EARTH WOULD I SEND A VALENTINE TO YOU??
YOU DIDN'T? BUT... BUT...
I'M TELLING!
..THEN WHO...??
MATCHMAKER, MATCHMAKER, MAKE ME A MATCH...
YOU!!
YOU WROTE THAT CARD! YOU TRICKED ME!!
WHEEEEE! LOVE MAKES THE WORLD GO ROUND!
YOU'RE GONNA SEE STARS GO ROUND, I PROMISE!

I WISH I HAD AMAZING SUPER POWERS.
IF YOU WORK AND STUDY REAL HARD FOR YEARS AND YEARS, YOU COULD DEVELOP THE POWERS YOU ALREADY HAVE.
MAYBE I CAN FIND A RADIOACTIVE METEORITE THAT MUTATES ME INTO A LIVING LIQUID.
TRY TO FIND ONE THAT MUTATES YOU INTO SOMEONE WITH A WORK ETHIC.
WATTERSON

MOM AND DAD DON'T VALUE HARD WORK AND ORIGINALITY AS MUCH AS THEY SAY THEY DO.
WATTERSON

DING DONG ♪

HEH HEH HEH!

OH! OOP!...UM...HI, MRS. DERKINS. I WAS HOPING SUSIE WOULD ANSWER THE...UH...I MEAN, UM, I'M SELLING HUGE SNOWBALLS. WOULD YOU LIKE TO BUY ONE?

MY "PLAN A's" ARE GREAT, BUT MY "PLAN B's" LEAVE A LOT TO BE DESIRED.

POW!

LOOK OUT!

MY SNOWBALLS GO FASTER THAN THE SPEED OF SOUND.

THEY DO NOT, YOU BIG LIAR!

I WISH THIS SLED HAD A SPEEDOMETER SO WE COULD KNOW HOW FAST WE'RE GOING.
I SUPPOSE WE COULD MEASURE THE HILL, TIME OUR DESCENT, CALCULATE OUR RATE IN FEET PER MINUTE, AND CONVERT THAT INTO MILES PER HOUR.
THAT SOUNDS LIKE MATH.
UM, YES..
SUDDENLY I STOPPED CARING.

WHAT'S **THIS** SNOWMAN?
HE'S A PALEONTOLOGIST.
HE'S LOOKING FOR CRETACEOUS SNOW DINOSAURS.
WHY DOES HE LOOK SO SAD?
HE REALIZED THAT SNOW DOESN'T FOSSILIZE. IT JUST MELTS.
YOUR SNOWMEN LEAD TRAGIC LIVES.
WELL, THEY'RE NOT VERY BRIGHT.

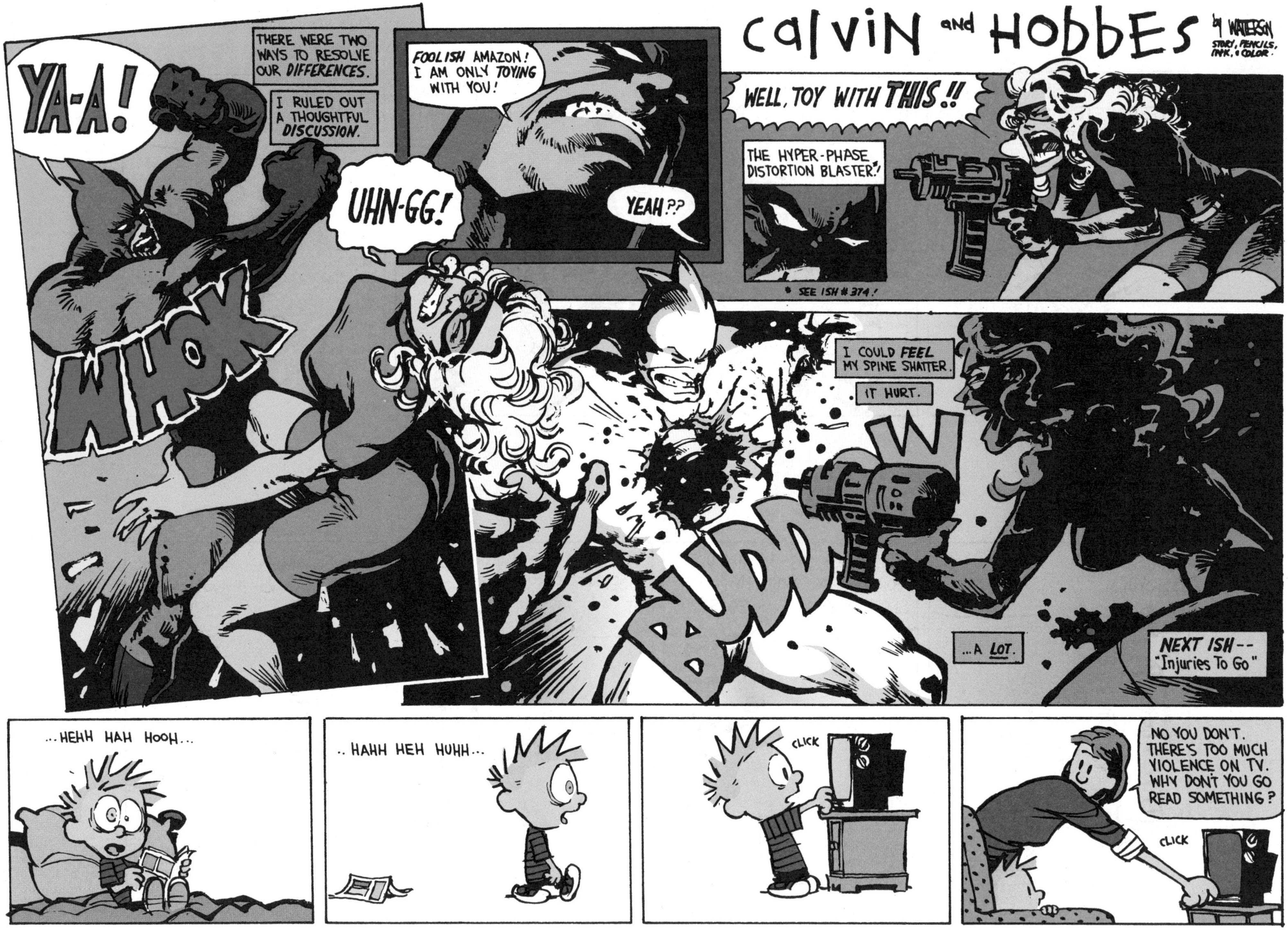

calvin and HOBBES
by WATERSN
STORY, PENCILS, INK, & COLOR.
YA-A!
THERE WERE TWO WAYS TO RESOLVE OUR DIFFERENCES.
I RULED OUT A THOUGHTFUL DISCUSSION.
WHOK
UHN-GG!
FOOLISH AMAZON! I AM ONLY TOYING WITH YOU!
YEAH??
WELL, TOY WITH THIS!!
THE HYPER-PHASE DISTORTION BLASTER!*
* SEE ISH #374!
I COULD FEEL MY SPINE SHATTER.
IT HURT.
BWDOW
...A LOT.
NEXT ISH -- "Injuries To Go"
...HEHH HAH HOOH...
..HAHH HEH HUHH...
CLICK
NO YOU DON'T. THERE'S TOO MUCH VIOLENCE ON TV. WHY DON'T YOU GO READ SOMETHING?
CLICK

CALVIN, I'M LATE FOR WORK!
XING

HOW MUCH IS THAT TIGER IN THE WINDOW? THE ONE WHO DOES NOTHING BUT SLEEP? WE'LL SPREAD HIM OUT FLAT IN THE REC ROOM AND HAVE A NEW RUG IF HE'S CHEAP!

YES, CALVIN?

WHY AREN'T YOU TEACHING US THE GENDERS OF NOUNS?

IS "DESK" MASCULINE? IS "CHAIR" FEMININE? FOREIGN KIDS KNOW, BUT **WE** DON'T! NO WONDER WE CAN'T COMPETE IN A GLOBAL MARKET! I DEMAND SEX EDUCATION!

..I WONDER IF HER DOCTOR KNOWS SHE MIXES ALL THOSE MEDICATIONS.

YAWWNN

TRIFLE NOT WITH TIRED TIGERS.

I BET I CAN KNOCK DAD'S HAT OFF WITH THIS SNOWBALL.
I BET YOU CAN'T.
OH YEAH ?! HOW MUCH?
A HUNDRED DOLLARS.
YOU'RE ON, FUZZBRAIN. GET OUT YOUR WALLET!
BOY, FIVE INCHES HIGHER WOULD'VE DONE IT. YOU ALWAYS GET ME IN TROUBLE.
YOU OWE ME $2,500 SO FAR.

WHY SHOULD OTHER PEOPLE BENEFIT FROM MY HARD WORK?

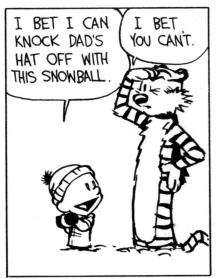

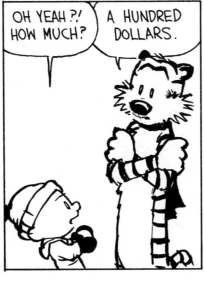

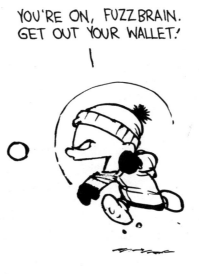

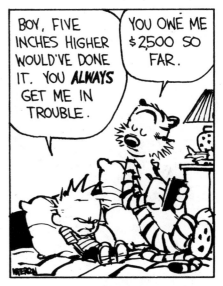

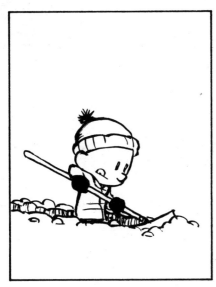

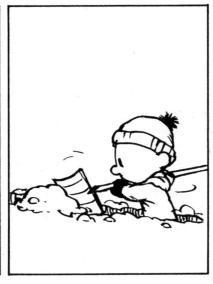

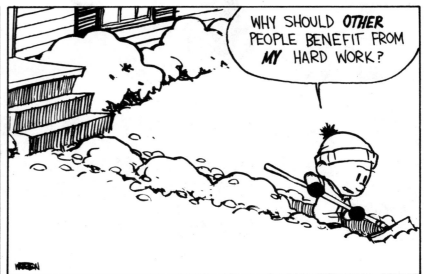

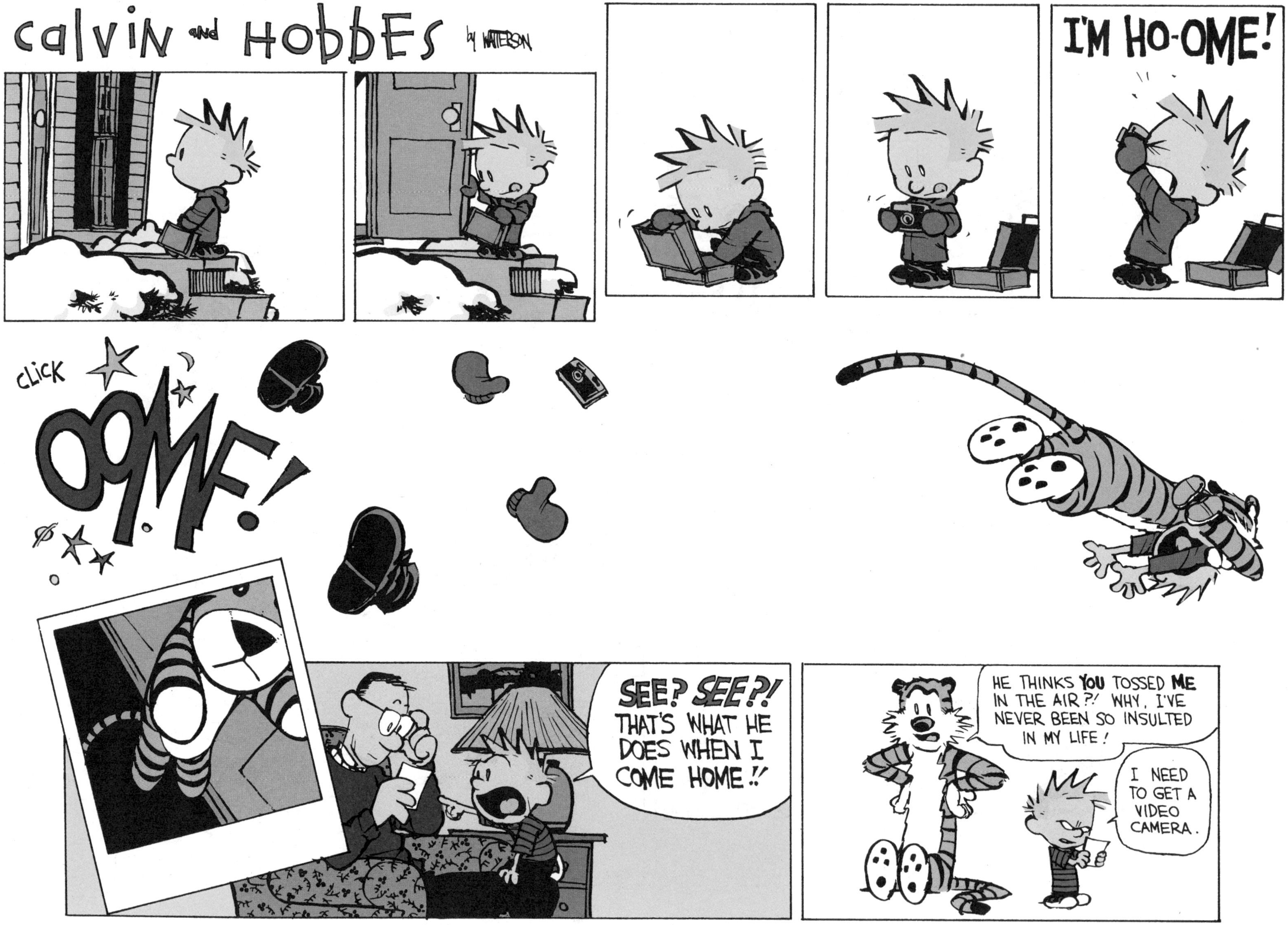
calvin and HOBBES by WATTERSON
I'M HO-OME!
CLICK
OOMF!
SEE? SEE?! THAT'S WHAT HE DOES WHEN I COME HOME!!
HE THINKS YOU TOSSED ME IN THE AIR?! WHY, I'VE NEVER BEEN SO INSULTED IN MY LIFE!
I NEED TO GET A VIDEO CAMERA.

SHOULD I STAY INSIDE OR GO OUTSIDE?

IT'S AWFULLY COLD OUT, BUT I SUPPOSE I COULD BUNDLE UP. IT LOOKS WINDY THOUGH. BUT STILL, I'D LIKE TO GO SLEDDING. THEN AGAIN, MAYBE I'D RATHER STAY IN. ON THE OTHER HAND...

GO OUT AND CLOSE THE DOOR!

THE MORE INDECISIVE I AM, THE FASTER THINGS GET DECIDED.

I LIKE FOLLOWING THE NEWS! NEWS ORGANIZATIONS KNOW I WON'T SIT STILL FOR ANY SERIOUS DISCUSSION OF COMPLEX AND BORING ISSUES.

THEY GIVE ME WHAT I WANT: ANTICS, EMOTIONAL CONFRONTATION, SOUND BITES, SCANDAL, SOB STORIES AND POPULARITY POLLS ALL PACKAGED AS A SOAP OPERA AND HORSE RACE! IT'S VERY ENTERTAINING.

THEN COMMENTATORS WONDER WHY THE PUBLIC IS CYNICAL ABOUT POLITICS.

YOU CAN TELL THIS IS AN IN-DEPTH STORY, BECAUSE IT'S GOT AN ARTICLE NEXT TO THE CHART.

I SAW A SIGN ON A RESTAURANT DOOR THAT SAID, "NO SHIRT, NO SHOES, NO SERVICE."
BUT IT DIDN'T SAY ANYTHING ABOUT **PANTS**! IF I WENT IN WEARING SHOES AND A SHIRT, BUT NO PANTS, THEY'D HAVE TO SERVE ME!
THEY'D PROBABLY SERVE YOU WITH A COURT SUMMONS.
C'MON, LET'S SEE IF MOM WILL TAKE US OUT FOR DINNER!

THERE!
WHATCHA DOIN'?
I'VE HIDDEN A CACHE OF SNOWBALLS BEHIND EVERY TREE IN THE YARD!
NOW WHEN MY ENEMIES COME AFTER ME, I NEED ONLY RUN TO THE NEAREST TREE TO BE INSTANTLY ARMED.
INGENIOUS.
NOW I NEED TO MAKE SOME ENEMIES.
I'LL BE ONE.

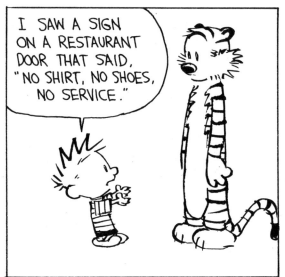

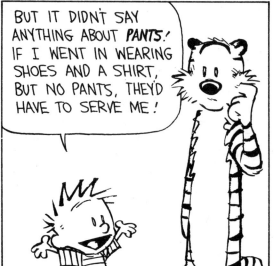

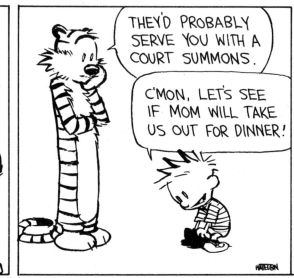

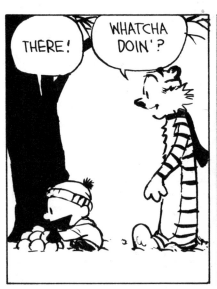

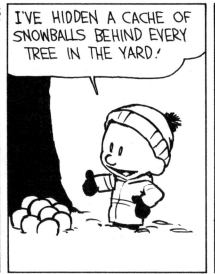

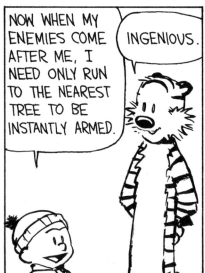

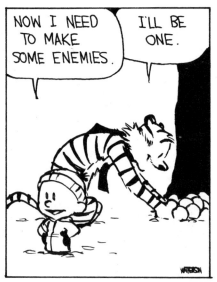

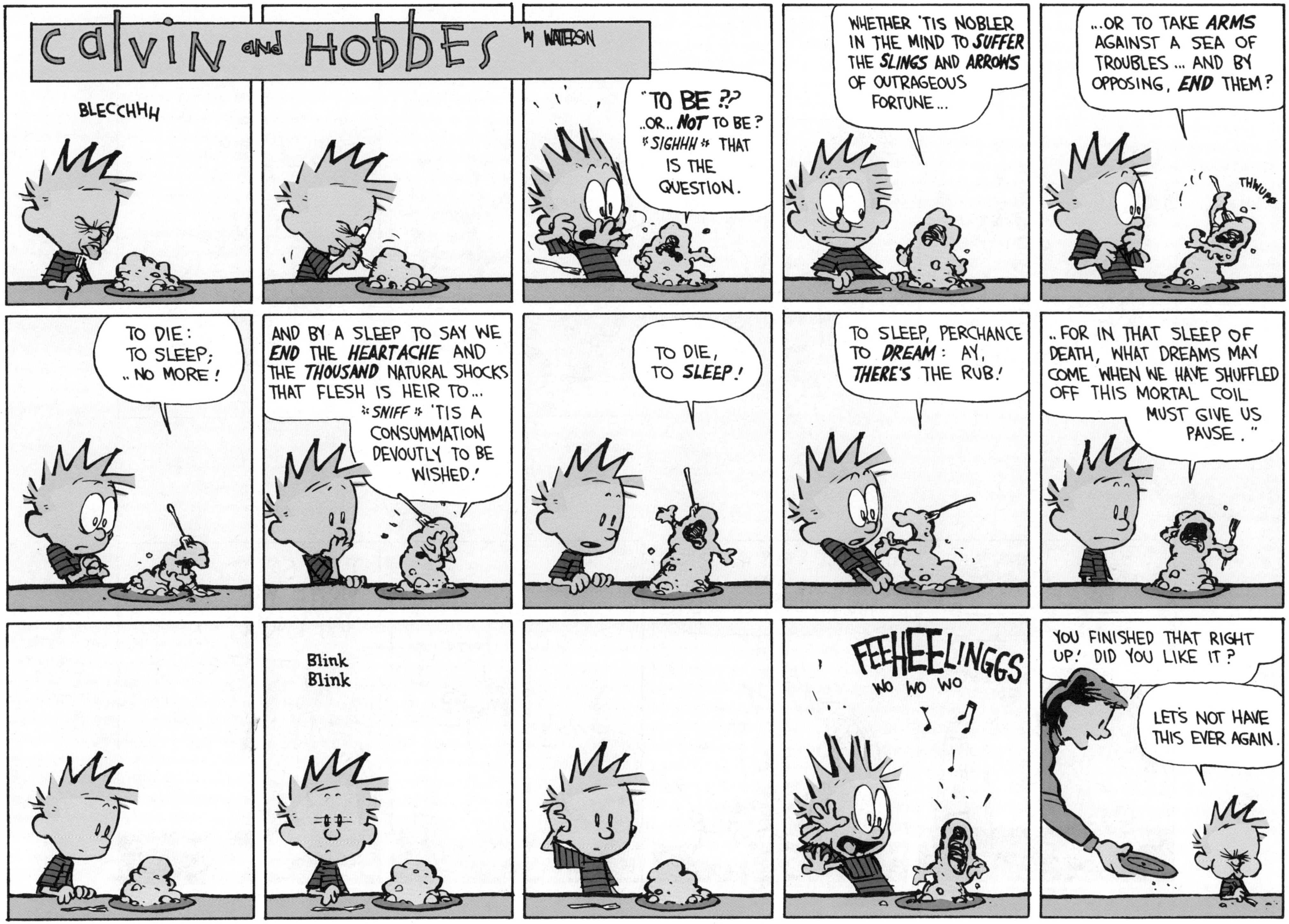
Calvin and HobbEs
by WATTERSON
BLECCHHH
"TO BE ?? ..OR.. NOT TO BE? *SIGHHH* THAT IS THE QUESTION.
WHETHER 'TIS NOBLER IN THE MIND TO SUFFER THE SLINGS AND ARROWS OF OUTRAGEOUS FORTUNE...
...OR TO TAKE ARMS AGAINST A SEA OF TROUBLES ... AND BY OPPOSING, END THEM?
THWUPP
TO DIE: TO SLEEP; .. NO MORE!
AND BY A SLEEP TO SAY WE END THE HEARTACHE AND THE THOUSAND NATURAL SHOCKS THAT FLESH IS HEIR TO...
SNIFF 'TIS A CONSUMMATION DEVOUTLY TO BE WISHED.'
TO DIE, TO SLEEP!
TO SLEEP, PERCHANCE TO DREAM: AY, THERE'S THE RUB!
.. FOR IN THAT SLEEP OF DEATH, WHAT DREAMS MAY COME WHEN WE HAVE SHUFFLED OFF THIS MORTAL COIL MUST GIVE US PAUSE."
Blink
Blink
FEEHEELINGGS
WO WO WO
YOU FINISHED THAT RIGHT UP! DID YOU LIKE IT?
LET'S NOT HAVE THIS EVER AGAIN.

IT OFFENDS THE HUMAN EGO THAT NATURE IS INDIFFERENT TO US.

NATURE DOESN'T CARE IF PEOPLE LIVE OR DIE. IT REFUSES TO BE TAMED. IT DOES WHATEVER IT WANTS AND ACTS LIKE PEOPLE DON'T MATTER. IT WON'T CONFIRM OUR RIGHT TO BE HERE.

THAT DRIVES PEOPLE CRAZY. WE CAN'T STAND BEING IGNORED. IT'S INSULTING AND ...HEY!

YAWWNN

I THINK THAT'S ALSO WHY SOME PEOPLE DON'T LIKE CATS.

I'M WRITING A NOVEL.

WHAT'S IT ABOUT?

IT'S ABOUT A GUY WHO FLICKS THROUGH TV CHANNELS WITH HIS REMOTE CONTROL.

THEY SAY TO WRITE WHAT YOU KNOW!

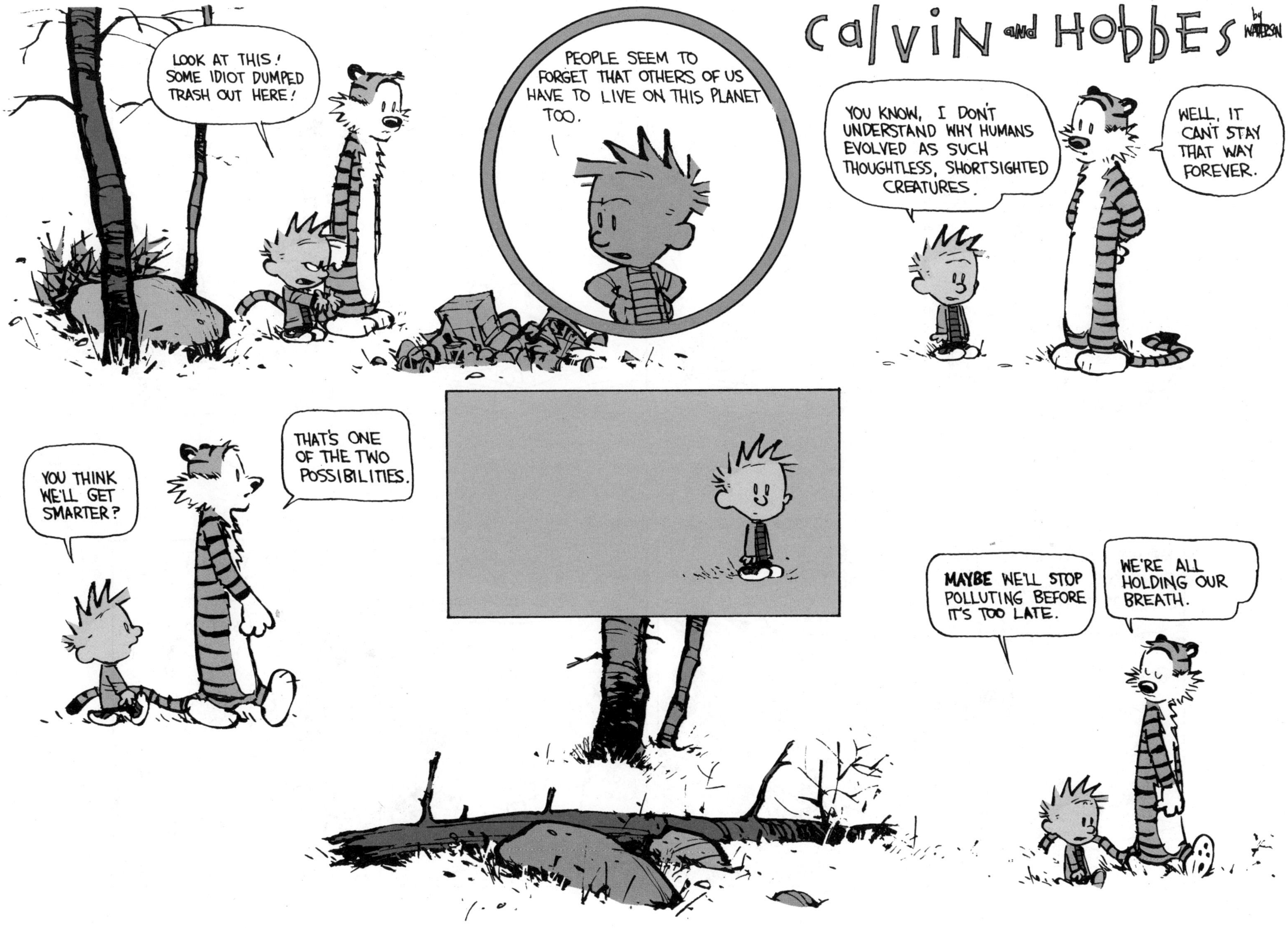
Calvin and Hobbes by Watterson
LOOK AT THIS! SOME IDIOT DUMPED TRASH OUT HERE!
PEOPLE SEEM TO FORGET THAT OTHERS OF US HAVE TO LIVE ON THIS PLANET TOO.
YOU KNOW, I DON'T UNDERSTAND WHY HUMANS EVOLVED AS SUCH THOUGHTLESS, SHORTSIGHTED CREATURES.
WELL, IT CAN'T STAY THAT WAY FOREVER.
YOU THINK WE'LL GET SMARTER?
THAT'S ONE OF THE TWO POSSIBILITIES.
MAYBE WE'LL STOP POLLUTING BEFORE IT'S TOO LATE.
WE'RE ALL HOLDING OUR BREATH.

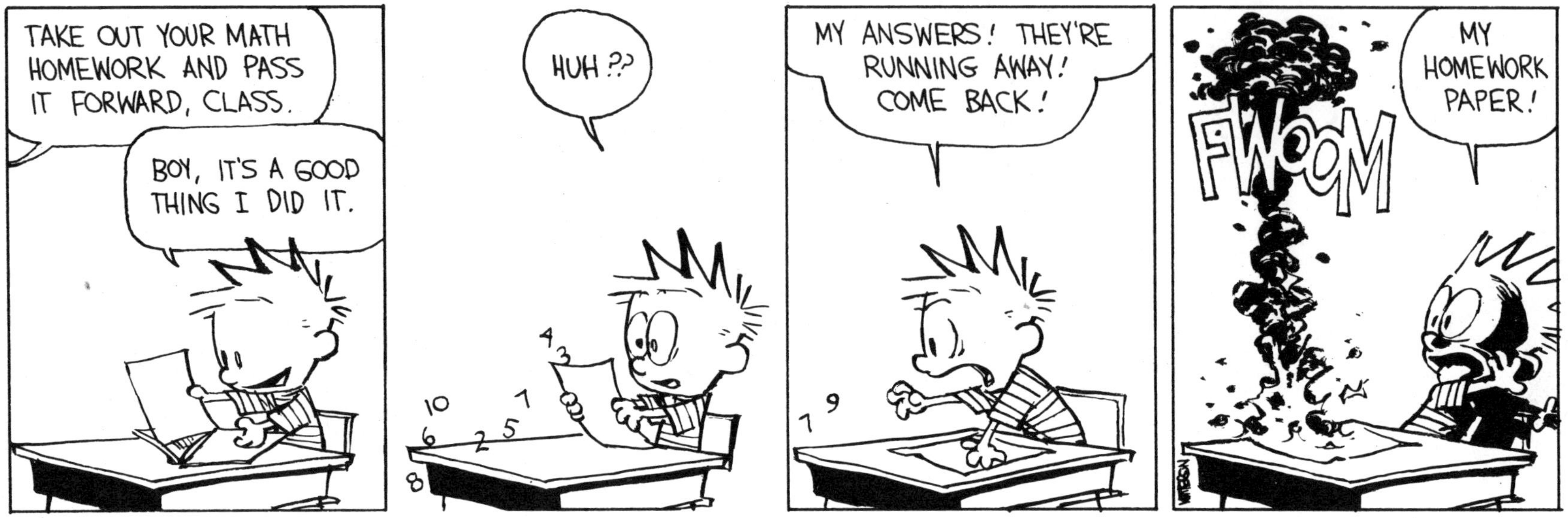
TAKE OUT YOUR MATH HOMEWORK AND PASS IT FORWARD, CLASS.
BOY, IT'S A GOOD THING I DID IT.
HUH ??
MY ANSWERS! THEY'RE RUNNING AWAY! COME BACK!
FWOOM
MY HOMEWORK PAPER!

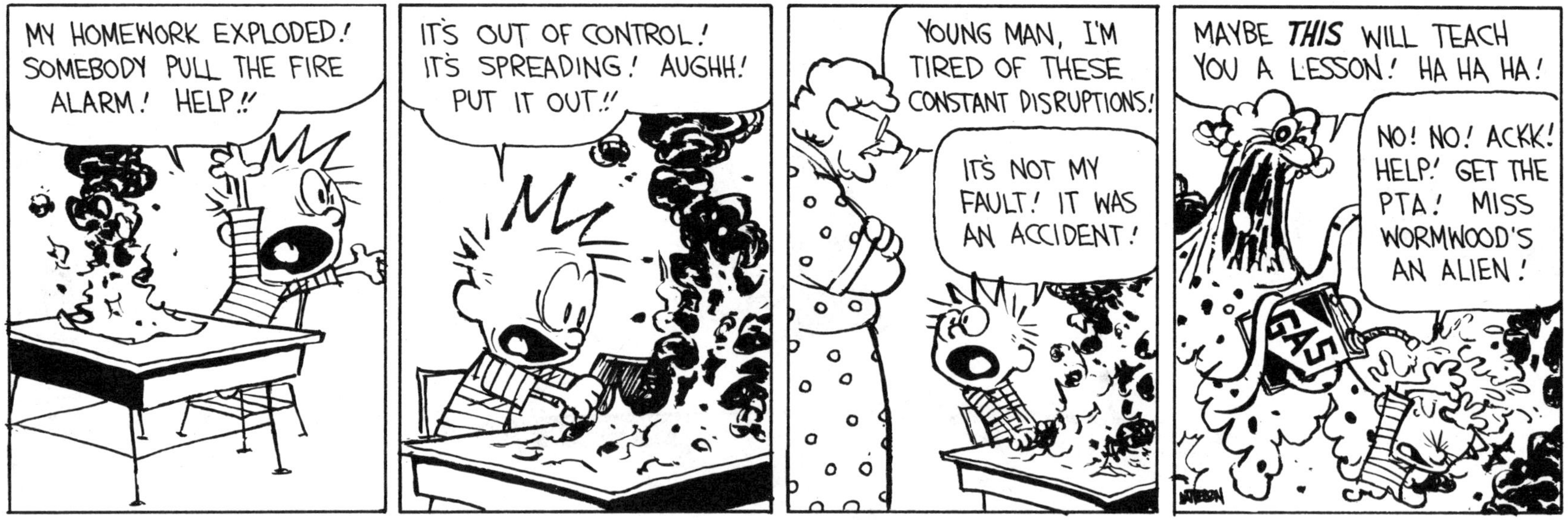
MY HOMEWORK EXPLODED! SOMEBODY PULL THE FIRE ALARM! HELP!!
IT'S OUT OF CONTROL! IT'S SPREADING! AUGHH! PUT IT OUT!!
YOUNG MAN, I'M TIRED OF THESE CONSTANT DISRUPTIONS!
IT'S NOT MY FAULT! IT WAS AN ACCIDENT!
MAYBE **THIS** WILL TEACH YOU A LESSON! HA HA HA!
NO! NO! ACKK! HELP! GET THE PTA! MISS WORMWOOD'S AN ALIEN!
GAS

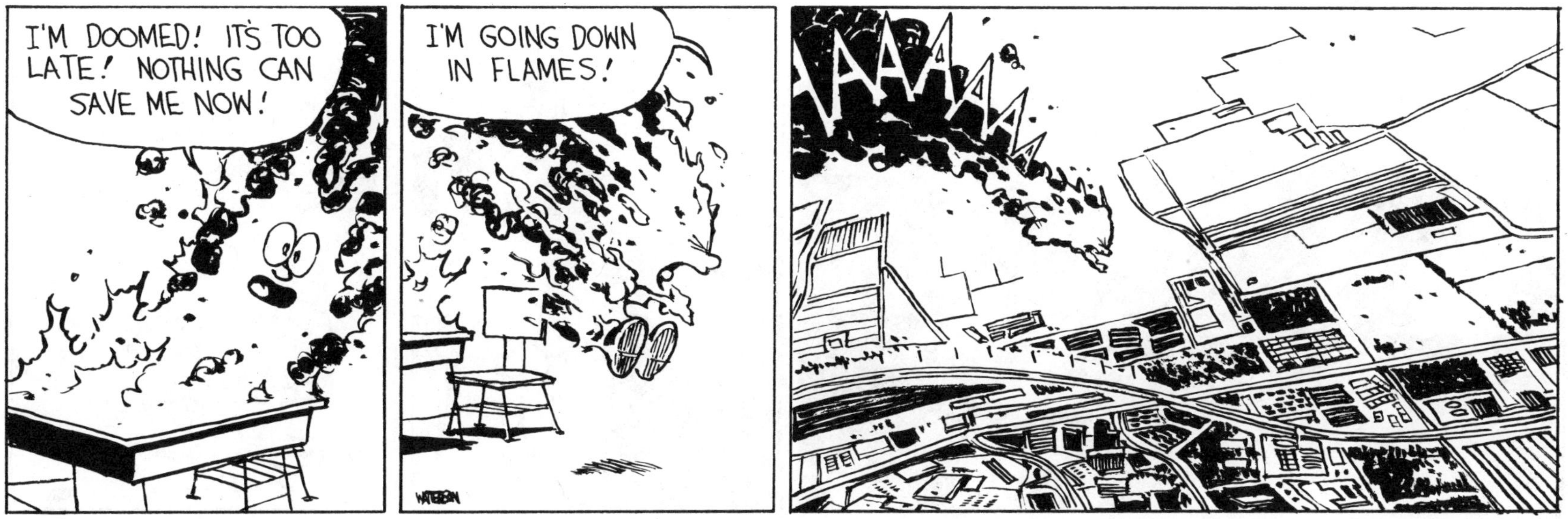
I'M DOOMED! IT'S TOO LATE! NOTHING CAN SAVE ME NOW!
I'M GOING DOWN IN FLAMES!

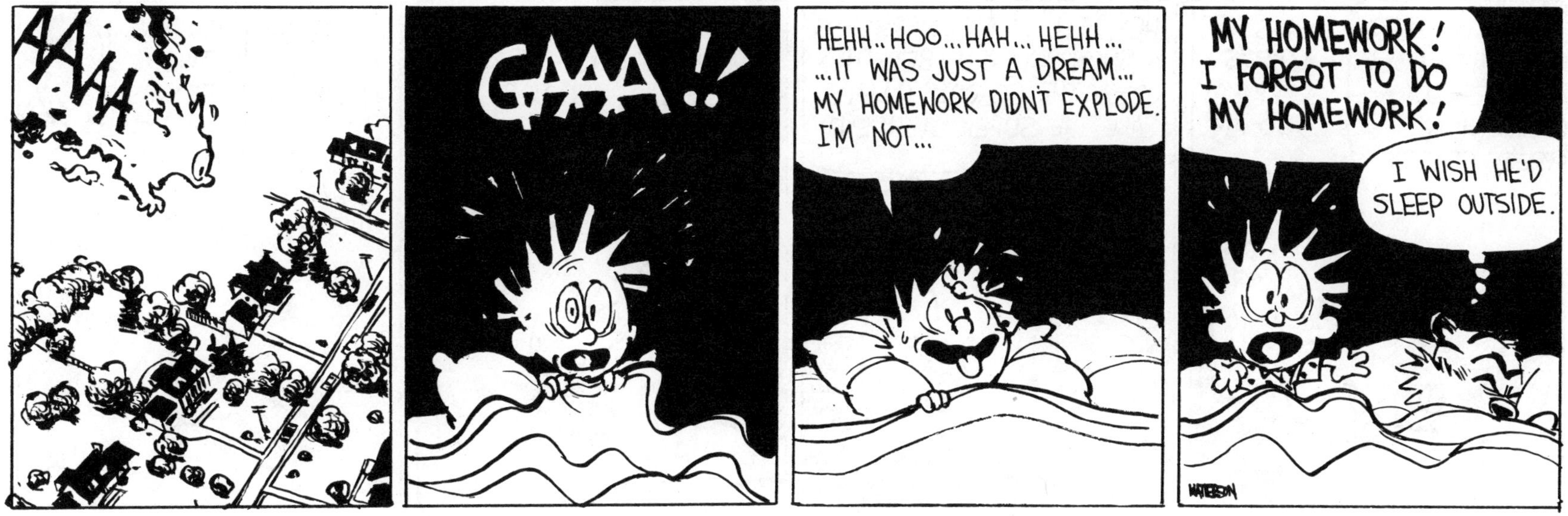
GAAA!!
HEHH.. HOO... HAH... HEHH... ...IT WAS JUST A DREAM... MY HOMEWORK DIDN'T EXPLODE. I'M NOT...
MY HOMEWORK! I FORGOT TO DO MY HOMEWORK!
I WISH HE'D SLEEP OUTSIDE.

HOBBES, WAKE UP! I FORGOT TO DO MY MATH HOMEWORK!
IT'S TWO IN THE MORNING.
BUT MISS WORMWOOD'S GOING TO COLLECT IT TOMORROW! IF I DON'T HAVE IT, SHE'LL KILL ME! I HAD A NIGHTMARE ABOUT IT!
C'MON, WE'LL HAVE TO DO THE ASSIGNMENT NOW, WHILE THERE'S STILL TIME!
THIS FEELS LIKE A NIGHTMARE TOO.
DO YOU THINK IF WE WOKE UP MOM, SHE'D LET US HAVE COFFEE?

WOW, LISTEN TO THE WIND HOWL. IT'S REALLY SNOWING! PRETTY CREEPY.
THINGS ARE **ALWAYS** CREEPY AT 2:00 AM.
HEY, I'LL BET TOMORROW'S A SNOW DAY! I'LL BET THEY CLOSE THE SCHOOLS! LET'S CALL THE SUPERINTENDENT AND SEE!
IF TOMORROW'S A SNOW DAY, WE CAN GO RIGHT BACK TO BED!
..OR MAYBE WE WILL ANYWAY.
WHO *IS* THIS?!?
YOU HAVE TWO SECONDS TO IMPROVE MY MOOD.

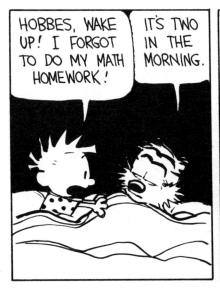

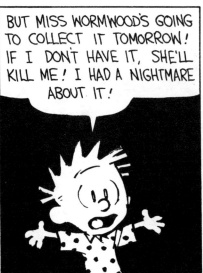

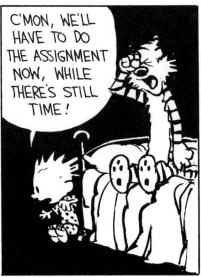

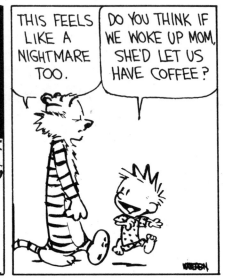

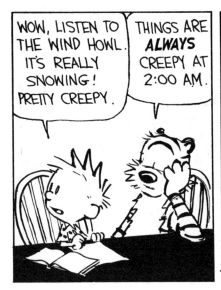

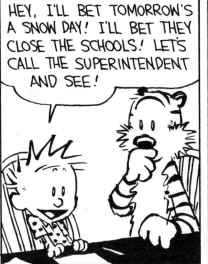

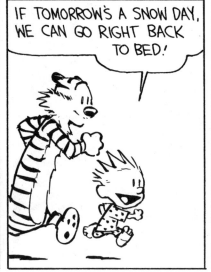

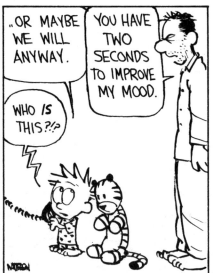

TIME TO GET UP, CALVIN.

IS IT A SNOW DAY? DID THEY CLOSE THE SCHOOLS?

I'VE GOT THE RADIO ON, SO WE'LL HEAR. GET READY ANYWAY, THOUGH.

OH MAN, I HOPE I HOPE I HOPE!

IF SCHOOL'S CLOSED, I'LL HAVE THE WHOLE DAY TO DO THE MATH HOMEWORK I FORGOT YESTERDAY. IF SCHOOL'S OPEN, I'M IN BIG TROUBLE.

SUDDENLY I FEEL EXTREMELY RELIGIOUS.

ANOTHER DEATHBED CONVERSION.

HA HA! THEY JUST ANNOUNCED THE SCHOOLS ARE CLOSED! IT'S A SNOW DAY! WHEEEEEEE!

YES! YES! YES! YES!

TALK ABOUT LUCK! NOW YOU CAN DO YOUR HOMEWORK AND YOU WON'T GET IN TROUBLE!

RIGHT, BUT THERE'S OVER TWO FEET OF SNOW THAT REQUIRES OUR IMMEDIATE AND UNDIVIDED ATTENTION.

FIRST THINGS FIRST.

MATH WILL STILL BE THERE WHEN THE SNOW MELTS.

DON'T YOU THINK YOU'D ENJOY THIS MORE IF YOU DID YOUR MATH ASSIGNMENT FIRST, SO IT WASN'T HANGING OVER YOUR HEAD?

I'M A PRACTICAL MAN, HOBBES. I DON'T WASTE TIME THINKING ABOUT HYPOTHETICAL SITUATIONS. I DEAL WITH THE WORLD HERE AND NOW.

AND THE INCONTROVERTIBLE FACT IS THAT I'M OUTSIDE IN THE SNOW! *THAT'S* REALITY! *THAT'S* WHAT I THINK ABOUT!

TOMORROW'S A REALITY TOO.

HYPOTHETICALLY, IT MIGHT BE ANOTHER SNOW DAY.

WHAT A BUSY DAY! I'M POOPED!

MOM SAYS THE ROADS ARE PRETTY CLEAR, SO SCHOOL WILL PROBABLY OPEN AGAIN TOMORROW.

NOW I WISH I'D DONE MY MATH HOMEWORK INSTEAD OF PLAYING OUTSIDE ALL DAY.

...OR I WISH I'D DONE IT BEFORE DINNER... OR AFTER DINNER... OR INSTEAD OF WATCHING TV... OR BEFORE BED. BUT NOW IT'S TOO LATE.

A DAY CAN REALLY SLIP BY WHEN YOU'RE DELIBERATELY AVOIDING WHAT YOU'RE SUPPOSED TO DO.

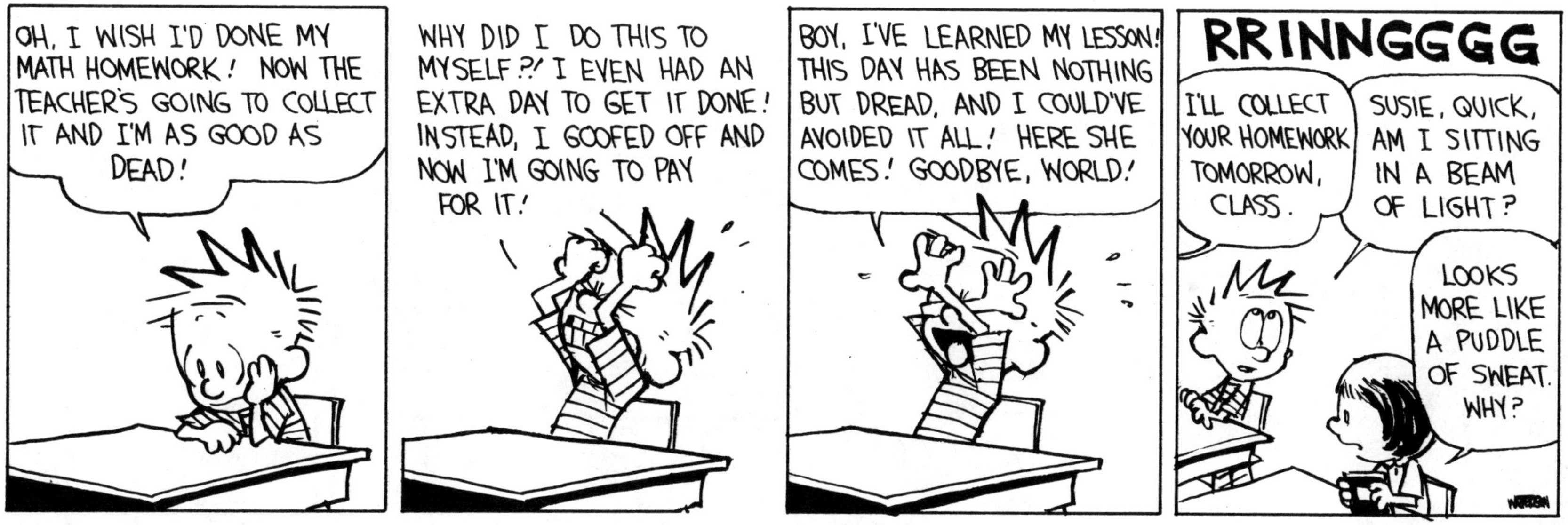
OH, I WISH I'D DONE MY MATH HOMEWORK! NOW THE TEACHER'S GOING TO COLLECT IT AND I'M AS GOOD AS DEAD!
WHY DID I DO THIS TO MYSELF?!' I EVEN HAD AN EXTRA DAY TO GET IT DONE! INSTEAD, I GOOFED OFF AND NOW I'M GOING TO PAY FOR IT!
BOY, I'VE LEARNED MY LESSON! THIS DAY HAS BEEN NOTHING BUT DREAD, AND I COULD'VE AVOIDED IT ALL! HERE SHE COMES! GOODBYE, WORLD!
RRINNGGGG
I'LL COLLECT YOUR HOMEWORK TOMORROW, CLASS.
SUSIE, QUICK, AM I SITTING IN A BEAM OF LIGHT?
LOOKS MORE LIKE A PUDDLE OF SWEAT. WHY?

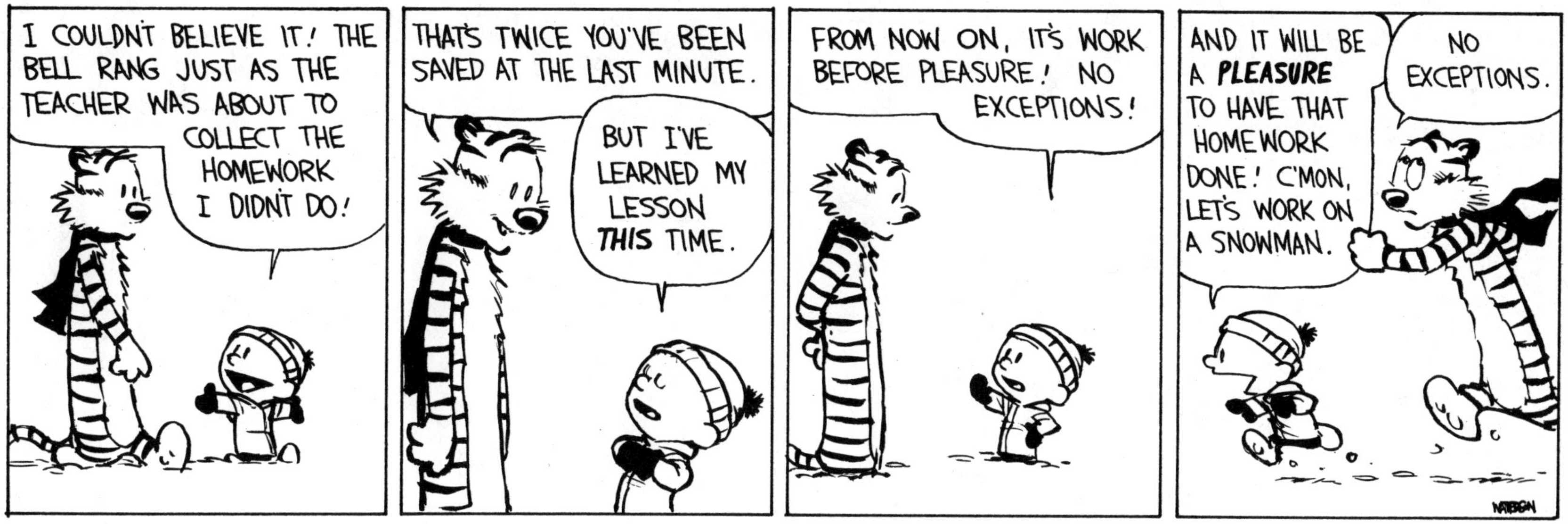
I COULDN'T BELIEVE IT! THE BELL RANG JUST AS THE TEACHER WAS ABOUT TO COLLECT THE HOMEWORK I DIDN'T DO!
THAT'S TWICE YOU'VE BEEN SAVED AT THE LAST MINUTE.
BUT I'VE LEARNED MY LESSON THIS TIME.
FROM NOW ON, IT'S WORK BEFORE PLEASURE! NO EXCEPTIONS!
AND IT WILL BE A PLEASURE TO HAVE THAT HOMEWORK DONE! C'MON, LET'S WORK ON A SNOWMAN.
NO EXCEPTIONS.

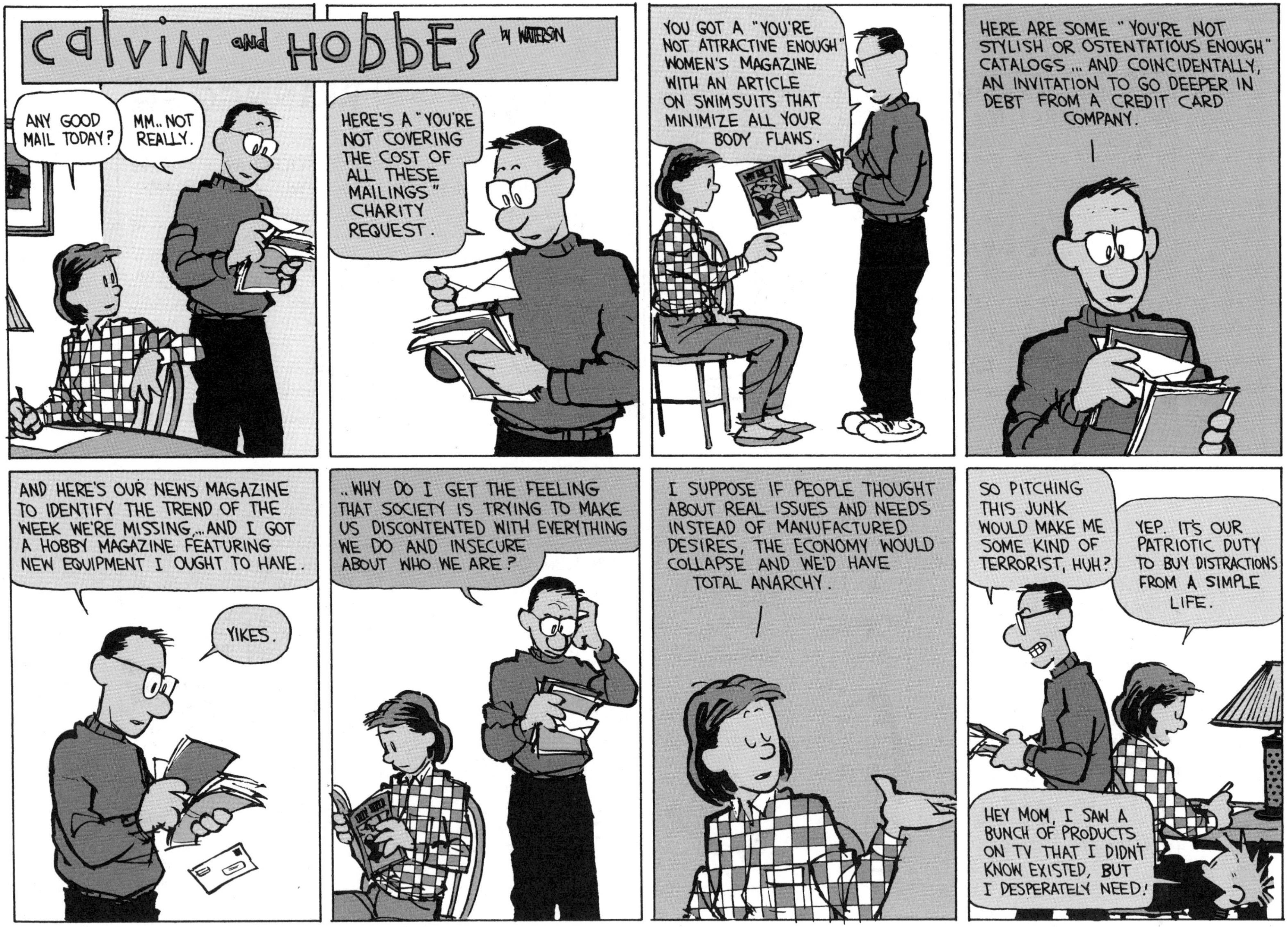
Calvin and Hobbes by WATTERSON
ANY GOOD MAIL TODAY?
MM.. NOT REALLY.
HERE'S A "YOU'RE NOT COVERING THE COST OF ALL THESE MAILINGS" CHARITY REQUEST.
YOU GOT A "YOU'RE NOT ATTRACTIVE ENOUGH" WOMEN'S MAGAZINE WITH AN ARTICLE ON SWIMSUITS THAT MINIMIZE ALL YOUR BODY FLAWS.
HERE ARE SOME "YOU'RE NOT STYLISH OR OSTENTATIOUS ENOUGH" CATALOGS ... AND COINCIDENTALLY, AN INVITATION TO GO DEEPER IN DEBT FROM A CREDIT CARD COMPANY.
AND HERE'S OUR NEWS MAGAZINE TO IDENTIFY THE TREND OF THE WEEK WE'RE MISSING,... AND I GOT A HOBBY MAGAZINE FEATURING NEW EQUIPMENT I OUGHT TO HAVE.
YIKES.
..WHY DO I GET THE FEELING THAT SOCIETY IS TRYING TO MAKE US DISCONTENTED WITH EVERYTHING WE DO AND INSECURE ABOUT WHO WE ARE?
I SUPPOSE IF PEOPLE THOUGHT ABOUT REAL ISSUES AND NEEDS INSTEAD OF MANUFACTURED DESIRES, THE ECONOMY WOULD COLLAPSE AND WE'D HAVE TOTAL ANARCHY.
SO PITCHING THIS JUNK WOULD MAKE ME SOME KIND OF TERRORIST, HUH?
YEP. IT'S OUR PATRIOTIC DUTY TO BUY DISTRACTIONS FROM A SIMPLE LIFE.
HEY MOM, I SAW A BUNCH OF PRODUCTS ON TV THAT I DIDN'T KNOW EXISTED, BUT I DESPERATELY NEED!

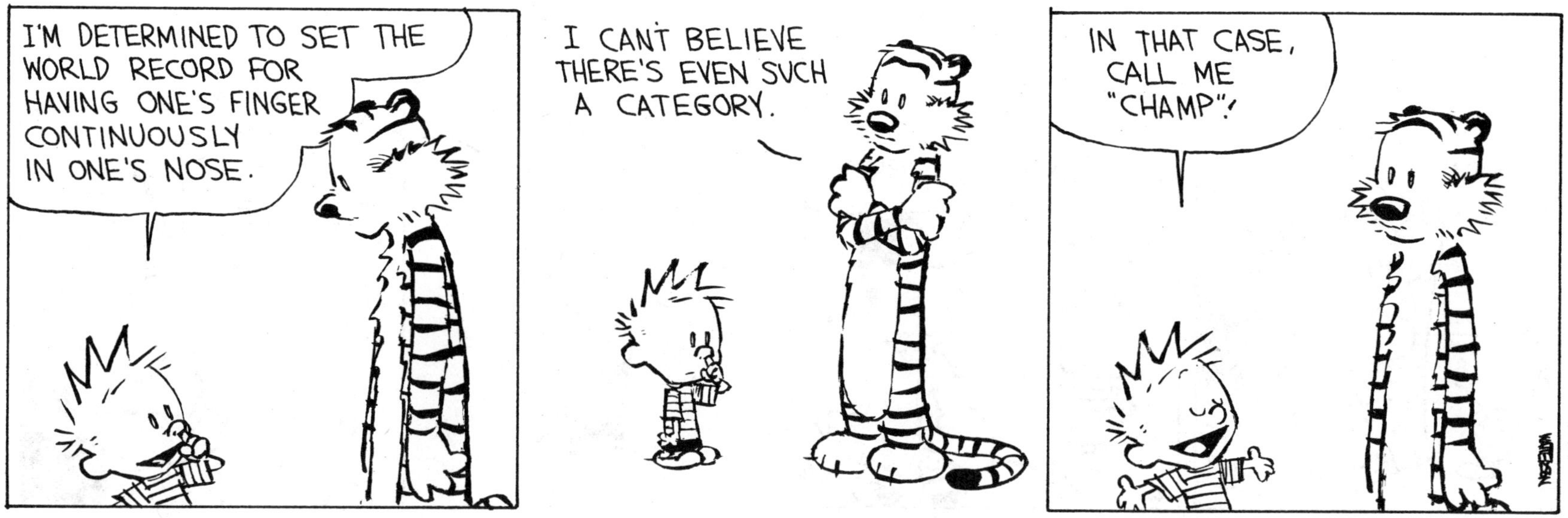
I'M DETERMINED TO SET THE WORLD RECORD FOR HAVING ONE'S FINGER CONTINUOUSLY IN ONE'S NOSE.
I CAN'T BELIEVE THERE'S EVEN SUCH A CATEGORY.
IN THAT CASE, CALL ME "CHAMP"!

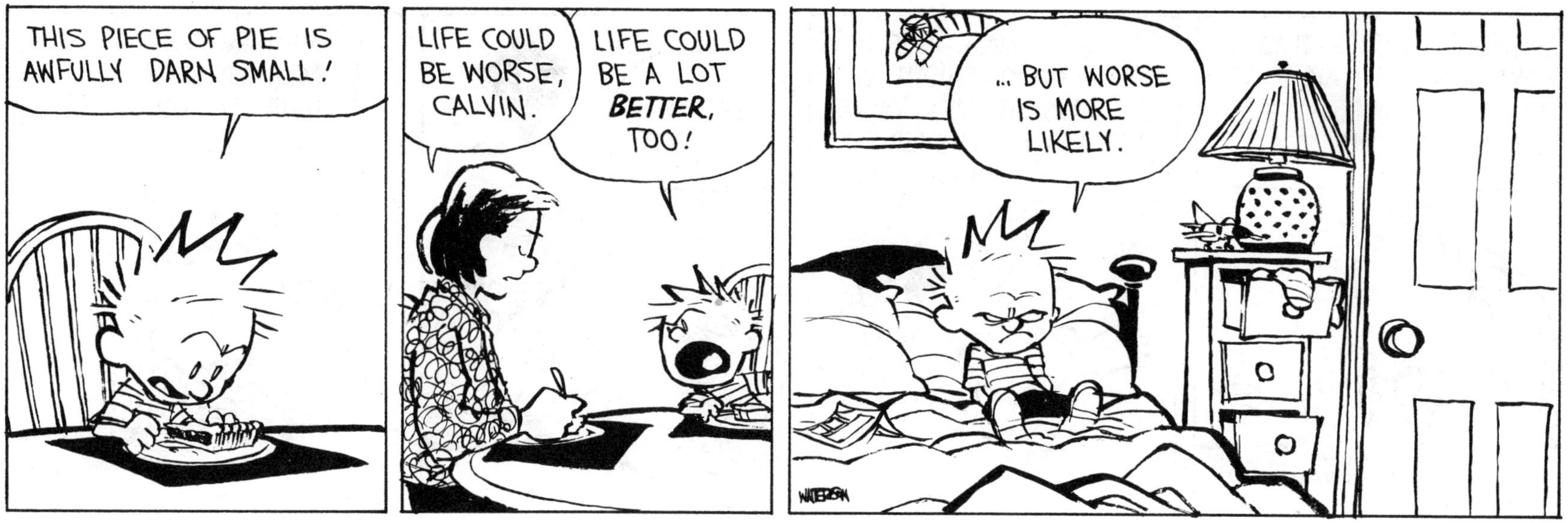
THIS PIECE OF PIE IS AWFULLY DARN SMALL!
LIFE COULD BE WORSE, CALVIN.
LIFE COULD BE A LOT **BETTER**, TOO!
... BUT WORSE IS MORE LIKELY.

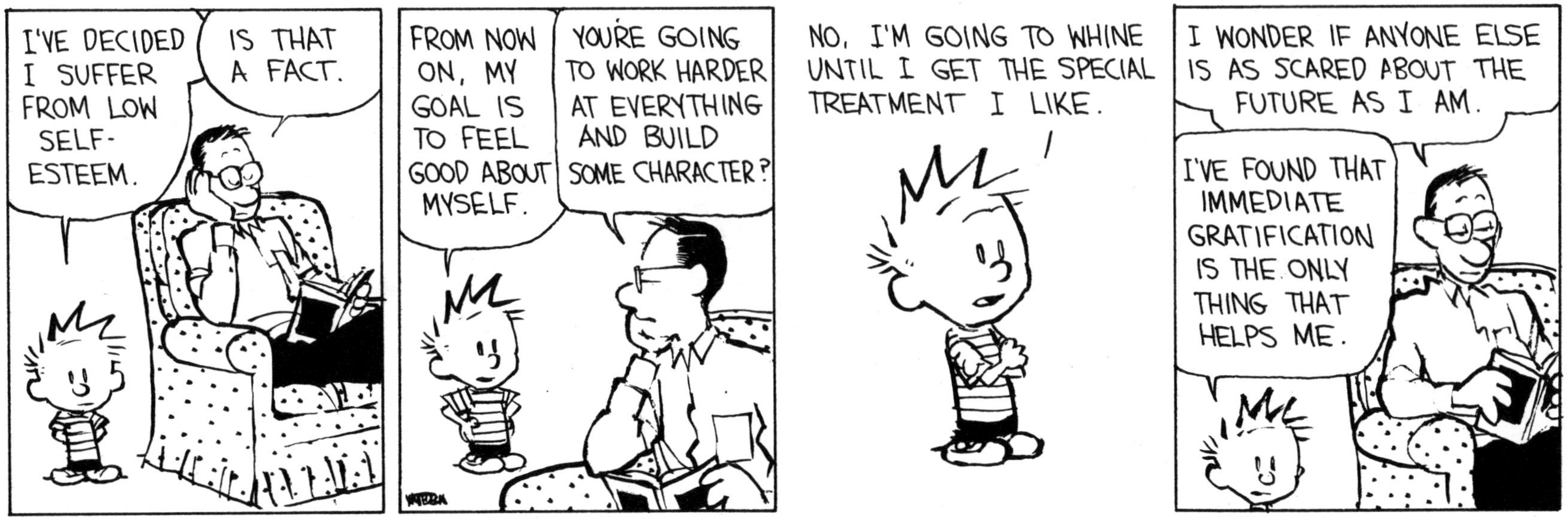
I'VE DECIDED I SUFFER FROM LOW SELF-ESTEEM.
IS THAT A FACT.
FROM NOW ON, MY GOAL IS TO FEEL GOOD ABOUT MYSELF.
YOU'RE GOING TO WORK HARDER AT EVERYTHING AND BUILD SOME CHARACTER?
NO, I'M GOING TO WHINE UNTIL I GET THE SPECIAL TREATMENT I LIKE.
I WONDER IF ANYONE ELSE IS AS SCARED ABOUT THE FUTURE AS I AM.
I'VE FOUND THAT IMMEDIATE GRATIFICATION IS THE ONLY THING THAT HELPS ME.

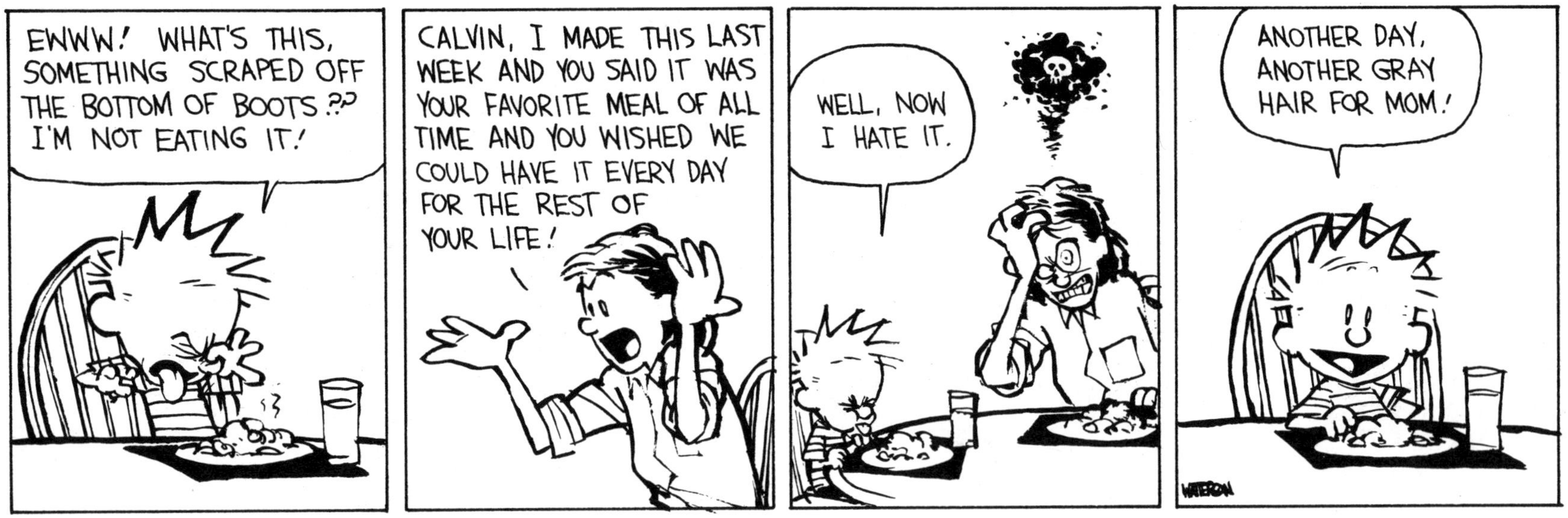
EWWW! WHAT'S THIS, SOMETHING SCRAPED OFF THE BOTTOM OF BOOTS?? I'M NOT EATING IT!
CALVIN, I MADE THIS LAST WEEK AND YOU SAID IT WAS YOUR FAVORITE MEAL OF ALL TIME AND YOU WISHED WE COULD HAVE IT EVERY DAY FOR THE REST OF YOUR LIFE!
WELL, NOW I HATE IT.
ANOTHER DAY, ANOTHER GRAY HAIR FOR MOM!

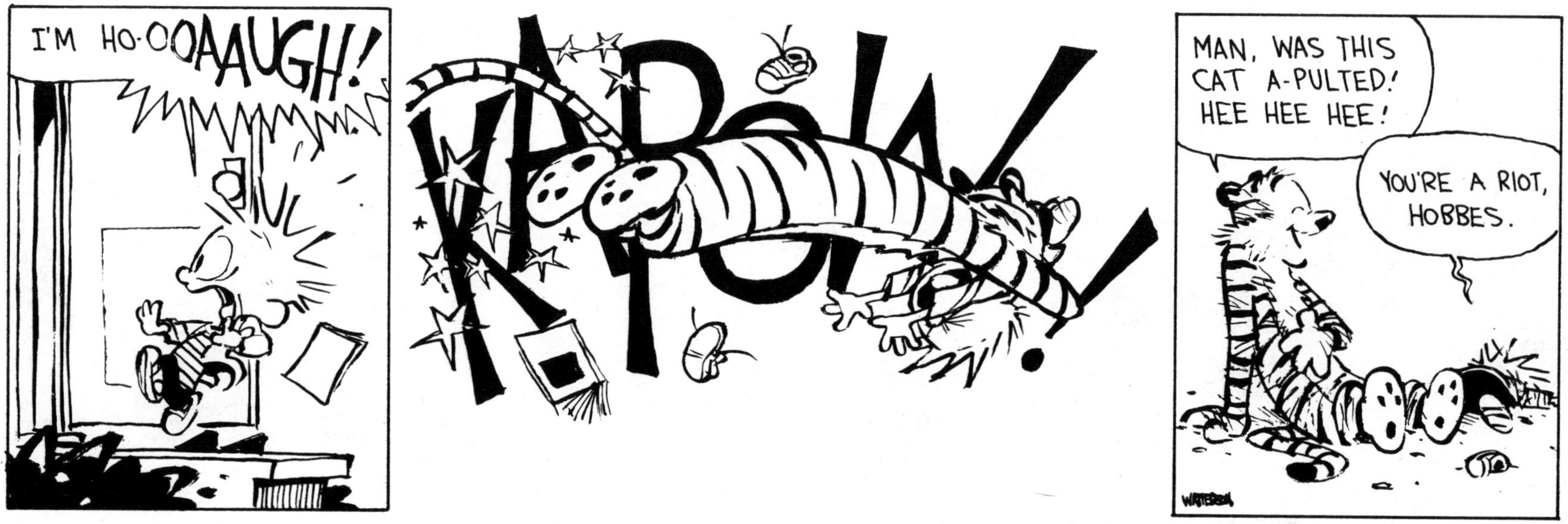
I'M HO-OOAAUGH!
KAPOW!
MAN, WAS THIS CAT A-PULTED! HEE HEE HEE!
YOU'RE A RIOT, HOBBES.

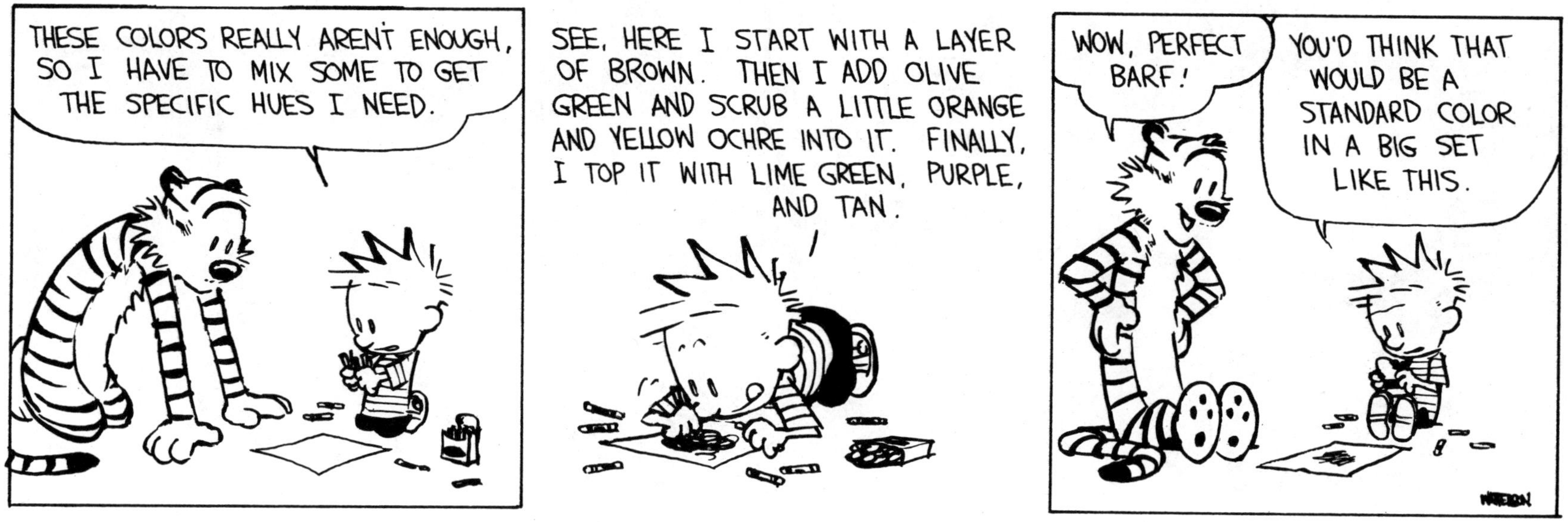
THESE COLORS REALLY AREN'T ENOUGH, SO I HAVE TO MIX SOME TO GET THE SPECIFIC HUES I NEED.
SEE, HERE I START WITH A LAYER OF BROWN. THEN I ADD OLIVE GREEN AND SCRUB A LITTLE ORANGE AND YELLOW OCHRE INTO IT. FINALLY, I TOP IT WITH LIME GREEN, PURPLE, AND TAN.
WOW, PERFECT BARF!
YOU'D THINK THAT WOULD BE A STANDARD COLOR IN A BIG SET LIKE THIS.

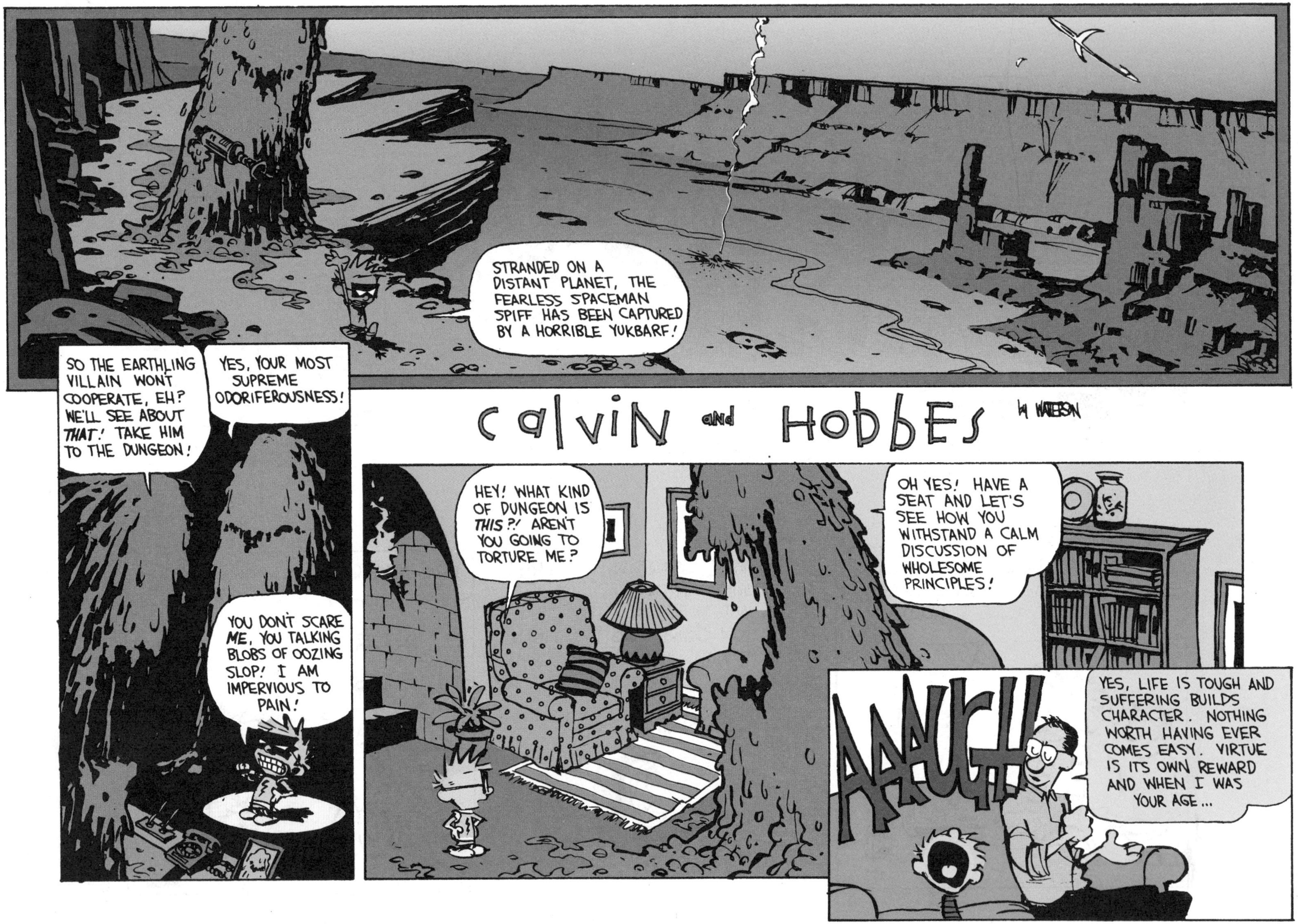

STRANDED ON A DISTANT PLANET, THE FEARLESS SPACEMAN SPIFF HAS BEEN CAPTURED BY A HORRIBLE YUKBARF!
SO THE EARTHLING VILLAIN WON'T COOPERATE, EH? WE'LL SEE ABOUT THAT! TAKE HIM TO THE DUNGEON!
YES, YOUR MOST SUPREME ODORIFEROUSNESS!
YOU DON'T SCARE ME, YOU TALKING BLOBS OF OOZING SLOP! I AM IMPERVIOUS TO PAIN!
calvin and HOBBES by WATERSON
HEY! WHAT KIND OF DUNGEON IS THIS?! AREN'T YOU GOING TO TORTURE ME?
OH YES! HAVE A SEAT AND LET'S SEE HOW YOU WITHSTAND A CALM DISCUSSION OF WHOLESOME PRINCIPLES!
AAAUGH!!
YES, LIFE IS TOUGH AND SUFFERING BUILDS CHARACTER. NOTHING WORTH HAVING EVER COMES EASY. VIRTUE IS ITS OWN REWARD AND WHEN I WAS YOUR AGE...

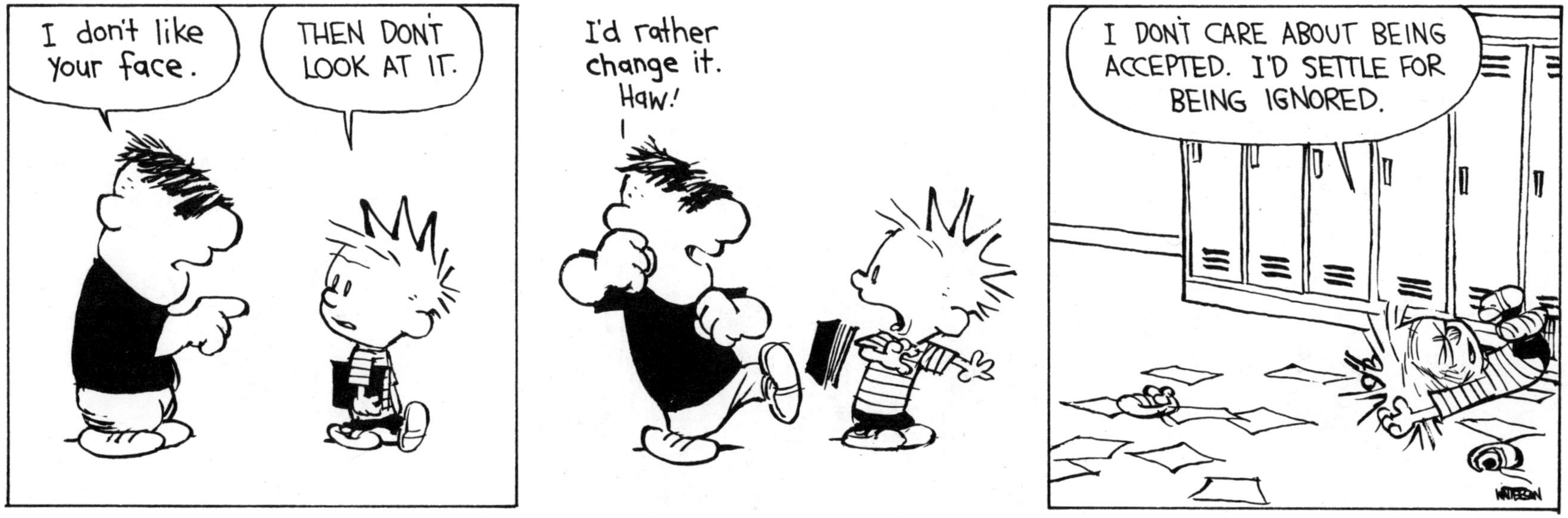
I don't like your face.
THEN DON'T LOOK AT IT.
I'd rather change it. Haw!
I DON'T CARE ABOUT BEING ACCEPTED. I'D SETTLE FOR BEING IGNORED.

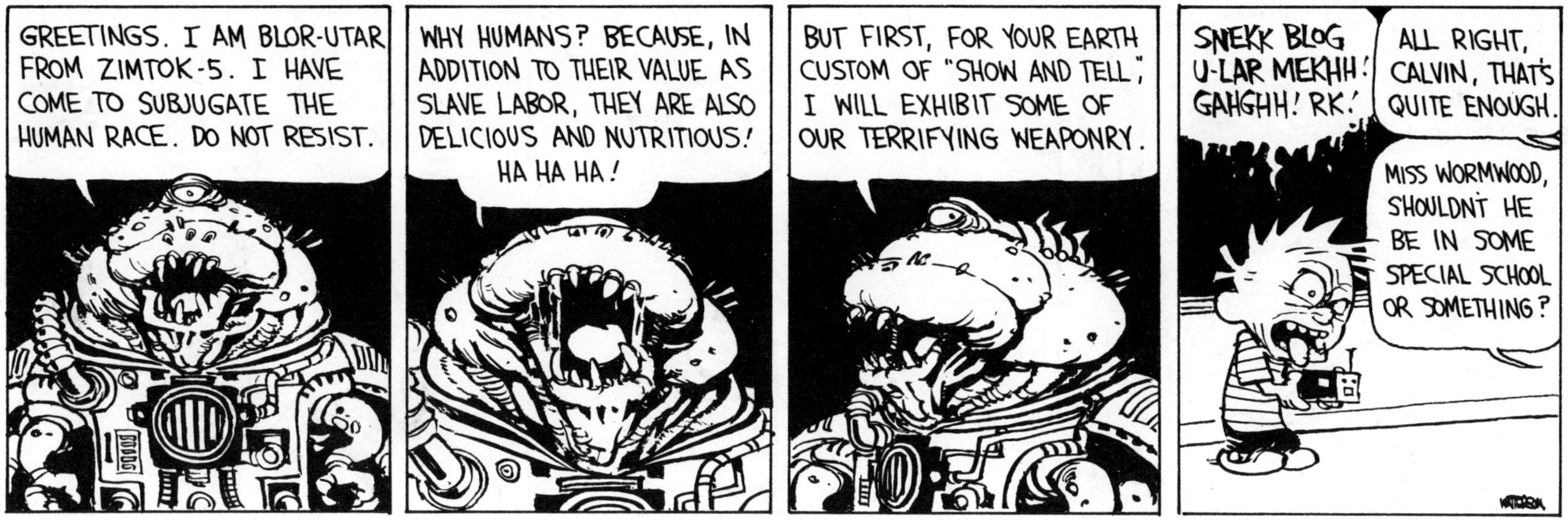
GREETINGS. I AM BLOR-UTAR FROM ZIMTOK-5. I HAVE COME TO SUBJUGATE THE HUMAN RACE. DO NOT RESIST.
WHY HUMANS? BECAUSE, IN ADDITION TO THEIR VALUE AS SLAVE LABOR, THEY ARE ALSO DELICIOUS AND NUTRITIOUS! HA HA HA!
BUT FIRST, FOR YOUR EARTH CUSTOM OF "SHOW AND TELL," I WILL EXHIBIT SOME OF OUR TERRIFYING WEAPONRY.
SNEKK BLOG U-LAR MEKHH! GAHGHH! RK!
ALL RIGHT, CALVIN, THAT'S QUITE ENOUGH.
MISS WORMWOOD, SHOULDN'T HE BE IN SOME SPECIAL SCHOOL OR SOMETHING?

WHEN IT SNOWS, YOU CAN GO
SLEDDING. WHEN IT'S WINDY,
YOU CAN FLY KITES. WHEN IT'S
HOT, YOU CAN GO SWIMMING.

BUT WHEN IT'S
RAINING... SIGH...

..THE ONLY SPORT IS DRIVING
MOM CRAZY.

I THOUGHT I
HAD A GREAT
IDEA, BUT IT
NEVER REALLY
TOOK OFF.

IN FACT, IT
DIDN'T EVEN
GET ON THE
RUNWAY.

I GUESS YOU
COULD SAY IT
EXPLODED IN
THE HANGAR.

I'VE HAD IDEAS
LIKE THAT.

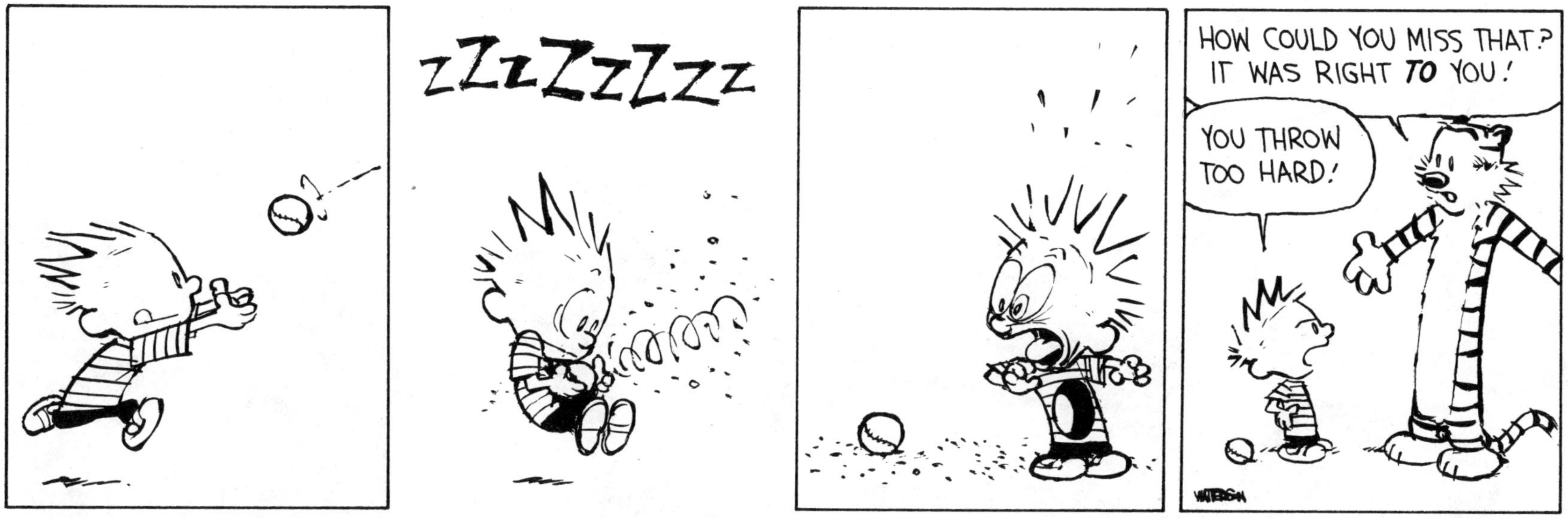
zZzZzZzz
HOW COULD YOU MISS THAT? IT WAS RIGHT TO YOU!
YOU THROW TOO HARD!

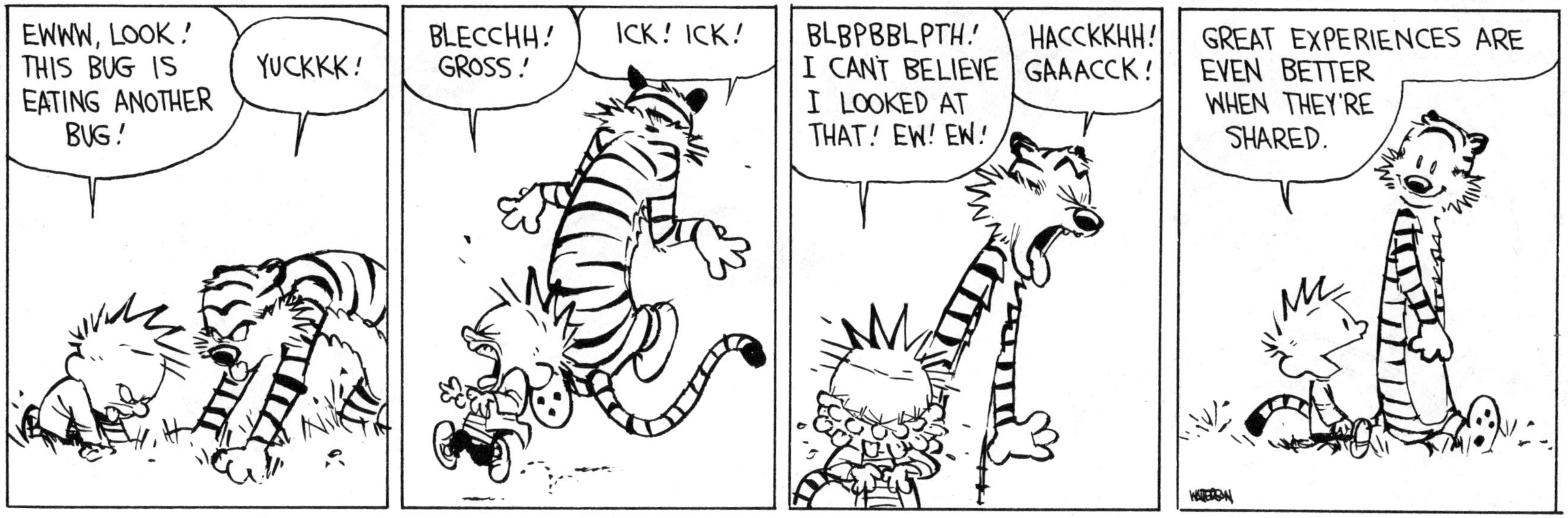
EWWW, LOOK! THIS BUG IS EATING ANOTHER BUG!
YUCKKK!
BLECCHH! GROSS!
ICK! ICK!
BLBPBBLPTH! I CAN'T BELIEVE I LOOKED AT THAT! EW! EW!
HACCKKHH! GAAACCK!
GREAT EXPERIENCES ARE EVEN BETTER WHEN THEY'RE SHARED.

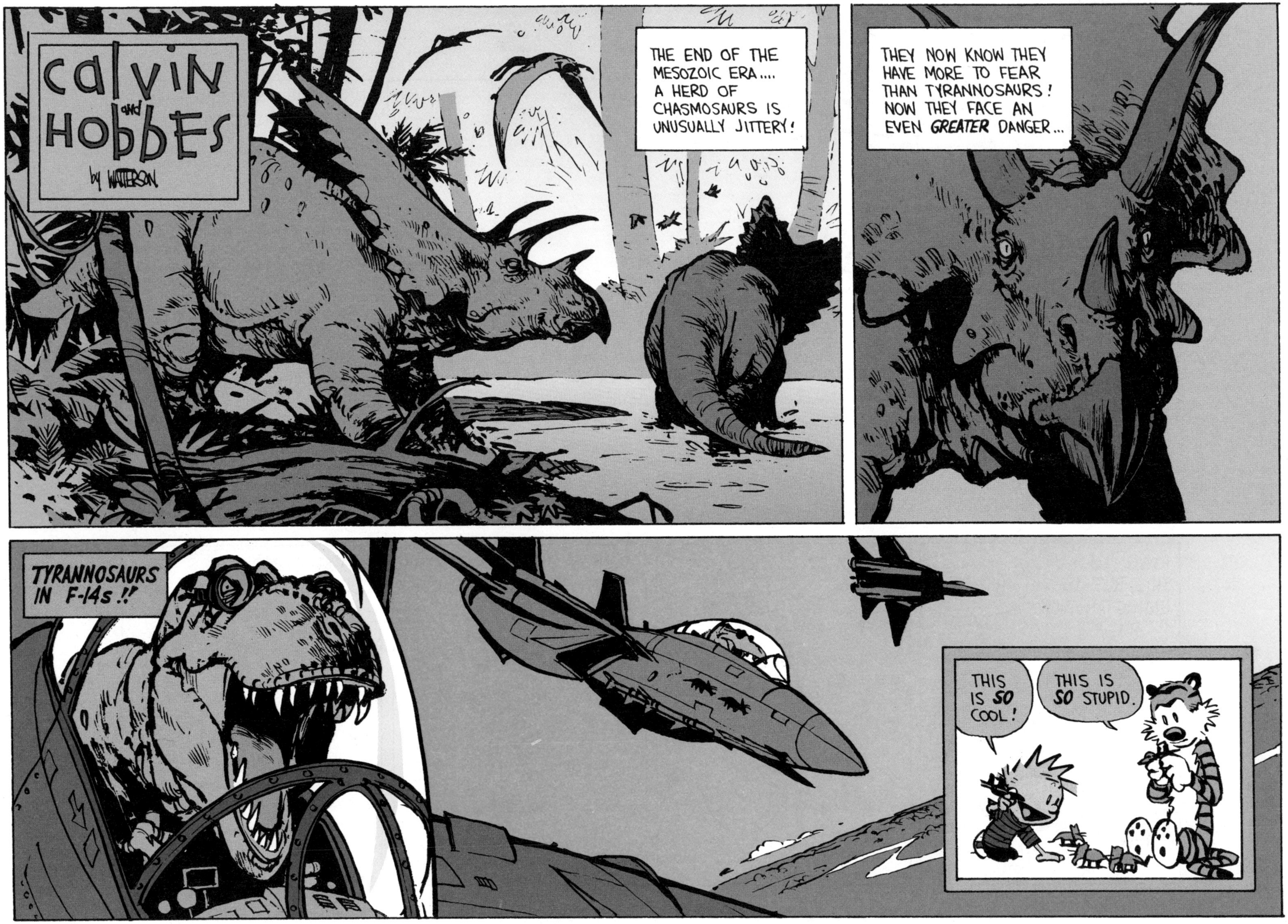
Calvin and Hobbes
by WATTERSON
THE END OF THE MESOZOIC ERA.... A HERD OF CHASMOSAURS IS UNUSUALLY JITTERY!
THEY NOW KNOW THEY HAVE MORE TO FEAR THAN TYRANNOSAURS! NOW THEY FACE AN EVEN **GREATER** DANGER...
TYRANNOSAURS IN F-14s!!
THIS IS **SO** COOL!
THIS IS **SO** STUPID.

HOW ARE YOU DOING ON YOUR NEW YEAR'S RESOLUTIONS?

I DIDN'T MAKE ANY.

SEE, IN ORDER TO IMPROVE ONESELF, ONE MUST HAVE SOME IDEA OF WHAT'S "GOOD." THAT IMPLIES CERTAIN VALUES.

BUT AS WE ALL KNOW, VALUES ARE RELATIVE. EVERY SYSTEM OF BELIEF IS EQUALLY VALID AND WE NEED TO TOLERATE DIVERSITY. VIRTUE ISN'T "BETTER" THAN VICE. IT'S JUST DIFFERENT.

I DON'T KNOW IF I CAN TOLERATE THAT MUCH TOLERANCE.

I REFUSE TO BE VICTIMIZED BY NOTIONS OF VIRTUOUS BEHAVIOR.

NO! NO! NO! I NEED MORE SLEEP!

I C-CAN'T KEEP M-MY EYES OPEN!

BED?! ALREADY?? BUT I'M WIDE AWAKE!!

MY INTERNAL CLOCK IS ON TOKYO TIME.

I SURE AM GREAT! I'M ONE OF THE GREATEST PEOPLE WHO EVER LIVED!
HOW LUCKY PEOPLE ARE TO KNOW SOMEONE AS GREAT AS ME! I'M GREAT IN SO MANY GREAT WAYS! IN FACT, I'M SO GREAT THAT MY GREATNESS IS...
YOU'RE NOT GREAT! YOU'RE THE MOST CONCEITED BLOWHARD I'VE EVER MET!
WHEN YOU'RE GREAT, PEOPLE OFTEN MISTAKE CANDOR FOR BRAGGING.

HERE, I'LL HANG UP YOUR COAT.
THANKS.
IF YOU'VE BEEN LOOKING FOR HOBBES, HE SOMEHOW GOT PUT IN THE CLOSET. I JUST FOUND HIM WAY BACK IN THERE.
WAITING FOR ME IN THE **CLOSET**, EH? TOO BAD YOUR LITTLE PLAN WAS ***THWARTED***!!
WHY DON'T YOU HANG UP YOUR COAT YOURSELF?!

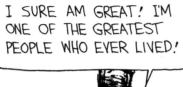

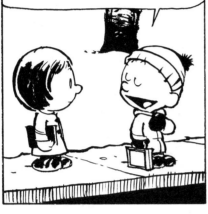

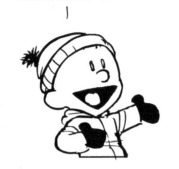

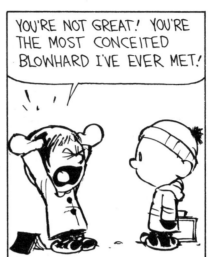

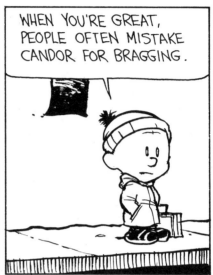

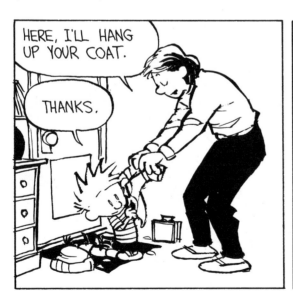

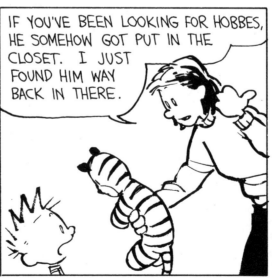

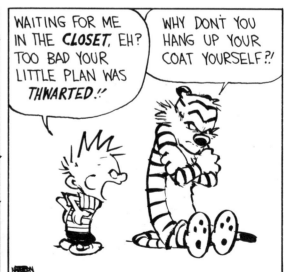

OH YEAH? DEFINE "WELL-ADJUSTED."

WHY DOES MAN CREATE?
IS IT MAN'S PURPOSE ON EARTH TO EXPRESS HIMSELF, TO BRING FORM TO THOUGHT, AND TO DISCOVER MEANING IN EXPERIENCE?
OR IS IT JUST SOMETHING TO DO WHEN HE'S BORED?

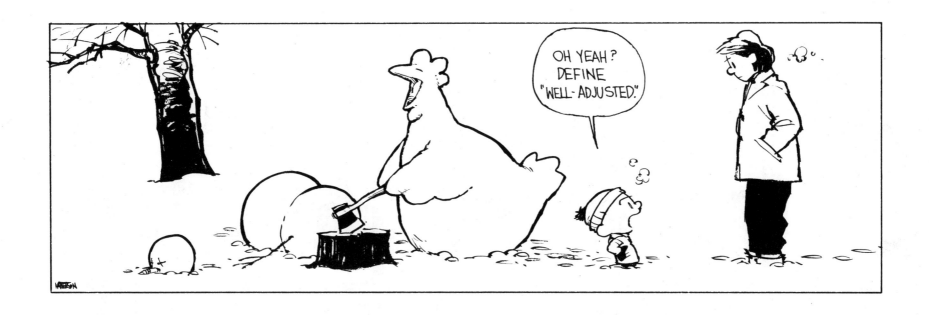

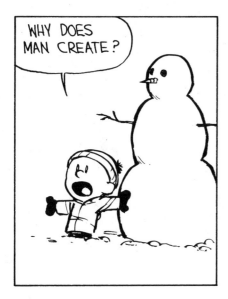

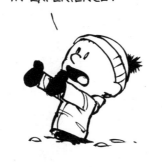

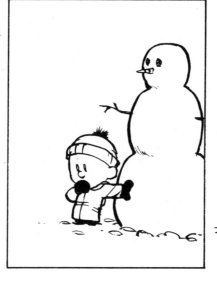

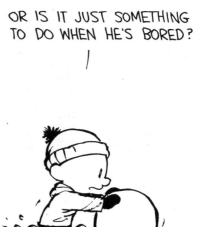

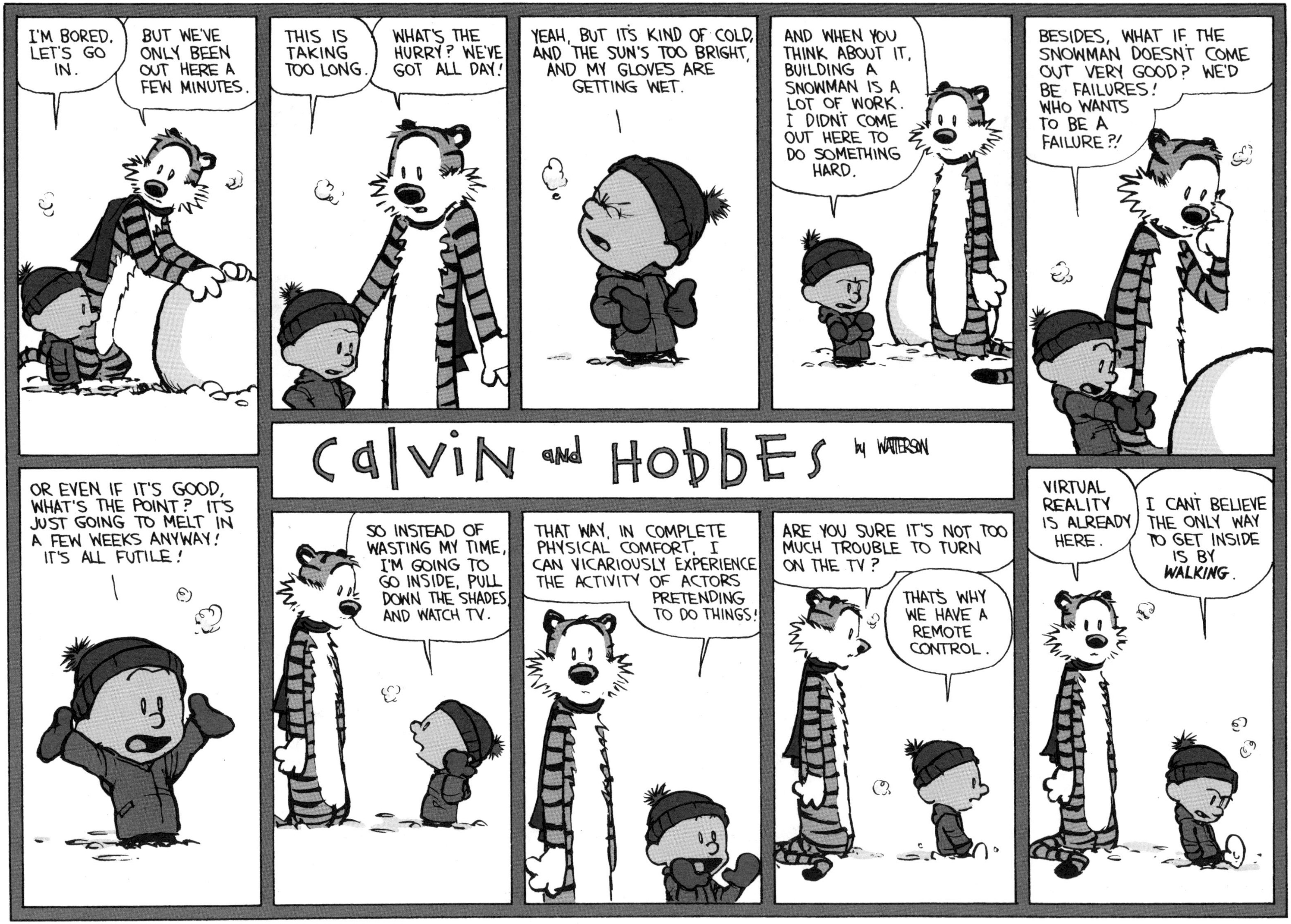
I'M BORED. LET'S GO IN.
BUT WE'VE ONLY BEEN OUT HERE A FEW MINUTES.
THIS IS TAKING TOO LONG.
WHAT'S THE HURRY? WE'VE GOT ALL DAY!
YEAH, BUT IT'S KIND OF COLD, AND THE SUN'S TOO BRIGHT, AND MY GLOVES ARE GETTING WET.
AND WHEN YOU THINK ABOUT IT, BUILDING A SNOWMAN IS A LOT OF WORK. I DIDN'T COME OUT HERE TO DO SOMETHING HARD.
BESIDES, WHAT IF THE SNOWMAN DOESN'T COME OUT VERY GOOD? WE'D BE FAILURES! WHO WANTS TO BE A FAILURE?!
CALVIN AND HOBBES
by WATTERSON
OR EVEN IF IT'S GOOD, WHAT'S THE POINT? IT'S JUST GOING TO MELT IN A FEW WEEKS ANYWAY! IT'S ALL FUTILE!
SO INSTEAD OF WASTING MY TIME, I'M GOING TO GO INSIDE, PULL DOWN THE SHADES AND WATCH TV.
THAT WAY, IN COMPLETE PHYSICAL COMFORT, I CAN VICARIOUSLY EXPERIENCE THE ACTIVITY OF ACTORS PRETENDING TO DO THINGS!
ARE YOU SURE IT'S NOT TOO MUCH TROUBLE TO TURN ON THE TV?
THAT'S WHY WE HAVE A REMOTE CONTROL.
VIRTUAL REALITY IS ALREADY HERE.
I CAN'T BELIEVE THE ONLY WAY TO GET INSIDE IS BY WALKING.

1. Explain Newton's First Law of Motion in your own words.
!
Yakka foob mog. Grug pubbawup zink wattoom gazork. Chumble spuzz.
I LOVE LOOPHOLES.
WATTERSON

I'M READY FOR ANYTHING!
ARE YOU READY FOR UNCONDITIONAL SURRENDER?
THAT ABOVE ALL ELSE.
WATTERSON

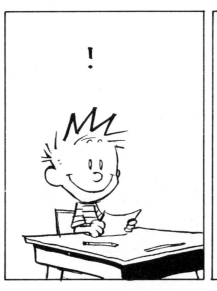

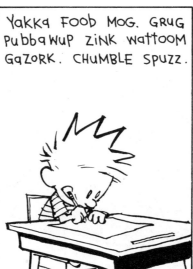

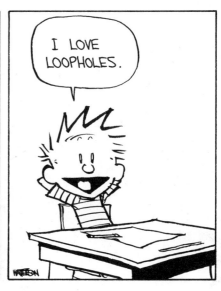

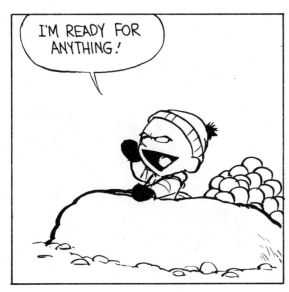

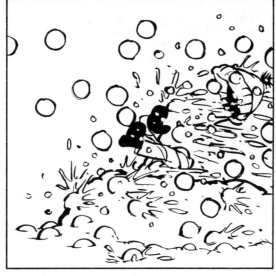

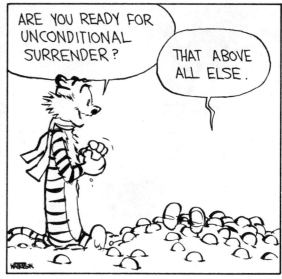

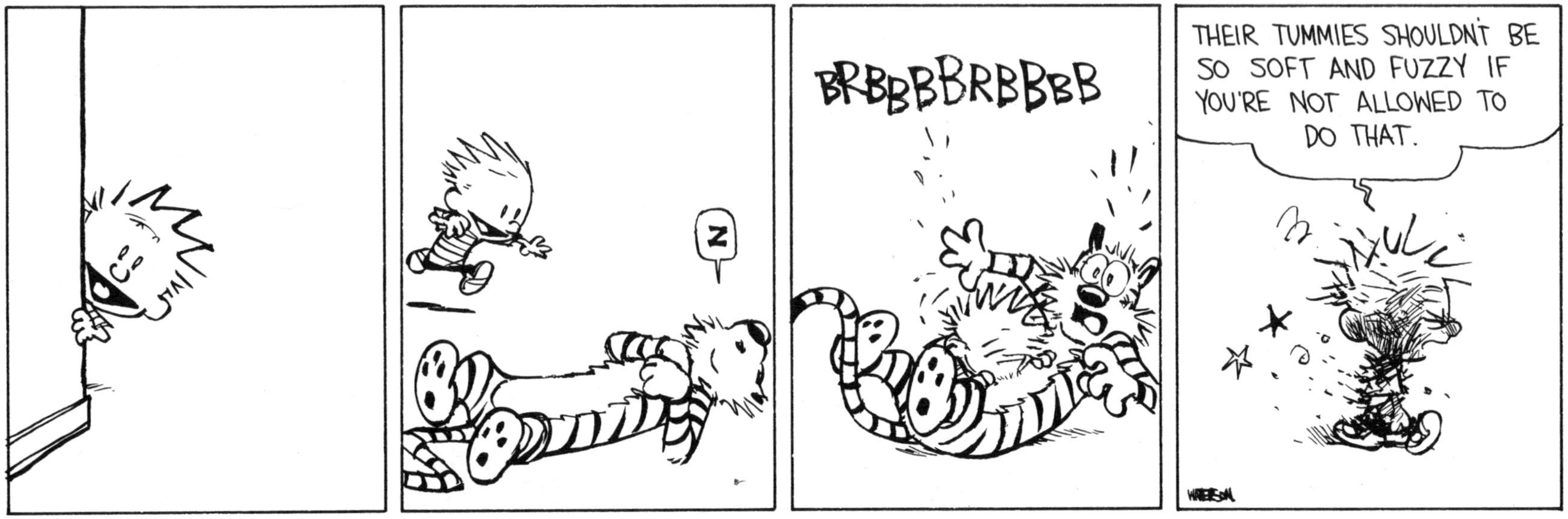
Z
BRBBBBRBBBB
THEIR TUMMIES SHOULDN'T BE SO SOFT AND FUZZY IF YOU'RE NOT ALLOWED TO DO THAT.

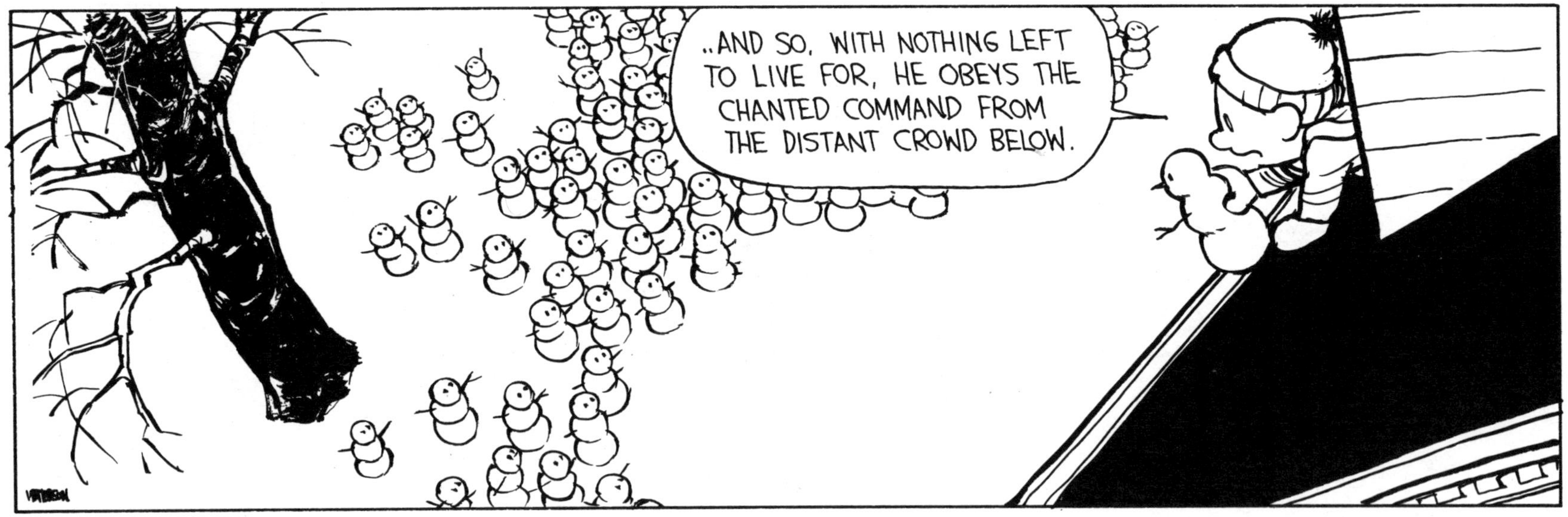
..AND SO, WITH NOTHING LEFT TO LIVE FOR, HE OBEYS THE CHANTED COMMAND FROM THE DISTANT CROWD BELOW.

NEXT, ON EYEWITNESS ACTION NEWS: BLOOD-SPATTERED SIDEWALKS AND SHROUD-COVERED BODIES! COULD THE NEXT VICTIM BE *YOU*??

WE'LL GET THE STORY FROM THE LIVING ROOMS OF SOBBING, HYSTERICAL RELATIVES AND WE'LL TELL YOU WHY *YOU* SHOULD BE PARALYZED WITH HELPLESS FEAR!

THAT'S EYEWITNESS ACTION NEWS! IT'S WHAT *YOU* NEED TO *KNOW!*

WHEN I GROW UP, I'M GOING TO BE A SCIENTIST.

I'LL DEDICATE MY CAREER TO THE PROPOSITION THAT MAN CAN RESHAPE THE UNIVERSE ACCORDING TO HIS OWN WHIMS.

I'LL PROBABLY GO INTO GENETIC ENGINEERING AND CREATE NEW LIFE FORMS.

YOU WANT TO PLAY GOD?

NOT EXACTLY. GOD NEVER BOTHERED TO PATENT HIS STUFF.

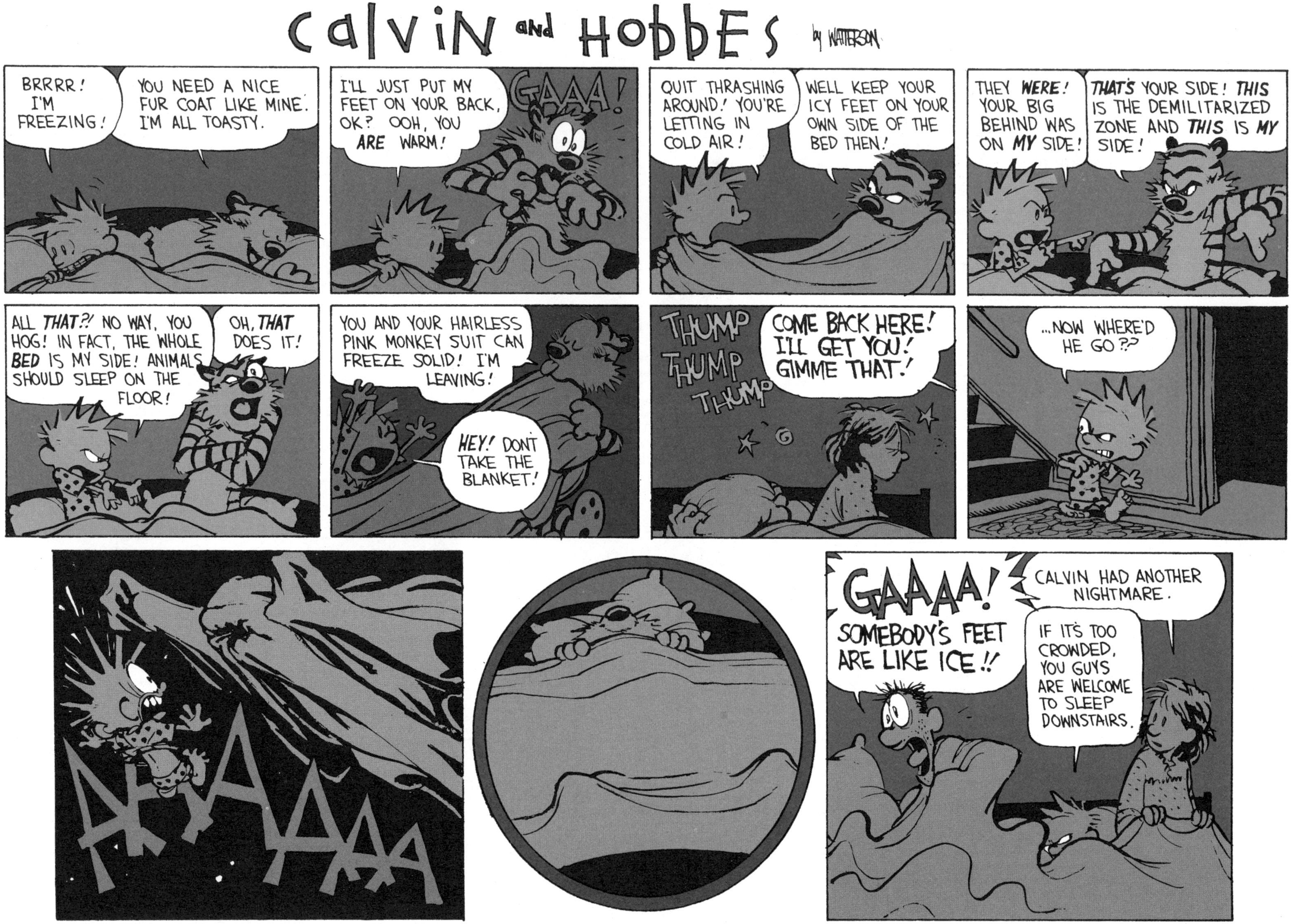
CALVIN AND HOBBES by WATTERSON
BRRRR! I'M FREEZING!
YOU NEED A NICE FUR COAT LIKE MINE. I'M ALL TOASTY.
I'LL JUST PUT MY FEET ON YOUR BACK, OK? OOH, YOU ARE WARM!
GAAA!
QUIT THRASHING AROUND! YOU'RE LETTING IN COLD AIR!
WELL KEEP YOUR ICY FEET ON YOUR OWN SIDE OF THE BED THEN!
THEY WERE! YOUR BIG BEHIND WAS ON MY SIDE!
THAT'S YOUR SIDE! THIS IS THE DEMILITARIZED ZONE AND THIS IS MY SIDE!
ALL THAT?! NO WAY, YOU HOG! IN FACT, THE WHOLE BED IS MY SIDE! ANIMALS SHOULD SLEEP ON THE FLOOR!
OH, THAT DOES IT!
YOU AND YOUR HAIRLESS PINK MONKEY SUIT CAN FREEZE SOLID! I'M LEAVING!
HEY! DON'T TAKE THE BLANKET!
THUMP THUMP THUMP
COME BACK HERE! I'LL GET YOU! GIMME THAT!
...NOW WHERE'D HE GO?!
AAAAAA
GAAAA! SOMEBODY'S FEET ARE LIKE ICE!!
CALVIN HAD ANOTHER NIGHTMARE.
IF IT'S TOO CROWDED, YOU GUYS ARE WELCOME TO SLEEP DOWNSTAIRS.

SOME DAYS YOU GET UP AND YOU ALREADY KNOW THAT THINGS AREN'T GOING TO GO WELL.

THEY'RE THE TYPE OF DAYS WHEN YOU SHOULD JUST GIVE IN, PUT YOUR PAJAMAS BACK ON, MAKE SOME HOT CHOCOLATE, AND READ COMIC BOOKS IN BED WITH THE COVERS UP UNTIL THE WORLD LOOKS MORE ENCOURAGING.

OF COURSE, THEY NEVER LET YOU DO THAT.

IS TODAY ONE OF THOSE DAYS?

IT SURE IS!!

ON GRAY DAYS, WHEN IT'S SNOWING OR RAINING, I THINK YOU SHOULD BE ABLE TO CALL UP A JUDGE AND TAKE AN OATH THAT YOU'LL JUST READ A GOOD BOOK ALL DAY, AND HE'D ALLOW YOU TO STAY HOME.

SO YOU'D ONLY GO TO SCHOOL ON SUNNY DAYS?

WELL NO, ON SUNNY DAYS THE JUDGE WOULD LET YOU PLAY OUTSIDE.

HE'S QUITE A GUY.

HE'D MAKE YOU GO TO SCHOOL IF IT WAS HOT, HAZY, AND HUMID WITH A LOT OF BUGS.

PSSST! WHAT'S 7+6?
THREE HUNDRED BILLION GAZILLION.
OH, THANKS FOR THE BIG HELP!
THAT'S A THREE, FOLLOWED BY 85 ZEROES.
AH! I KNEW THAT.

I'M THINKING OF STARTING MY OWN TALK RADIO SHOW.
I'LL SPOUT SIMPLISTIC OPINIONS FOR HOURS ON END, RIDICULE ANYONE WHO DISAGREES WITH ME, AND GENERALLY FOSTER DIVISIVENESS, CYNICISM, AND A LOWER LEVEL OF PUBLIC DIALOG!
IT WOULD SEEM YOU WERE BORN FOR THE JOB.
IMAGINE GETTING **PAID** TO ACT LIKE A SIX-YEAR-OLD!

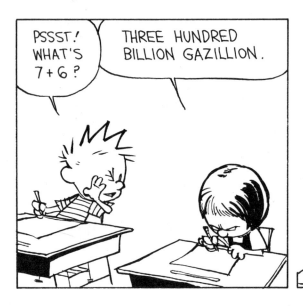

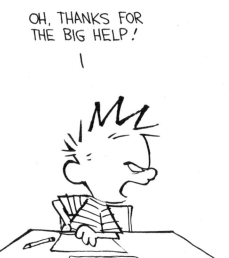

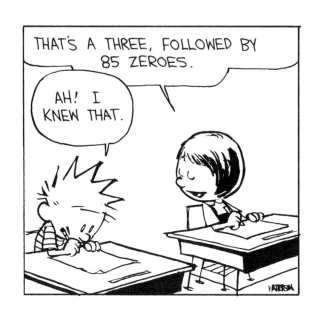

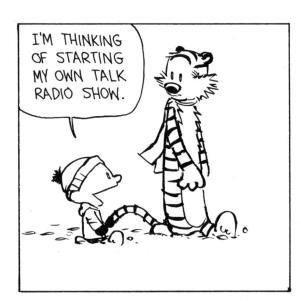

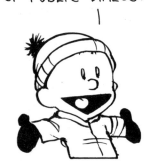

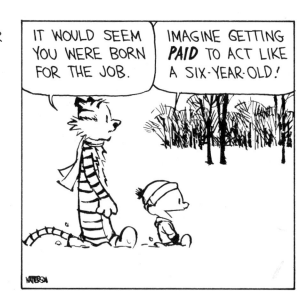

HEH HEH
HEH
HEH
HEH HEH HEH HEH HEH
OH BOY OH BOY OH BOY
HA HA HA HA HA HA
OBVIOUSLY I'VE TAPPED INTO SOME PRIMEVAL WELL OF THE HUMAN PSYCHE.

SNOW SHARKS?
THAT GUY'S A GONER.

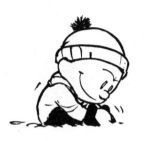

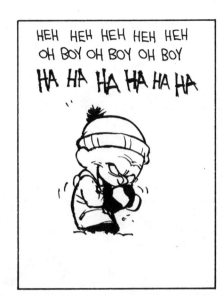

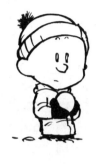

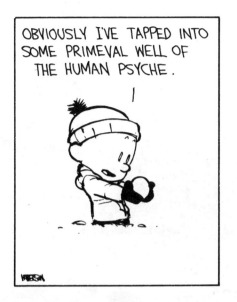

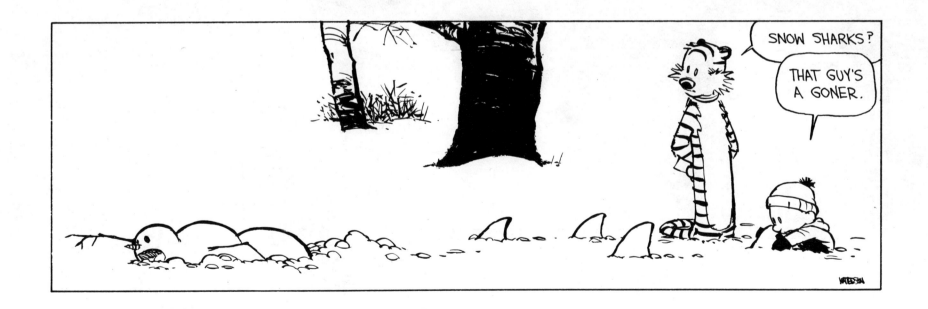

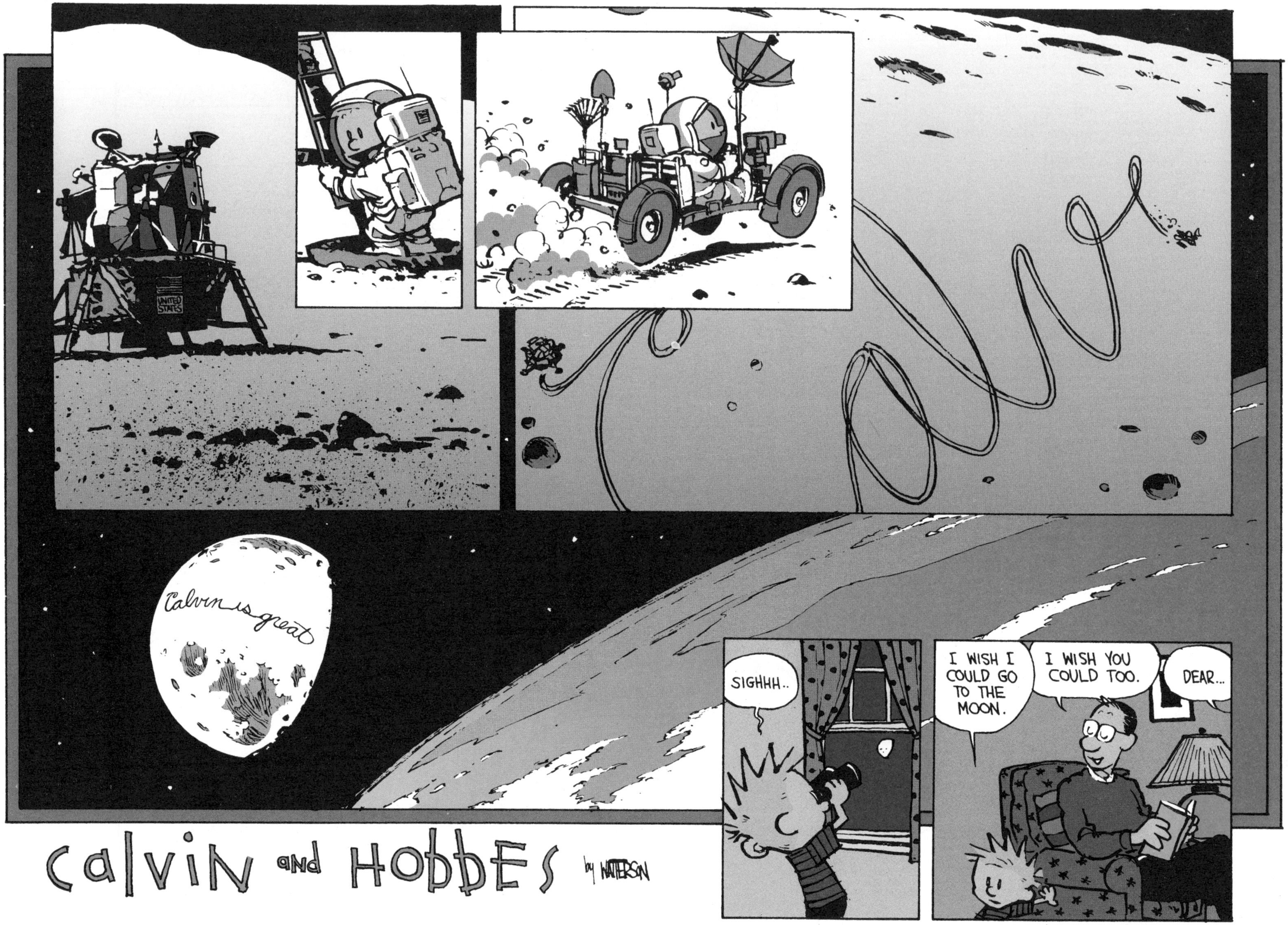
UNITED STATES
Calvin is great
SIGHHH..
I WISH I COULD GO TO THE MOON.
I WISH YOU COULD TOO.
DEAR...
Calvin and HOBBES
by WATTERSON

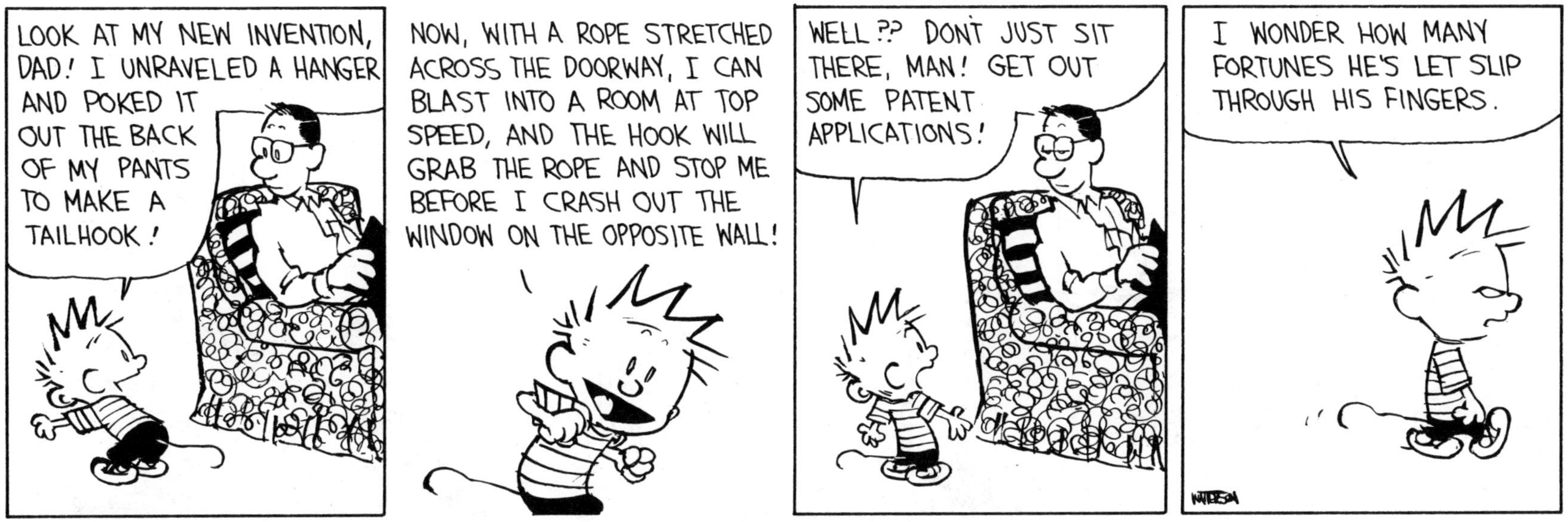
LOOK AT MY NEW INVENTION, DAD! I UNRAVELED A HANGER AND POKED IT OUT THE BACK OF MY PANTS TO MAKE A TAILHOOK!
NOW, WITH A ROPE STRETCHED ACROSS THE DOORWAY, I CAN BLAST INTO A ROOM AT TOP SPEED, AND THE HOOK WILL GRAB THE ROPE AND STOP ME BEFORE I CRASH OUT THE WINDOW ON THE OPPOSITE WALL!
WELL?? DON'T JUST SIT THERE, MAN! GET OUT SOME PATENT APPLICATIONS!
I WONDER HOW MANY FORTUNES HE'S LET SLIP THROUGH HIS FINGERS.

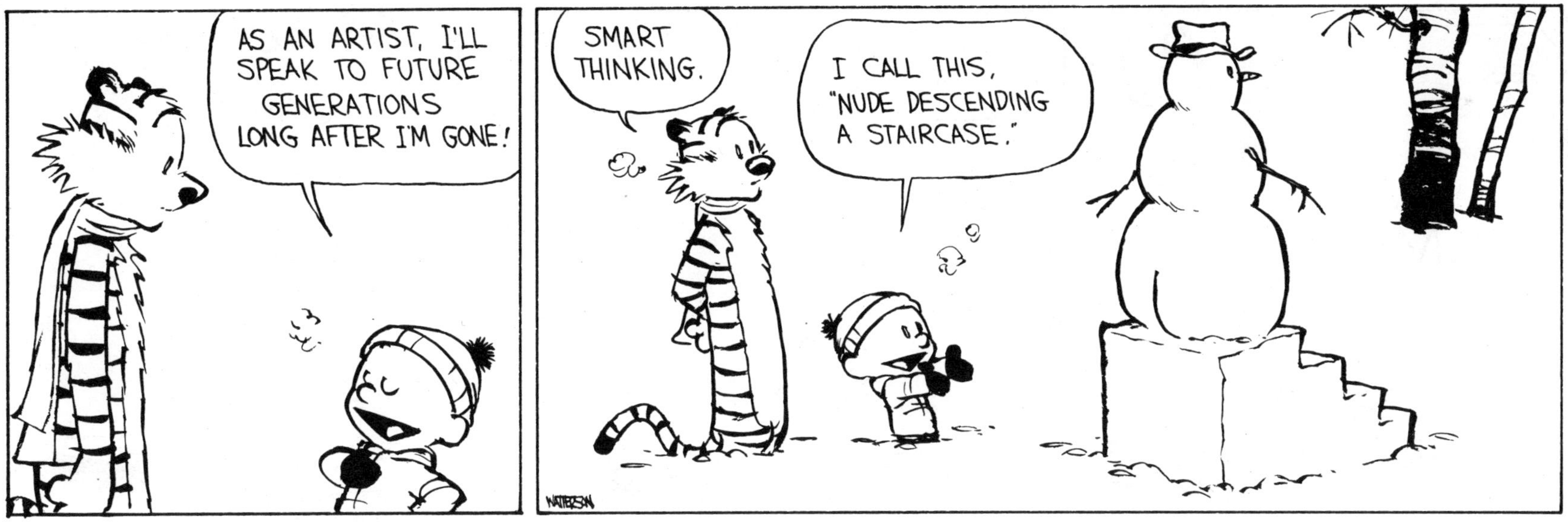
AS AN ARTIST, I'LL SPEAK TO FUTURE GENERATIONS LONG AFTER I'M GONE!
SMART THINKING.
I CALL THIS, "NUDE DESCENDING A STAIRCASE."

EVERYTHING IS SO DARN HARD!
I WISH I COULD JUST TAKE A PILL TO BE PERFECT AND I WISH I COULD JUST PUSH A BUTTON TO HAVE ANYTHING I WANT.
THE AMERICAN DREAM LIVES ON.
WHY SHOULD I HAVE TO **WORK** FOR EVERYTHING?! IT'S LIKE SAYING I DON'T DESERVE IT!

LOOK, IT'S ALMOST 11 O'CLOCK!
WOW, THE LAST TWO HOURS REALLY FLEW BY!
I HOPE THE TEACHER DIDN'T SAY ANYTHING IMPORTANT.

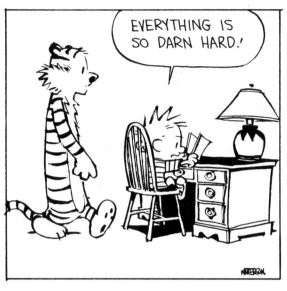

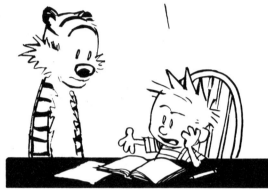

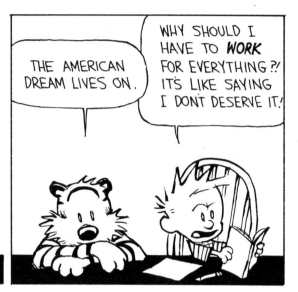

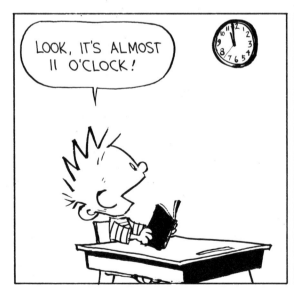

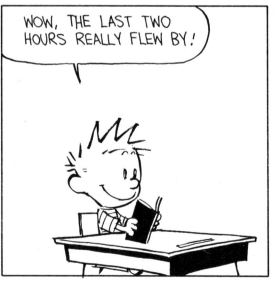

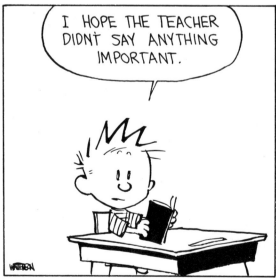

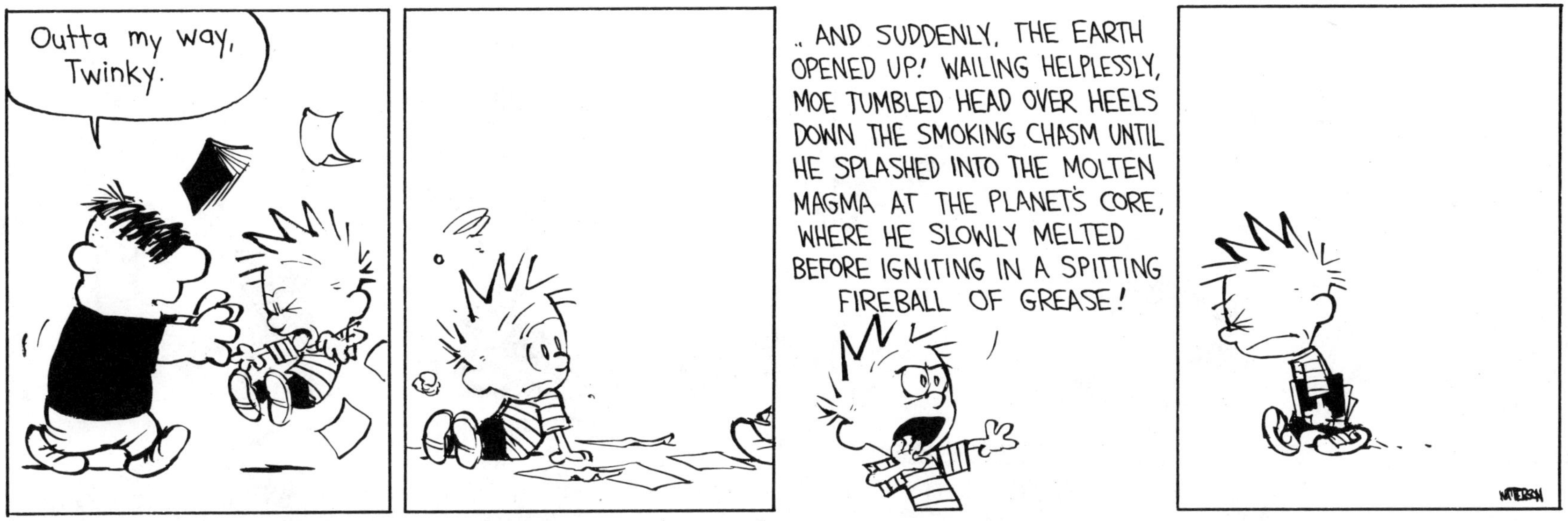
Outta my way, Twinky.
.. AND SUDDENLY, THE EARTH OPENED UP! WAILING HELPLESSLY, MOE TUMBLED HEAD OVER HEELS DOWN THE SMOKING CHASM UNTIL HE SPLASHED INTO THE MOLTEN MAGMA AT THE PLANET'S CORE, WHERE HE SLOWLY MELTED BEFORE IGNITING IN A SPITTING FIREBALL OF GREASE!

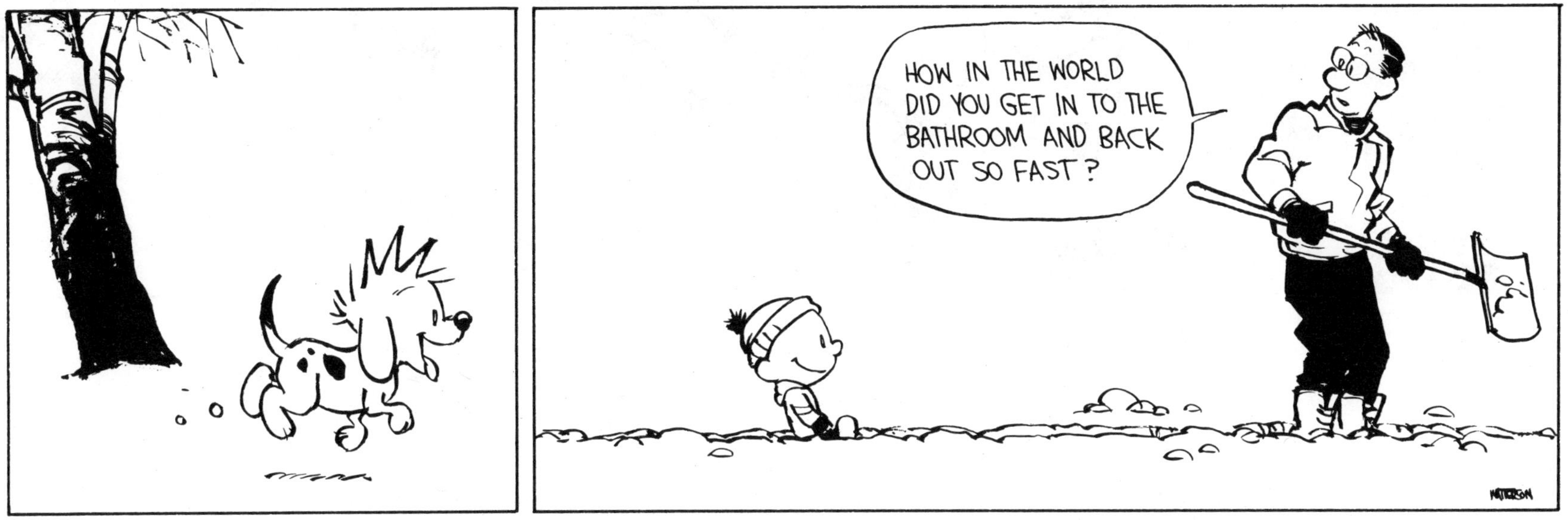
HOW IN THE WORLD DID YOU GET IN TO THE BATHROOM AND BACK OUT SO FAST?

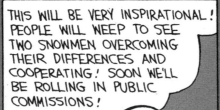

calvin and hobbes

by WATTERSON

THIS SCULPTURE WILL BE CALLED "THE SPIRIT OF COMPROMISE." WE'LL EACH MAKE A SNOWMAN AND HAVE THEM SHAKING HANDS.

GREAT.

THIS WILL BE VERY INSPIRATIONAL! PEOPLE WILL WEEP TO SEE TWO SNOWMEN OVERCOMING THEIR DIFFERENCES AND COOPERATING! SOON WE'LL BE ROLLING IN PUBLIC COMMISSIONS!

MAKE YOUR SNOWMAN'S ARM LONGER. HIS HAND WON'T REACH MY SNOWMAN'S HAND.

WHY SHOULD I MAKE A NEW ARM? JUST MAKE *YOURS* LONGER.

THEN IT WILL LOOK LIKE MY SNOWMAN HAD TO REACH FARTHER THAN YOURS DID. THEY SHOULD BE EQUAL.

THEN BUILD YOUR SNOWMAN CLOSER OVER HERE!

I'M NOT GOING TO START ALL OVER! JUST MAKE YOUR ARM LONGER!

I REFUSE! YOU CAN'T TELL ME WHAT TO DO!

IN THAT CASE, MY SNOWMAN REFUSES TO SHAKE WITH YOUR SNOWMAN!

SO WHAT!! *MY* SNOWMAN WON'T EVEN *TALK* TO YOURS! I'M TURNING HIS HEAD THE OTHER WAY!

HA! WHILE HE'S LOOKING OVER THERE, *MY* SNOWMAN WILL KICK *YOUR* SNOWMAN IN HIS BIG WHITE BUTT!

OH YEAH?! WELL MINE KNOCKS YOUR SNOWMAN'S HEAD OFF!

FINE! MY SNOWMAN FEEDS YOUR SNOWMAN HIS OWN NOSE!

WHY YOU!!

OW

LEGGO

OOF

STOP IT!

I DON'T THINK THIS SCULPTURE IS VERY GOOD.

IT'S A COMPROMISE.

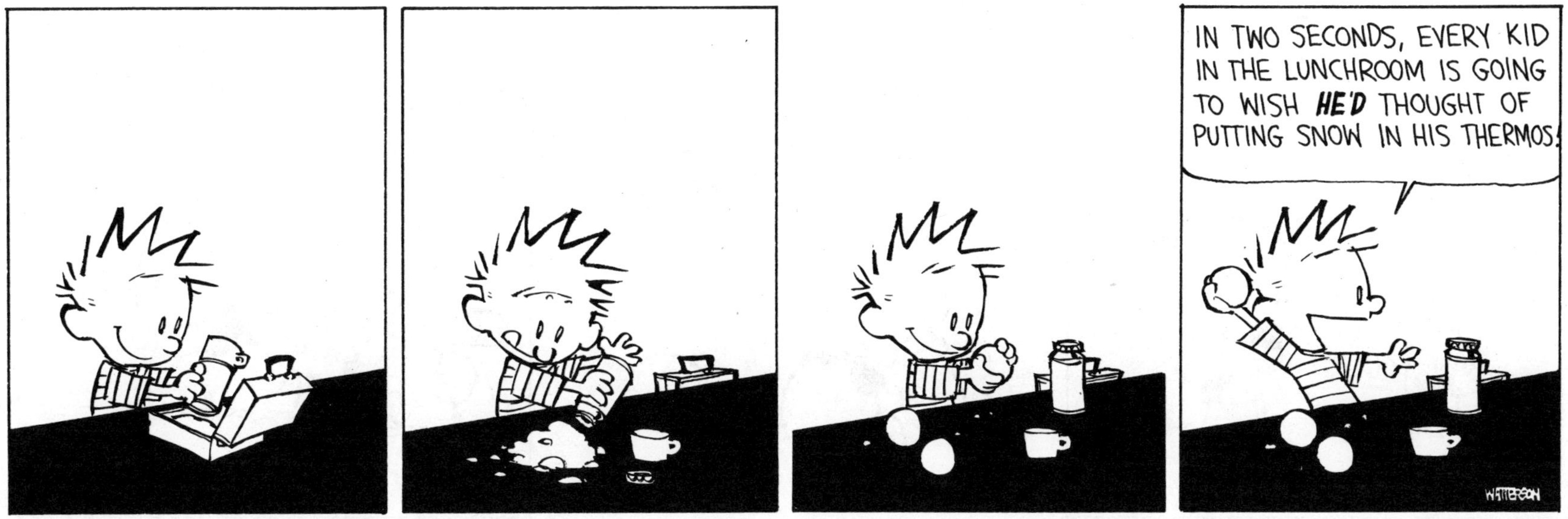
IN TWO SECONDS, EVERY KID IN THE LUNCHROOM IS GOING TO WISH HE'D THOUGHT OF PUTTING SNOW IN HIS THERMOS!
WATTERSON

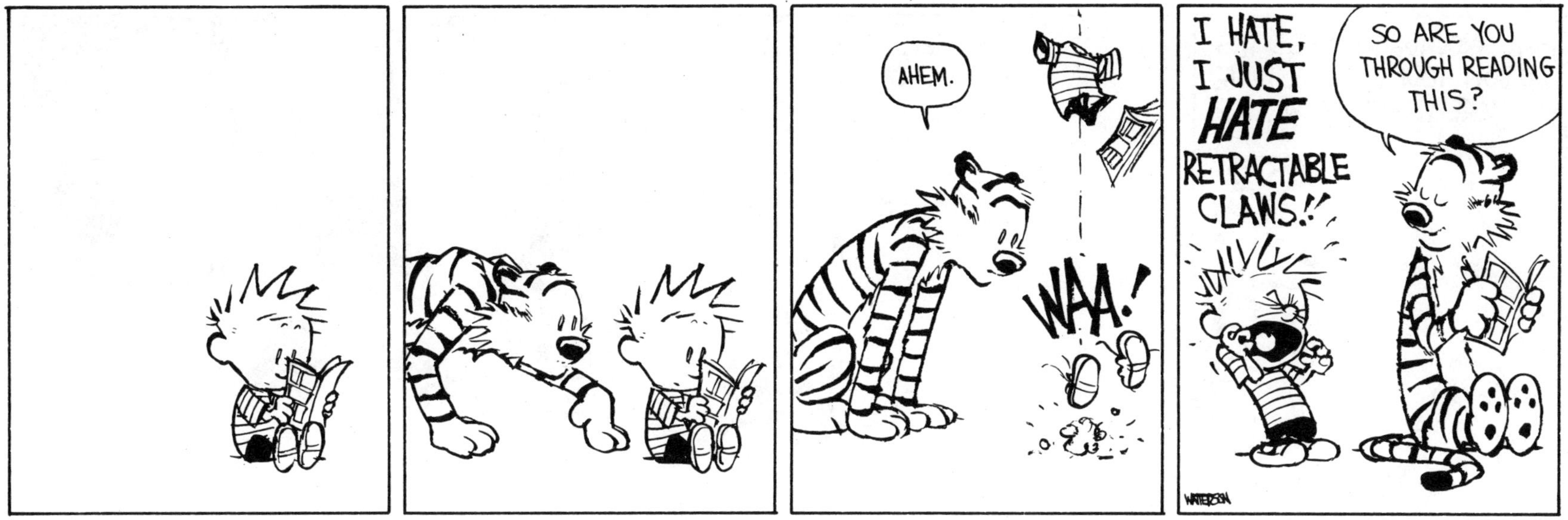
AHEM.
WAA!
I HATE, I JUST HATE RETRACTABLE CLAWS!!
SO ARE YOU THROUGH READING THIS?
WATTERSON

CALVIN!

IF A GROUNDHOG SEES HIS SHADOW TODAY, WE'LL HAVE SIX MORE WEEKS OF WINTER.
SO YELL IF YOU SEE ONE.

TIGER SPRAWLING IN THE SUN! FAST ASLEEP, HIS DAY IS DONE. LYING HERE, 'TWAS WARMTH HE SOUGHT. THE SUN HAS MADE HIS TUMMY HOT. ONE SAD FACT HE OVERLOOKED: HIS BRAIN IS NOW COMPLETELY COOKED!

DAD SAYS THERE'S NOTHING COZIER THAN A FIRE, BUT I DUNNO...

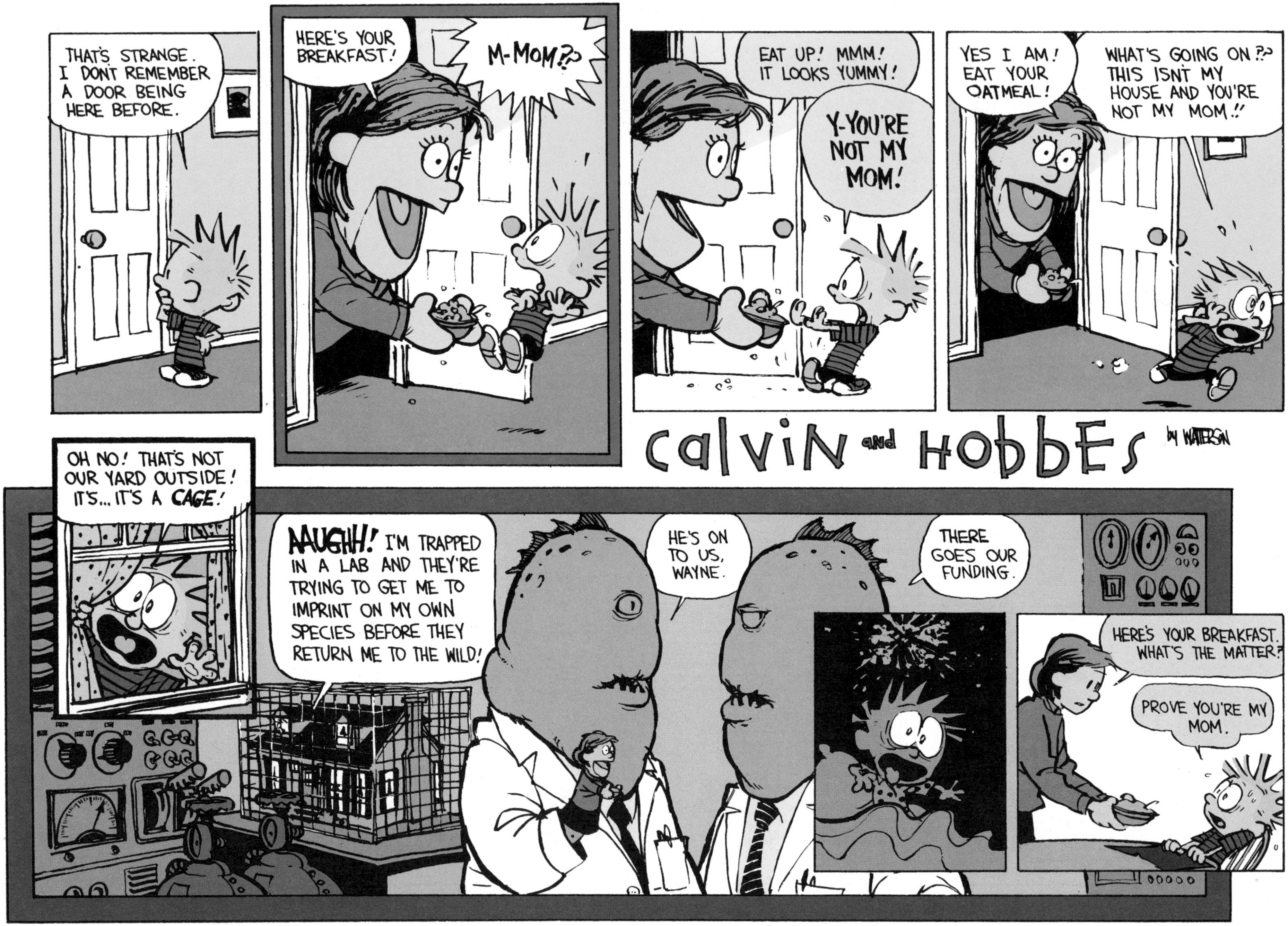
THAT'S STRANGE. I DON'T REMEMBER A DOOR BEING HERE BEFORE.
HERE'S YOUR BREAKFAST!
M-MOM?!?
EAT UP! MMM! IT LOOKS YUMMY!
Y-YOU'RE NOT MY MOM!
YES I AM! EAT YOUR OATMEAL!
WHAT'S GOING ON?!? THIS ISN'T MY HOUSE AND YOU'RE NOT MY MOM!!
Calvin and HOBBES
by WATTERSON
OH NO! THAT'S NOT OUR YARD OUTSIDE! IT'S... IT'S A CAGE!
AAUGHH! I'M TRAPPED IN A LAB AND THEY'RE TRYING TO GET ME TO IMPRINT ON MY OWN SPECIES BEFORE THEY RETURN ME TO THE WILD!
HE'S ON TO US, WAYNE.
THERE GOES OUR FUNDING.
HERE'S YOUR BREAKFAST. WHAT'S THE MATTER?
PROVE YOU'RE MY MOM.

ONE OF MY BABY TEETH CAME OUT!

I HAVE TO SAY, I'M NOT ENTIRELY COMFORTABLE HOLDING A PIECE OF MY OWN HEAD.

MOM SAYS THE TOOTH FAIRY MIGHT GIVE ME 50 CENTS FOR THIS TOOTH.

WOW!

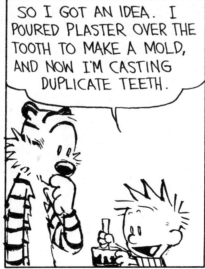

SO I GOT AN IDEA. I POURED PLASTER OVER THE TOOTH TO MAKE A MOLD, AND NOW I'M CASTING DUPLICATE TEETH.

I'LL PUT ONE UNDER THE PILLOW EVERY NIGHT, AND BY THE END OF THE YEAR, I'LL HAVE OVER 150 DOLLARS!

DO YOU THINK THE TOOTH FAIRY WILL BELIEVE YOUR MOUTH HAD 300 TEETH IN IT?

IF SHE'D RATHER HAVE AN OLD TOOTH THAN 50 CENTS, HOW BRIGHT CAN SHE BE?

LOOK AT THIS HILARIOUS CARTOON I DREW!
SEE, THIS SNOWMAN IS IN A SNOW CAR AND HE SAYS, "DARN IT, THE ENGINE FROZE UP!" HA HA HA HA! GET IT??
BUT IF THE CAR IS MADE OF SNOW, THE ENGINE WOULD **MELT** IF IT WASN'T FROZEN. EITHER WAY, IT WOULDN'T RUN.

AS I HAVE CREATED YOU, SO CAN I DESTROY YOU!
THEREFORE, IN RECOGNITION OF MY SUPREME POWER, YOU MUST WORSHIP ME!
YES, BOW BEFORE MIGHTY CALVIN AND TREMBLE, FOR I AM THE ETERNAL, ALL KNOWING...
PAFF

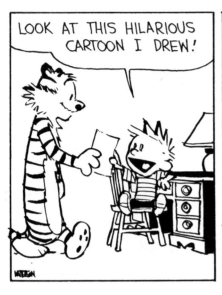

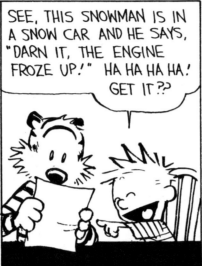

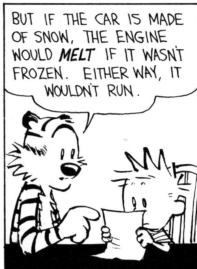

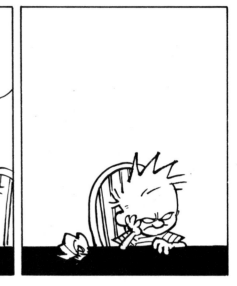

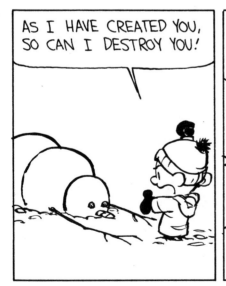

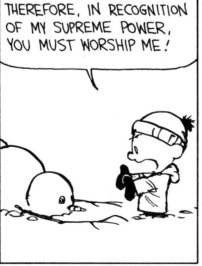

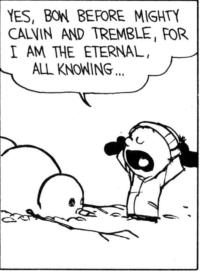

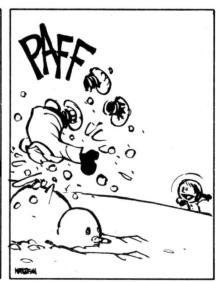

PIFF
I DIDN'T DO IT! I NEVER THREW THAT! YOU CAN'T PROVE I THREW IT!
BESIDES, I **MISSED**, DIDN'T I ?!
THE DEFENDANT PETITIONS THE COURT FOR A NEW TRIAL ON THE GROUNDS THAT HIS LAWYER IS INCOMPETENT.

HELLO?
IS YOUR MOTHER THERE?
WHO'S CALLING?? IS THIS ABOUT **ME**?! 'CAUSE IF IT IS, I DIDN'T **DO** IT! YOU GOT **NOTHING** ON ME, UNDERSTAND?! YOU CAN'T PROVE **ANY**THING! I TELL YOU I'M INNOCENT! JUST GIVE UP! YOU'LL NEVER GET ME!
OH, HERE MOM, IT'S FOR YOU.
HI, CAN I CALL YOU BACK?
GO AHEAD AND TALK. I CLEARED IT. IT'S COOL.

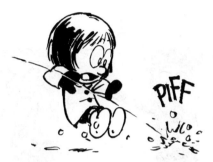

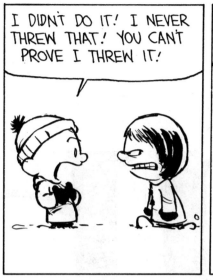

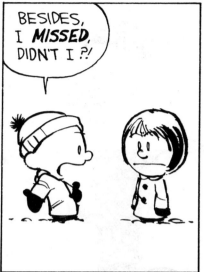

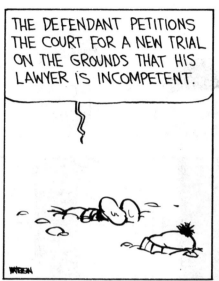

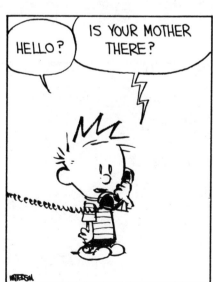

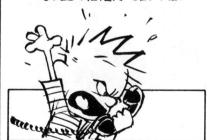

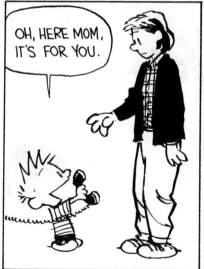

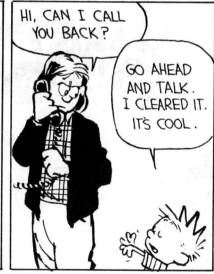

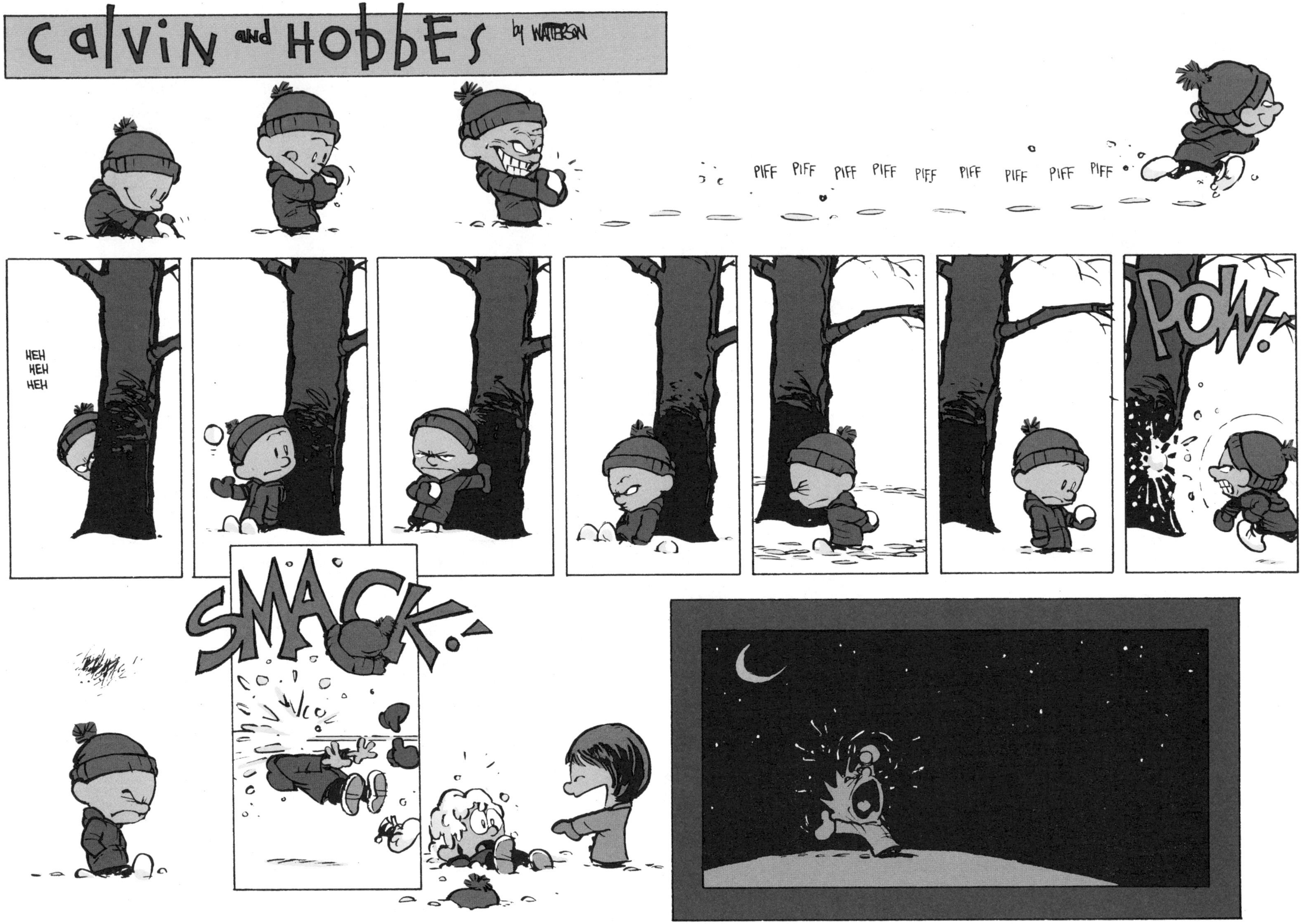
Calvin and HOBBES
by WATTERSON
PIFF PIFF PIFF PIFF PIFF PIFF PIFF PIFF PIFF
HEH
HEH
HEH
POW!
SMACK!

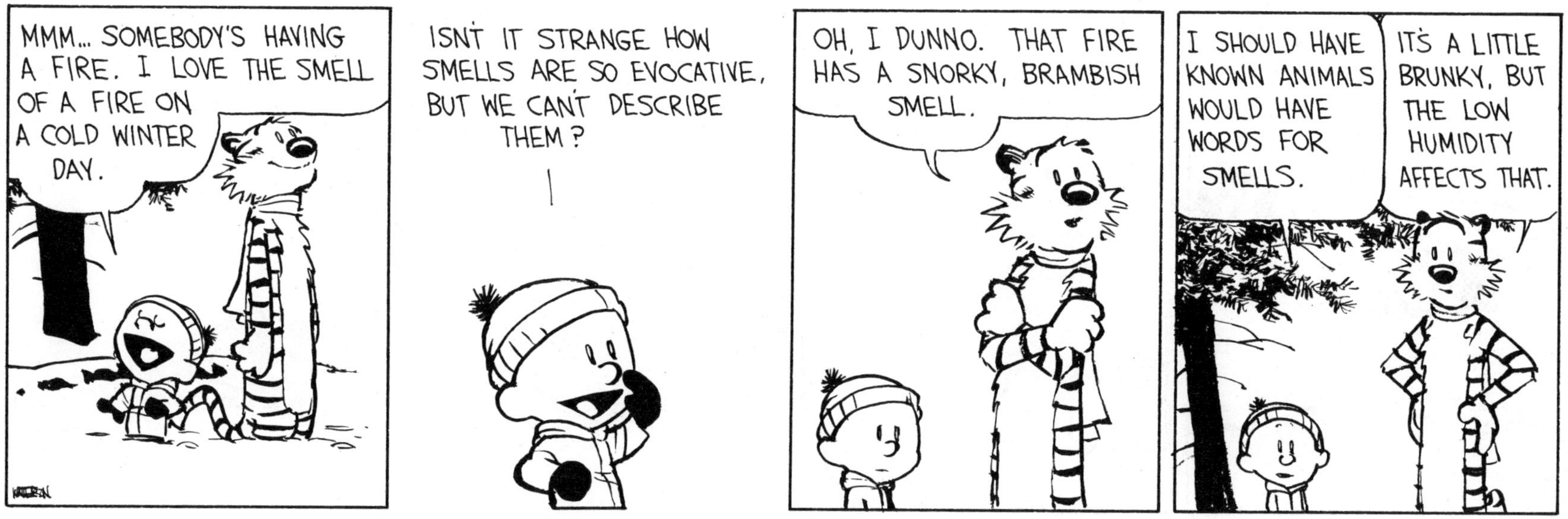
MMM... SOMEBODY'S HAVING A FIRE. I LOVE THE SMELL OF A FIRE ON A COLD WINTER DAY.
ISN'T IT STRANGE HOW SMELLS ARE SO EVOCATIVE, BUT WE CAN'T DESCRIBE THEM?
OH, I DUNNO. THAT FIRE HAS A SNORKY, BRAMBISH SMELL.
I SHOULD HAVE KNOWN ANIMALS WOULD HAVE WORDS FOR SMELLS.
IT'S A LITTLE BRUNKY, BUT THE LOW HUMIDITY AFFECTS THAT.

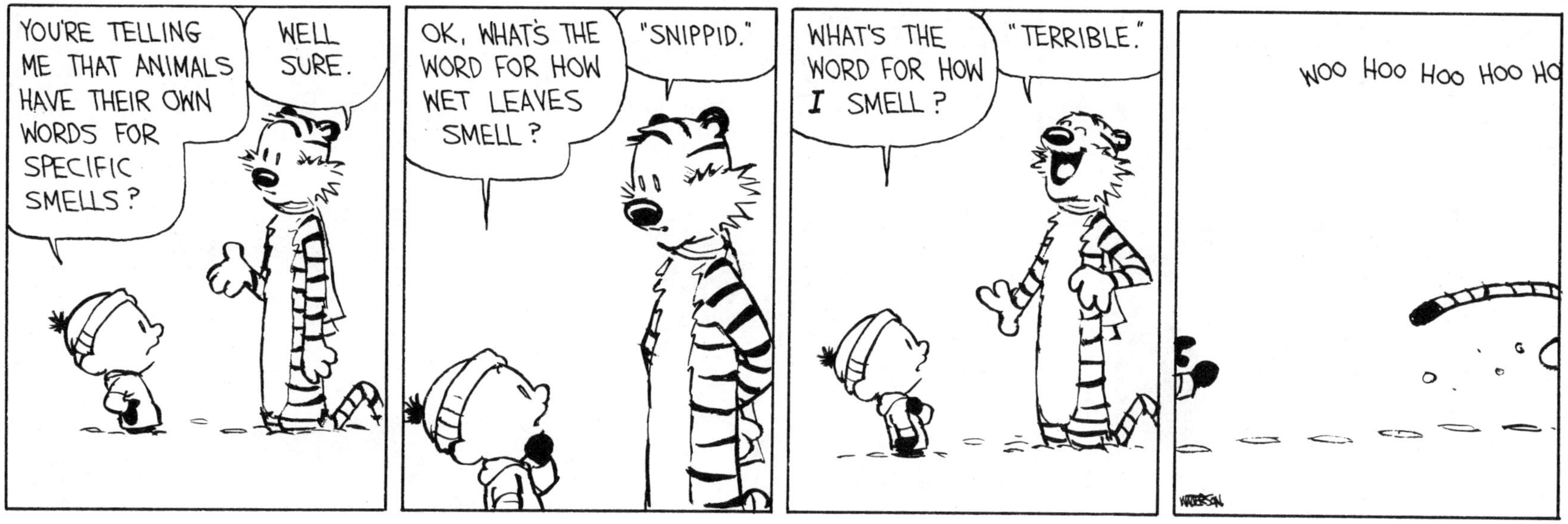
YOU'RE TELLING ME THAT ANIMALS HAVE THEIR OWN WORDS FOR SPECIFIC SMELLS?
WELL SURE.
OK, WHAT'S THE WORD FOR HOW WET LEAVES SMELL?
"SNIPPID."
WHAT'S THE WORD FOR HOW I SMELL?
"TERRIBLE."
WOO HOO HOO HOO HO

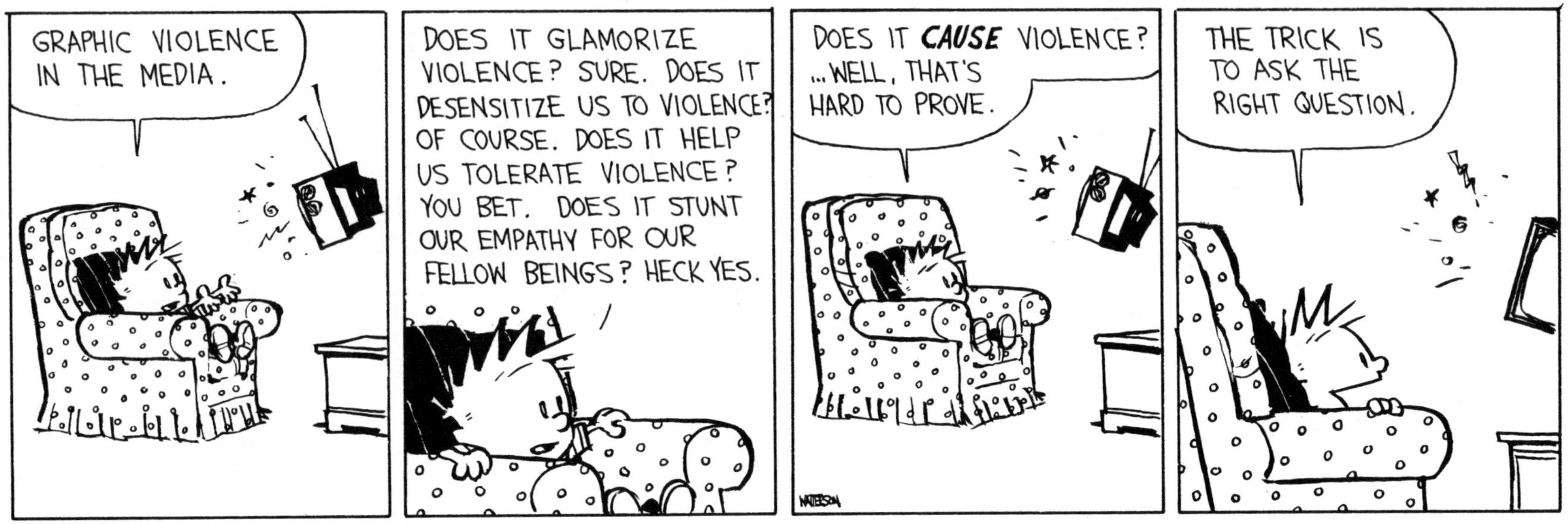
GRAPHIC VIOLENCE IN THE MEDIA.
DOES IT GLAMORIZE VIOLENCE? SURE. DOES IT DESENSITIZE US TO VIOLENCE? OF COURSE. DOES IT HELP US TOLERATE VIOLENCE? YOU BET. DOES IT STUNT OUR EMPATHY FOR OUR FELLOW BEINGS? HECK YES.
DOES IT **CAUSE** VIOLENCE? ...WELL, THAT'S HARD TO PROVE.
THE TRICK IS TO ASK THE RIGHT QUESTION.

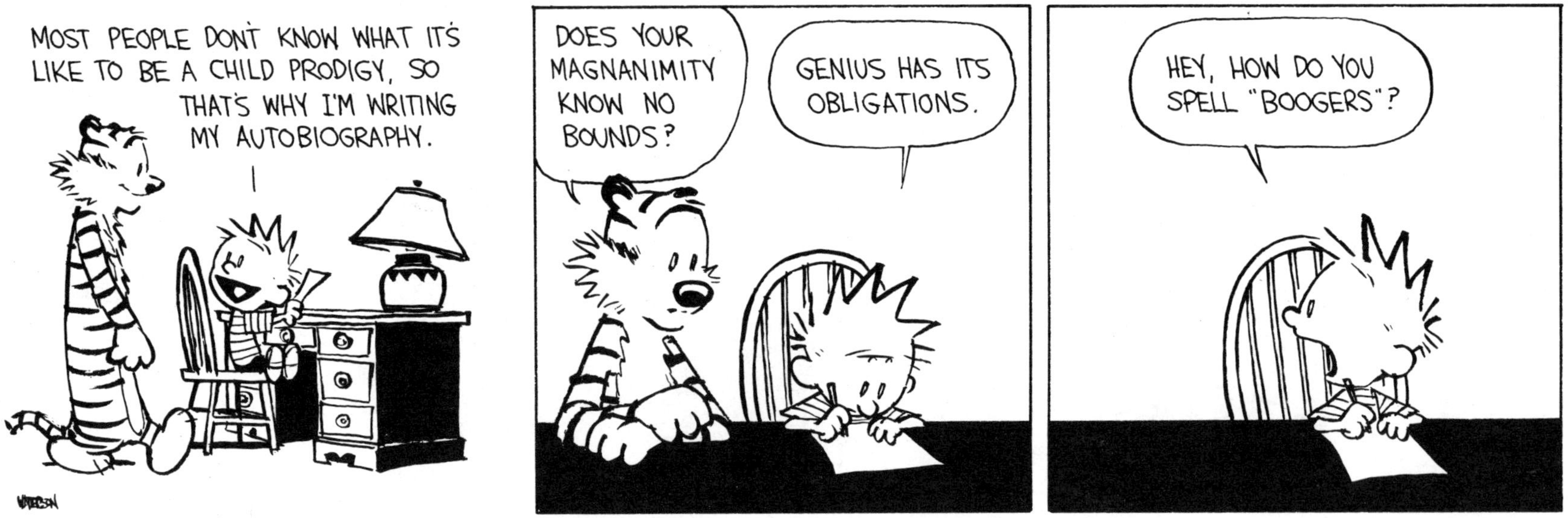
MOST PEOPLE DON'T KNOW WHAT IT'S LIKE TO BE A CHILD PRODIGY, SO THAT'S WHY I'M WRITING MY AUTOBIOGRAPHY.
DOES YOUR MAGNANIMITY KNOW NO BOUNDS?
GENIUS HAS ITS OBLIGATIONS.
HEY, HOW DO YOU SPELL "BOOGERS"?

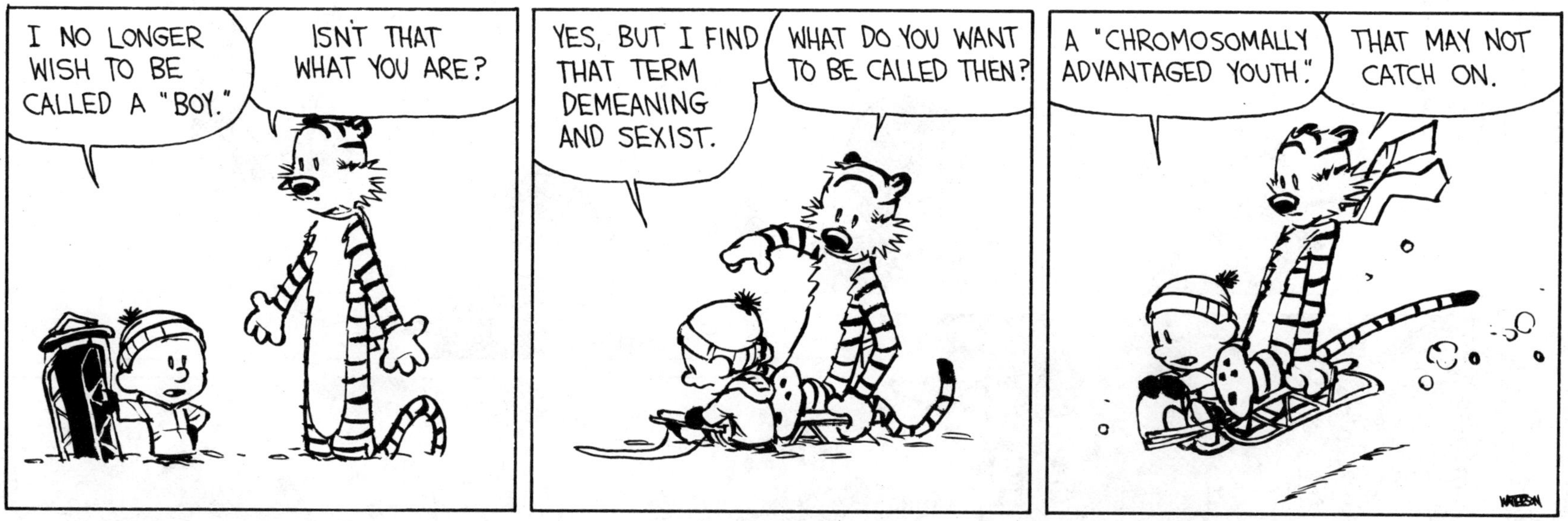
I NO LONGER WISH TO BE CALLED A "BOY."
ISN'T THAT WHAT YOU ARE?
YES, BUT I FIND THAT TERM DEMEANING AND SEXIST.
WHAT DO YOU WANT TO BE CALLED THEN?
A "CHROMOSOMALLY ADVANTAGED YOUTH."
THAT MAY NOT CATCH ON.
WATTERSON

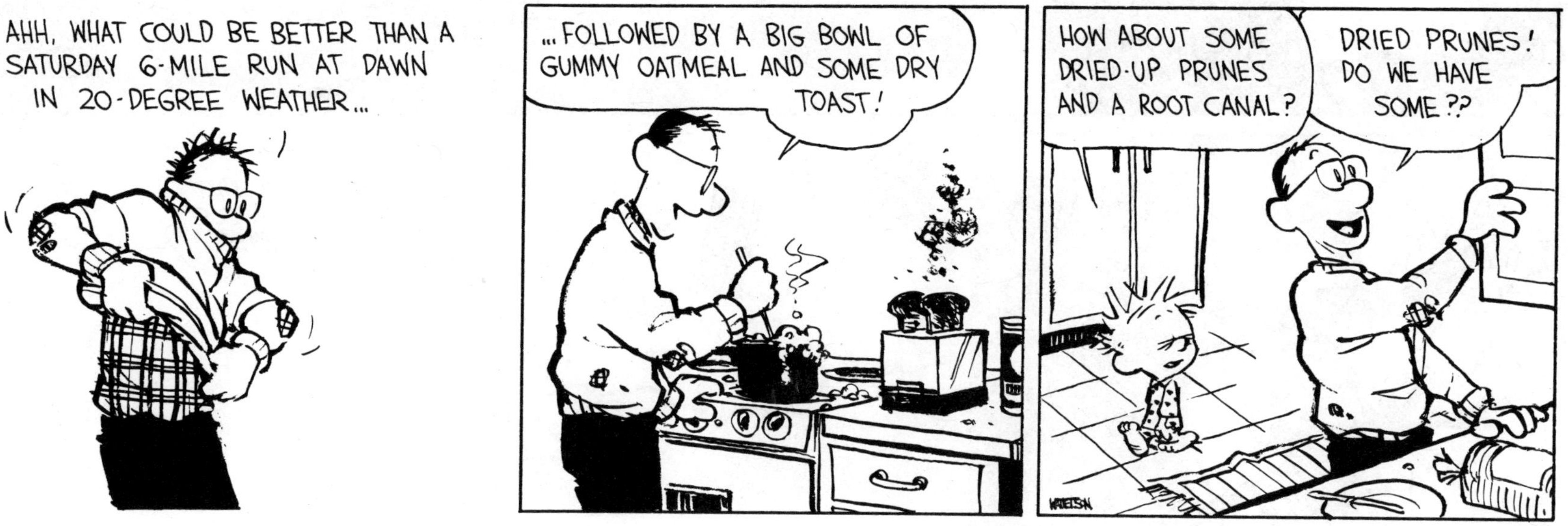
AHH, WHAT COULD BE BETTER THAN A SATURDAY 6-MILE RUN AT DAWN IN 20-DEGREE WEATHER...
...FOLLOWED BY A BIG BOWL OF GUMMY OATMEAL AND SOME DRY TOAST!
HOW ABOUT SOME DRIED-UP PRUNES AND A ROOT CANAL?
DRIED PRUNES! DO WE HAVE SOME??
WATTERSON

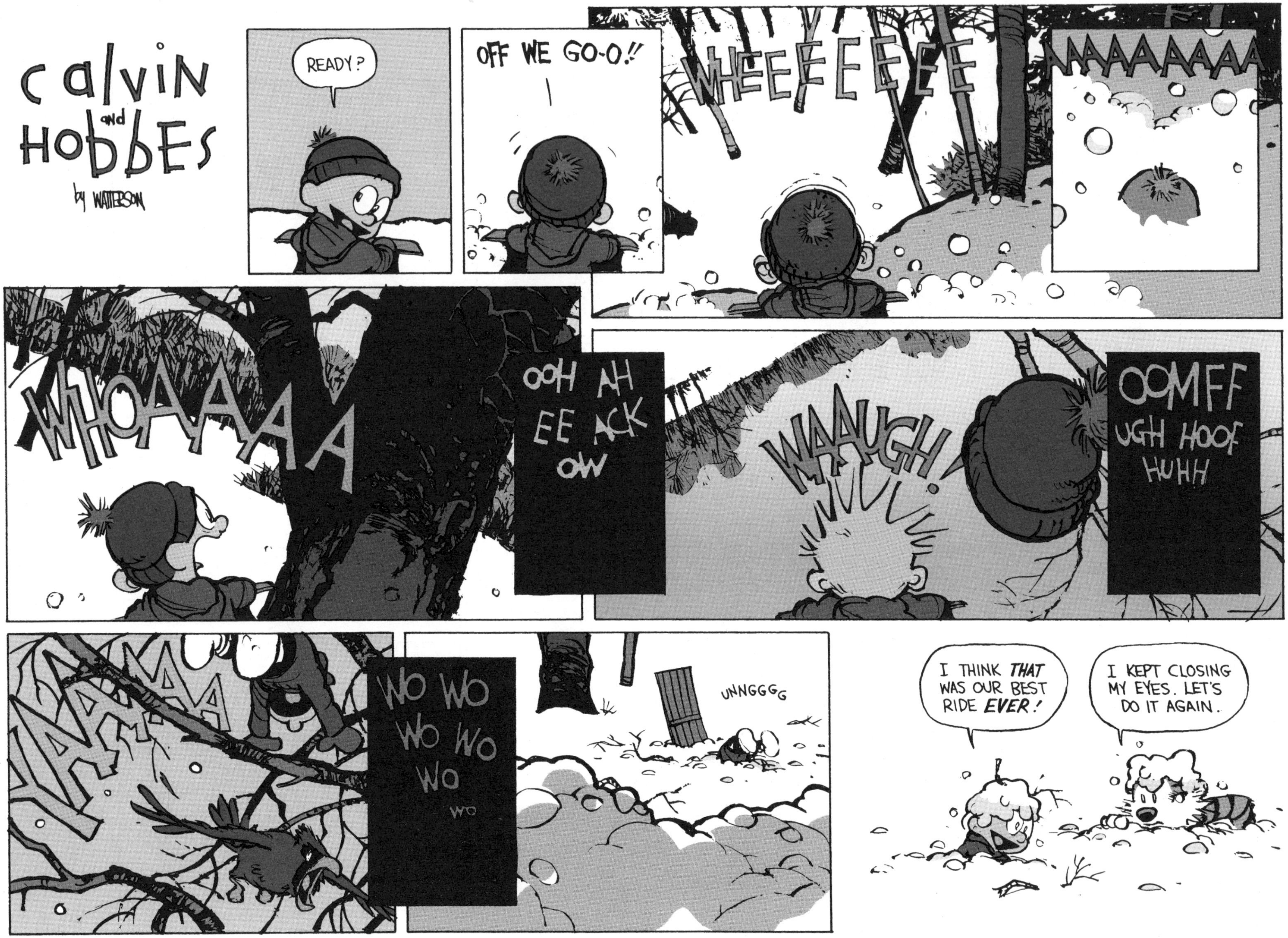
Calvin and Hobbes
by WATTERSON
READY?
OFF WE GO-O!!
WHEEEEEEE
AAAAAAAA
WHOAAAAA
OOH AH
EE ACK
OW
WAAUGH!
OOMFF
UGH HOOF
HUHH
YAAAAA
WO WO
WO WO
WO
WO
UNNGGGG
I THINK THAT WAS OUR BEST RIDE EVER!
I KEPT CLOSING MY EYES. LET'S DO IT AGAIN.

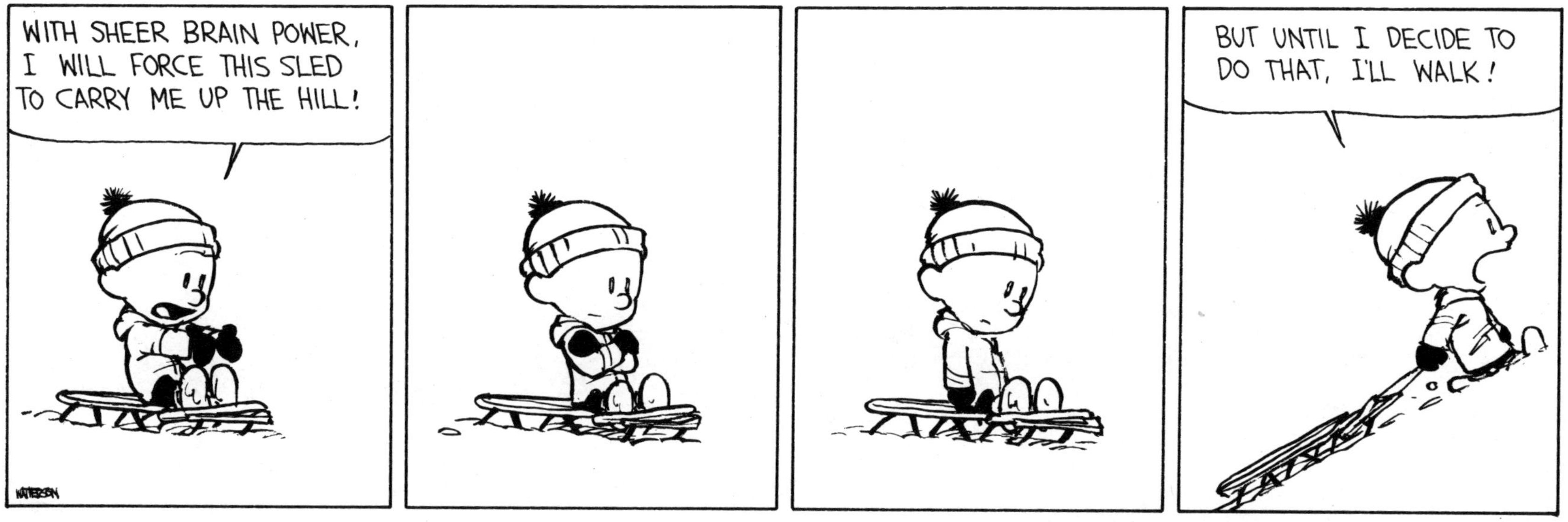
WITH SHEER BRAIN POWER, I WILL FORCE THIS SLED TO CARRY ME UP THE HILL!
BUT UNTIL I DECIDE TO DO THAT, I'LL WALK!

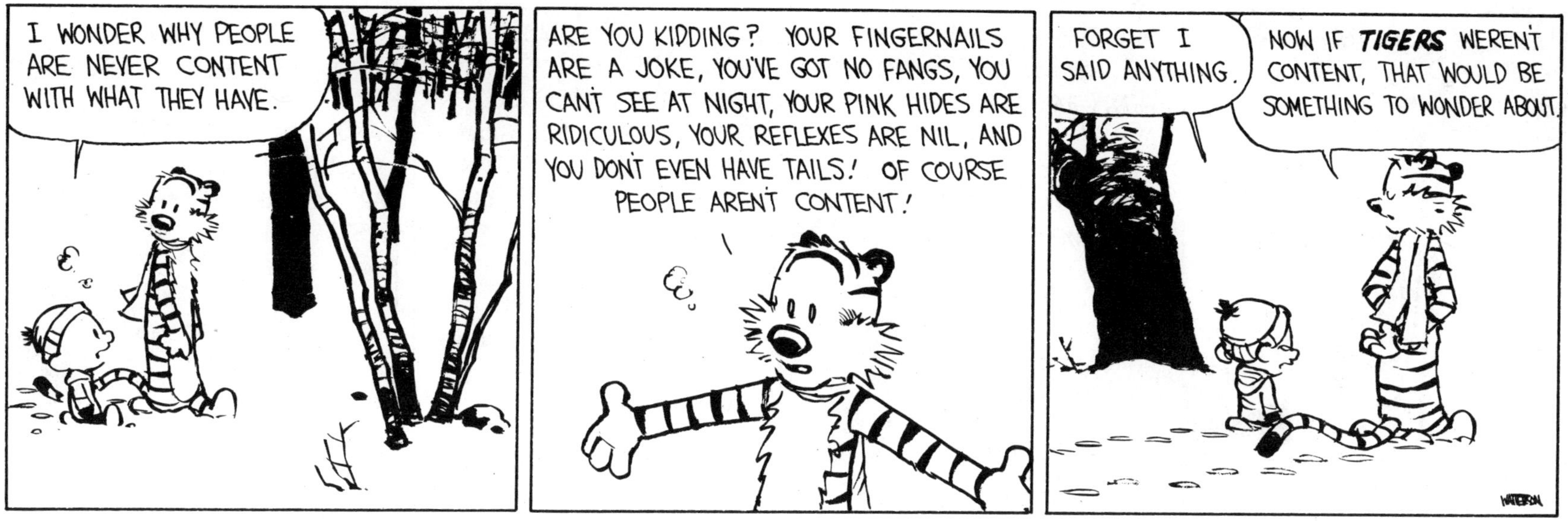
I WONDER WHY PEOPLE ARE NEVER CONTENT WITH WHAT THEY HAVE.
ARE YOU KIDDING? YOUR FINGERNAILS ARE A JOKE, YOU'VE GOT NO FANGS, YOU CAN'T SEE AT NIGHT, YOUR PINK HIDES ARE RIDICULOUS, YOUR REFLEXES ARE NIL, AND YOU DON'T EVEN HAVE TAILS! OF COURSE PEOPLE AREN'T CONTENT!
FORGET I SAID ANYTHING.
NOW IF **TIGERS** WEREN'T CONTENT, THAT WOULD BE SOMETHING TO WONDER ABOUT.

I LIKE HOMEWORK. HOMEWORK MAKES ME HAPPY.

I DON'T WANT TO GO OUTSIDE. I WANT TO DO MATH PROBLEMS.

BLEHHH

MY BRAIN ALWAYS REJECTS ATTITUDE TRANSPLANTS.

LOOK AT HOW PEOPLE ARE PORTRAYED IN COMIC STRIPS. THE WOMEN ARE INDECISIVE WHINERS, NAGGING SHREWS, AND BIMBOS!

AND THE MEN ARE NO BETTER. THEY'RE BEFUDDLED MORONS, HEAVY DRINKERS, GLUTTONS, AND LAZY GOOF-OFFS! EVERYONE IS INCOMPETENT, UNAPPRECIATED, AND UNSUCCESSFUL!

WHAT KIND OF INSIDIOUS SOCIAL PROGRAMMING *IS* THIS?! NO WONDER THE WORLD'S SUCH A MESS! I DEMAND POLITICALLY CORRECT, MORALLY UPLIFTING ROLE MODELS IN THE FUNNIES!

YES, WE ALL KNOW HOW FUNNY GOOD ROLE MODELS ARE.

AND LOOK, ALL THE KIDS ARE OBNOXIOUS BRATS!

WOULDN'T IT BE COOL IF YOU SNEEZED AND THE SPRAY FROM YOUR NOSE INSTANTLY FROZE?

YOU COULD BREAK IT OFF YOUR FACE AND HAVE A 3-D SCULPTURE OF YOUR SNEEZE!

...WELL, I THINK IT WOULD BE COOL.

PEOPLE WONDER WHY CATS ARE SOLITARY.

CALVIN, STOP RUNNING THROUGH THE HOUSE!

THE LAW IS ON THE BOOKS, BUT IT WOULD TAKE ALL THEIR RESOURCES TO ENFORCE IT.

CALVIN!

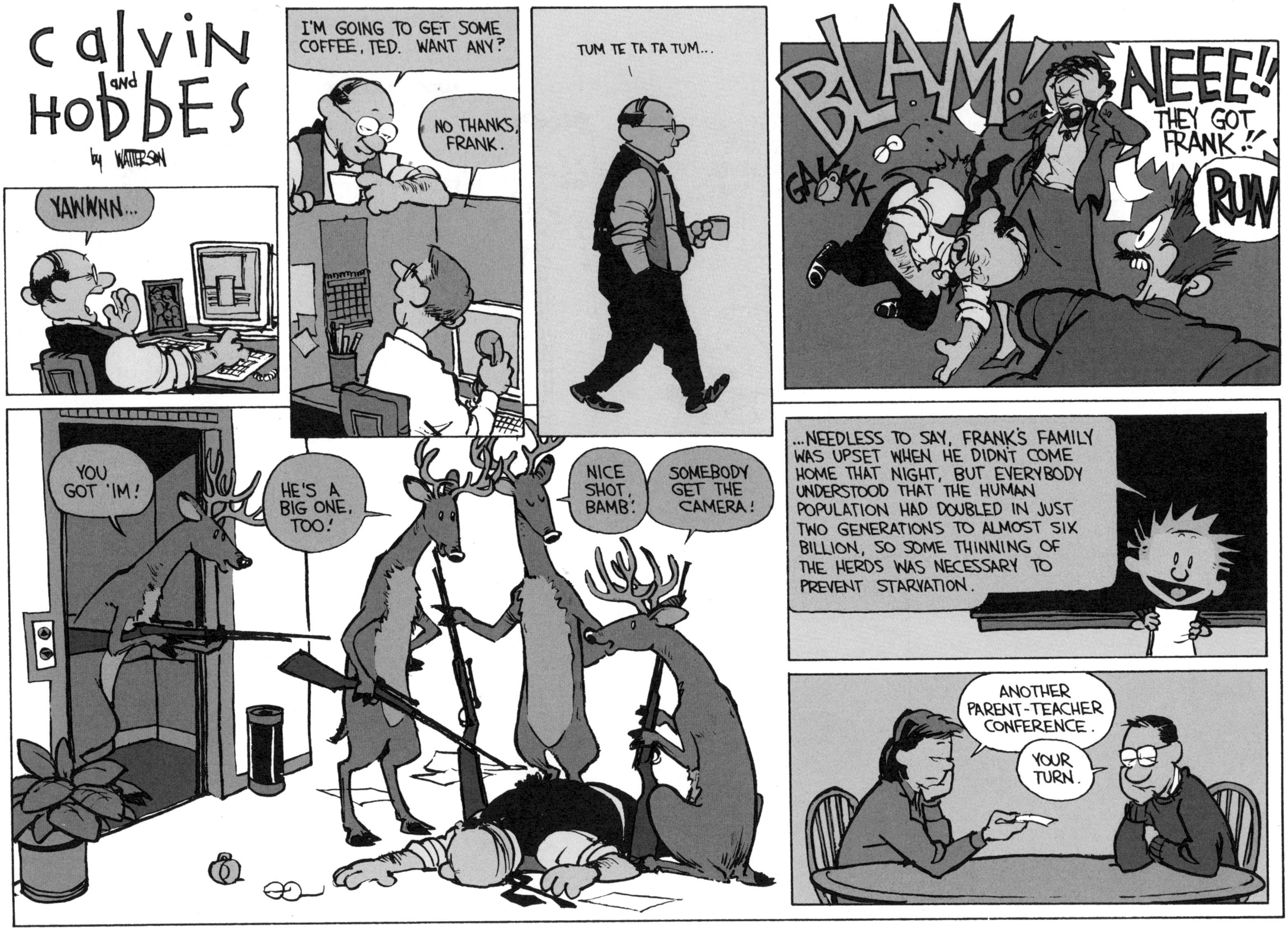
Calvin and Hobbes
by WATTERSON
YAWNNN...
I'M GOING TO GET SOME COFFEE, TED. WANT ANY?
NO THANKS, FRANK.
TUM TE TA TA TUM...
BLAM!
GAKKK
AIEEE!! THEY GOT FRANK!!
RUN
YOU GOT 'IM!
HE'S A BIG ONE, TOO!
NICE SHOT, BAMB!
SOMEBODY GET THE CAMERA!
...NEEDLESS TO SAY, FRANK'S FAMILY WAS UPSET WHEN HE DIDN'T COME HOME THAT NIGHT, BUT EVERYBODY UNDERSTOOD THAT THE HUMAN POPULATION HAD DOUBLED IN JUST TWO GENERATIONS TO ALMOST SIX BILLION, SO SOME THINNING OF THE HERDS WAS NECESSARY TO PREVENT STARVATION.
ANOTHER PARENT-TEACHER CONFERENCE.
YOUR TURN.

VROOOOMM
BEEP BEEP BEEP BEEP

SPLUTCHH

ACKK! NOT SO MUCH! NOT SO MUCH! I HATE THIS STUFF!

PIPE DOWN AND EAT.

What happened in Concord in 1775?

LET'S BE HONEST. YOU'RE asking ME aBout CONCORD? I RELY ON THE BUS DRIVER to FIND MY OWN HOUSE FROM HERE. CONCORD COULD BE ON NEPTUNE FOR aLL I KNOW.

AND WHAT HAPPENED 220 YEARS aGO?? I'M a KID. I DON'T KNOW WHAT'S GOING ON NOW. I DON'T HAVE a SHRED OF CONTEXT FOR aNY OF THIS. IT'S HOPELESS, MISS WORMWOOD, HOPELESS.

WE BOTH TRY TO DEMORALIZE EACH OTHER.

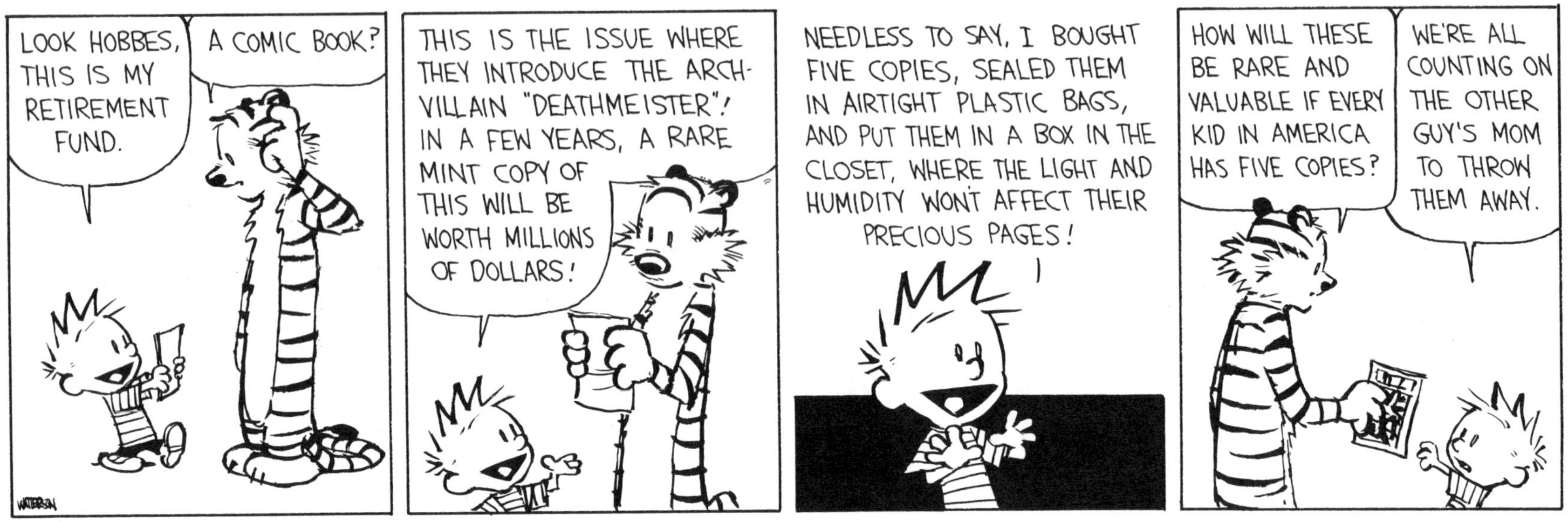
LOOK HOBBES, THIS IS MY RETIREMENT FUND.
A COMIC BOOK?
THIS IS THE ISSUE WHERE THEY INTRODUCE THE ARCH-VILLAIN "DEATHMEISTER"! IN A FEW YEARS, A RARE MINT COPY OF THIS WILL BE WORTH MILLIONS OF DOLLARS!
NEEDLESS TO SAY, I BOUGHT FIVE COPIES, SEALED THEM IN AIRTIGHT PLASTIC BAGS, AND PUT THEM IN A BOX IN THE CLOSET, WHERE THE LIGHT AND HUMIDITY WON'T AFFECT THEIR PRECIOUS PAGES!
HOW WILL THESE BE RARE AND VALUABLE IF EVERY KID IN AMERICA HAS FIVE COPIES?
WE'RE ALL COUNTING ON THE OTHER GUY'S MOM TO THROW THEM AWAY.

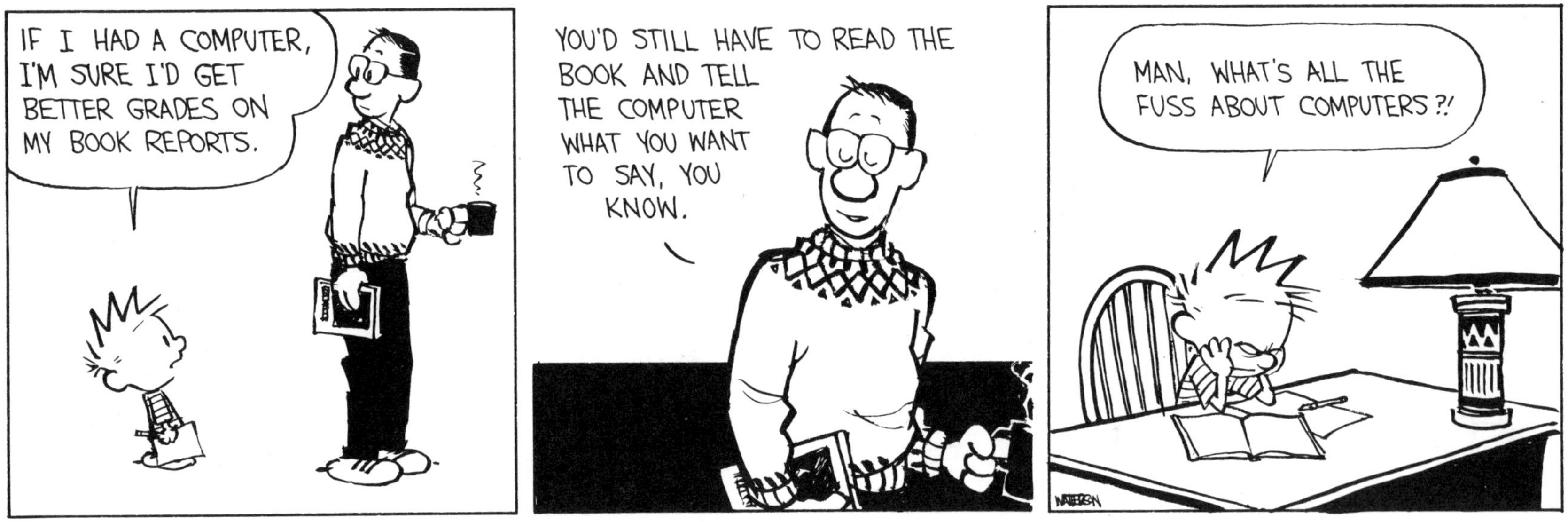
IF I HAD A COMPUTER, I'M SURE I'D GET BETTER GRADES ON MY BOOK REPORTS.
YOU'D STILL HAVE TO READ THE BOOK AND TELL THE COMPUTER WHAT YOU WANT TO SAY, YOU KNOW.
MAN, WHAT'S ALL THE FUSS ABOUT COMPUTERS?!

WANT TO BUY MY LATEST INVENTION?
WHAT IS IT?
IT'S A WRITER'S BLOCK! YOU PUT IT ON TOP OF YOUR DESK AND THEN YOU CAN'T WRITE THERE ANY MORE!
I MUST BE YEARS AHEAD OF MY TIME.

WHAT'S THE MATTER, HONEY? YOU LOOK DOWN IN THE DUMPS.
I DON'T HAVE A HAIRY CHEST.
MOM SAYS SOME BABES DON'T CARE.
THPTPBT! RIGHT.

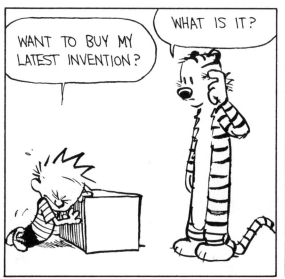

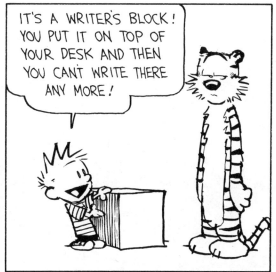

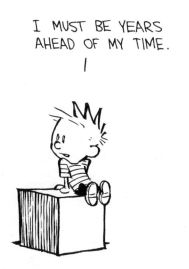

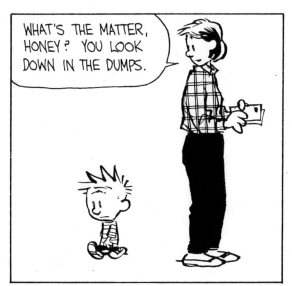

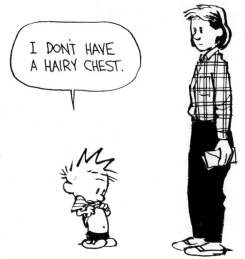

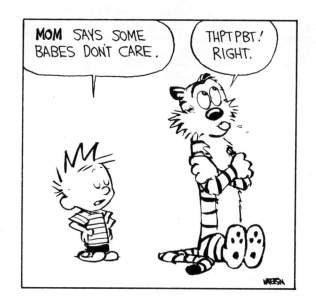

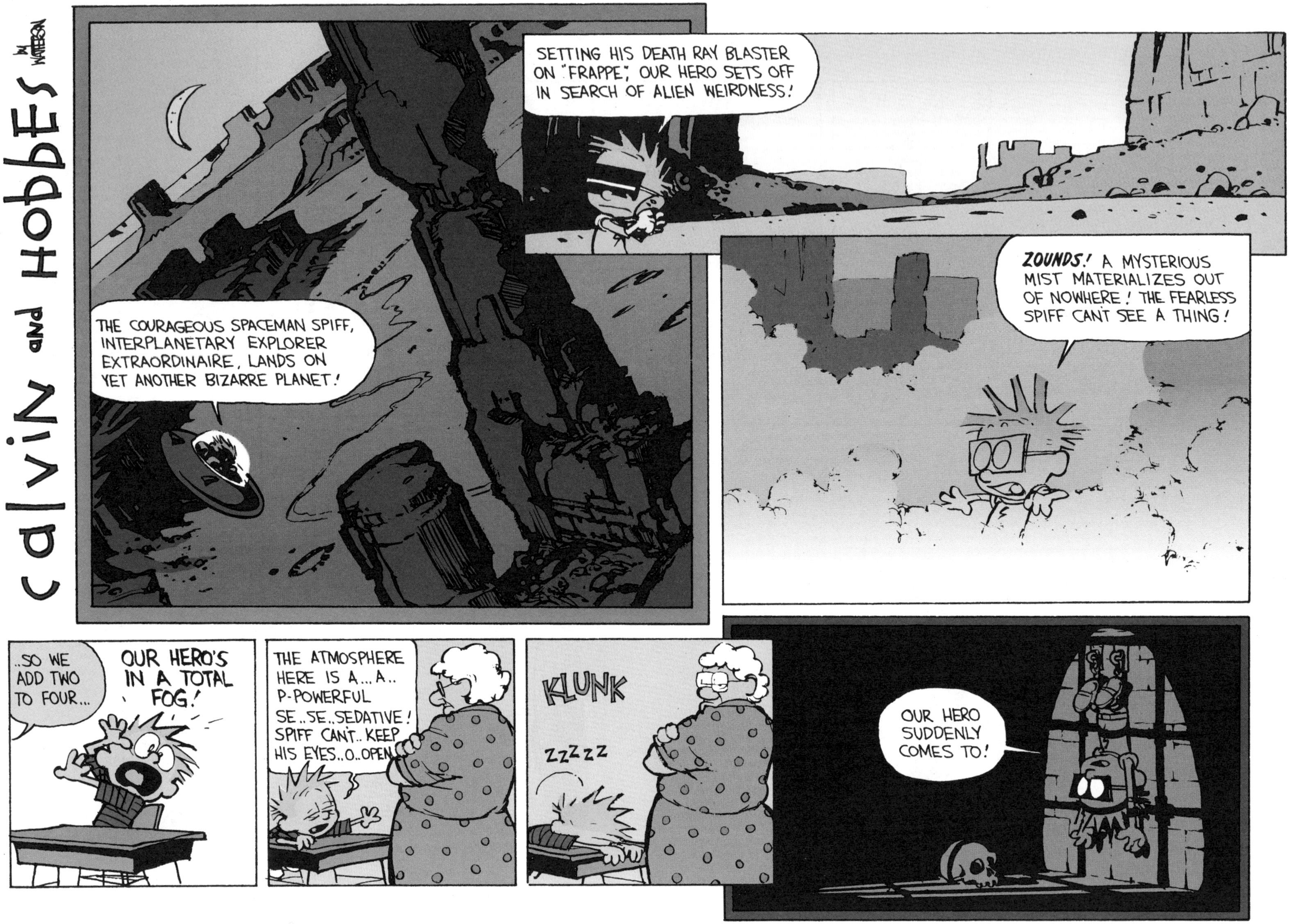
calvin and HOBBES
by WATTERSON
THE COURAGEOUS SPACEMAN SPIFF, INTERPLANETARY EXPLORER EXTRAORDINAIRE, LANDS ON YET ANOTHER BIZARRE PLANET!
SETTING HIS DEATH RAY BLASTER ON "FRAPPE," OUR HERO SETS OFF IN SEARCH OF ALIEN WEIRDNESS!
ZOUNDS! A MYSTERIOUS MIST MATERIALIZES OUT OF NOWHERE! THE FEARLESS SPIFF CAN'T SEE A THING!
..SO WE ADD TWO TO FOUR...
OUR HERO'S IN A TOTAL FOG!
THE ATMOSPHERE HERE IS A... A.. P-POWERFUL SE..SE..SEDATIVE! SPIFF CAN'T.. KEEP HIS EYES..O..OPEN..
KLUNK
ZZZZZ
OUR HERO SUDDENLY COMES TO!

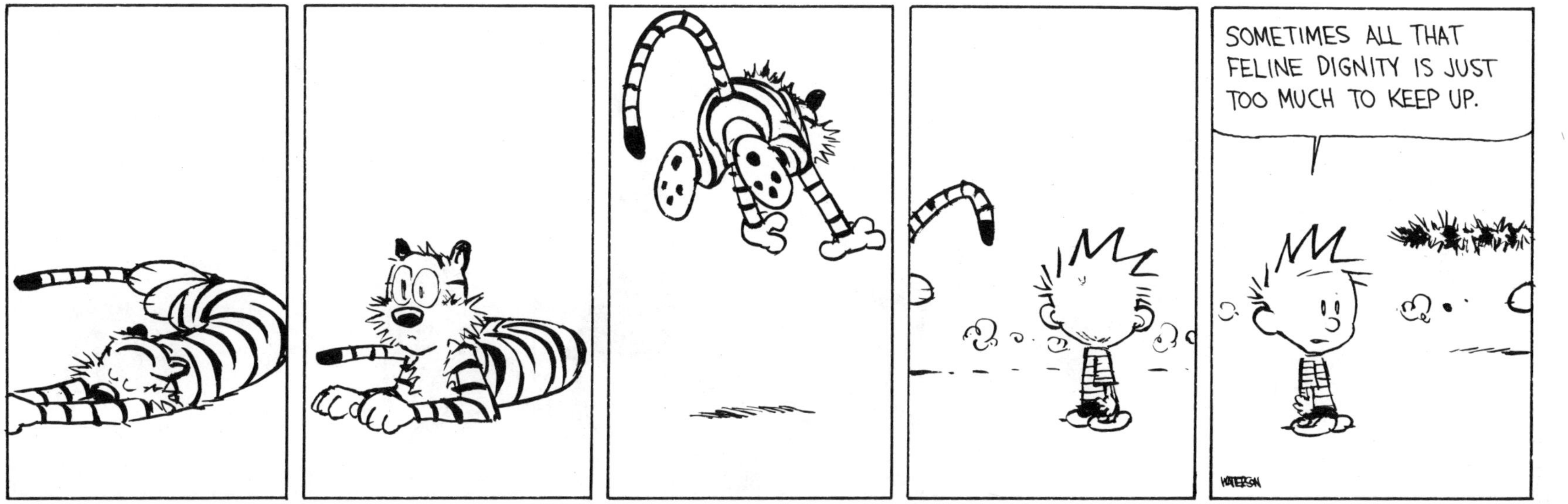
SOMETIMES ALL THAT FELINE DIGNITY IS JUST TOO MUCH TO KEEP UP.

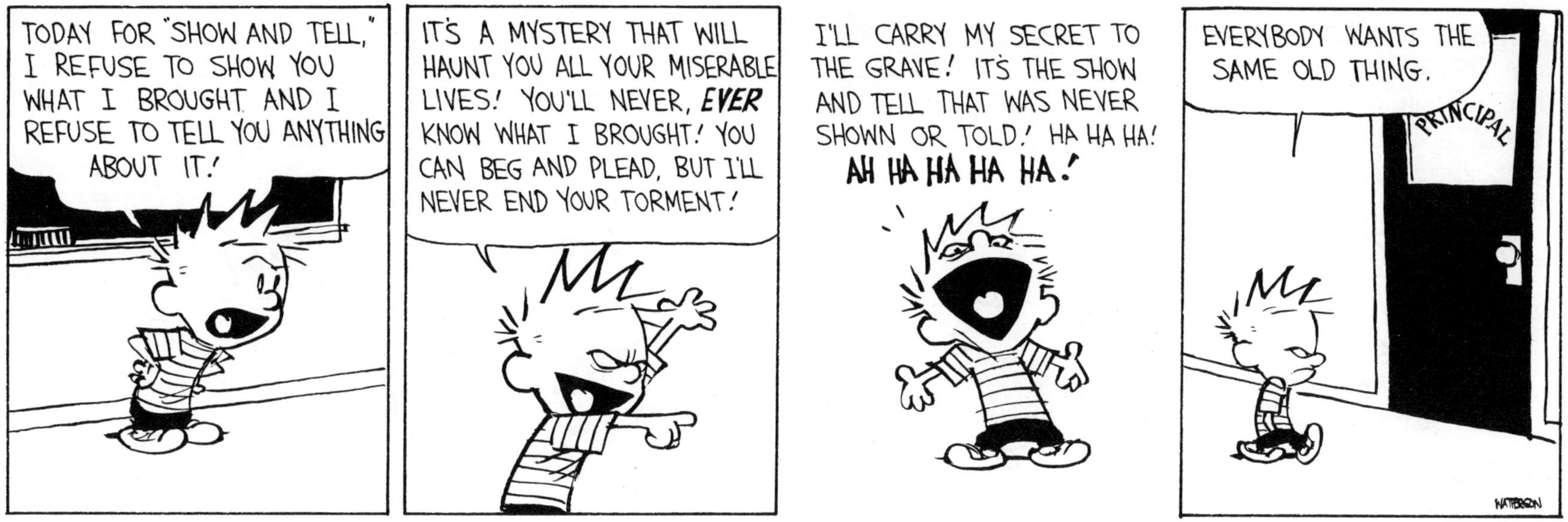
TODAY FOR "SHOW AND TELL," I REFUSE TO SHOW YOU WHAT I BROUGHT AND I REFUSE TO TELL YOU ANYTHING ABOUT IT!
IT'S A MYSTERY THAT WILL HAUNT YOU ALL YOUR MISERABLE LIVES! YOU'LL NEVER, EVER KNOW WHAT I BROUGHT! YOU CAN BEG AND PLEAD, BUT I'LL NEVER END YOUR TORMENT!
I'LL CARRY MY SECRET TO THE GRAVE! IT'S THE SHOW AND TELL THAT WAS NEVER SHOWN OR TOLD! HA HA HA! AH HA HA HA HA!
EVERYBODY WANTS THE SAME OLD THING.
PRINCIPAL

CIGARS ARE ALL THE RAGE, DAD. YOU SHOULD SMOKE CIGARS!

FLATULENCE COULD BE ALL THE RAGE, BUT IT WOULD STILL BE DISGUSTING.

I SEE.

NICELY PUT, DEAR.

A BOX OF NEW CRAYONS! NOW THEY'RE ALL POINTY, LINED UP IN ORDER, BRIGHT AND PERFECT!

SOON THEY'LL BE A BUNCH OF GROUND-DOWN, ROUNDED, INDISTINGUISHABLE STUMPS, MISSING THEIR WRAPPERS AND SMUDGED WITH OTHER COLORS.

SOMETIMES LIFE SEEMS UNBEARABLY TRAGIC.

OK, THAT'S PLENTY OF TELEVISION. TURN IT OFF.

I'LL MOPE AND WHINE AND ARGUE! I'LL GET IN THE WAY! I'LL GET IN TROUBLE! I'LL TEAR AROUND! YOU WON'T HAVE A MOMENT'S PEACE IF YOU MAKE ME TURN OFF THE TV!

I NOTICED SHE HAD TO THINK ABOUT IT.

HELLO? YES, I'D LIKE TO SPEAK WITH THE CHIEF OF POLICE.

HELLO, CHIEF? IS IT A **LAW** THAT YOUR SOCKS HAVE TO MATCH ANYTHING ELSE YOU'RE WEARING?

HEY MOM, LISTEN TO THIS!

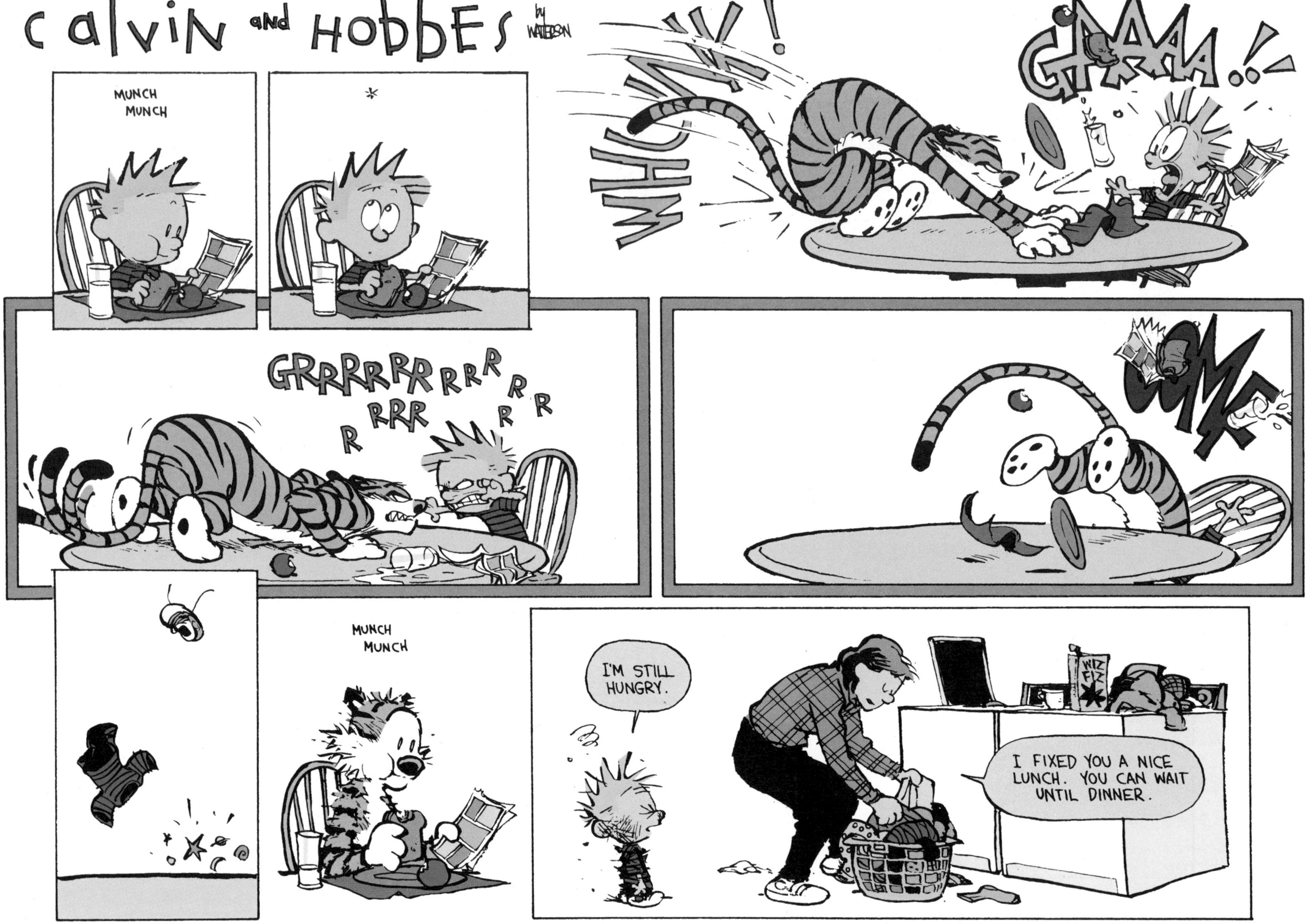
Calvin and Hobbes
by WATTERSON
MUNCH
MUNCH
*
WHUMPH!
GAAAA..!!
GRRRRRRRRRRRR
RRR
R
R R
OOMF
MUNCH
MUNCH
I'M STILL HUNGRY.
I FIXED YOU A NICE LUNCH. YOU CAN WAIT UNTIL DINNER.

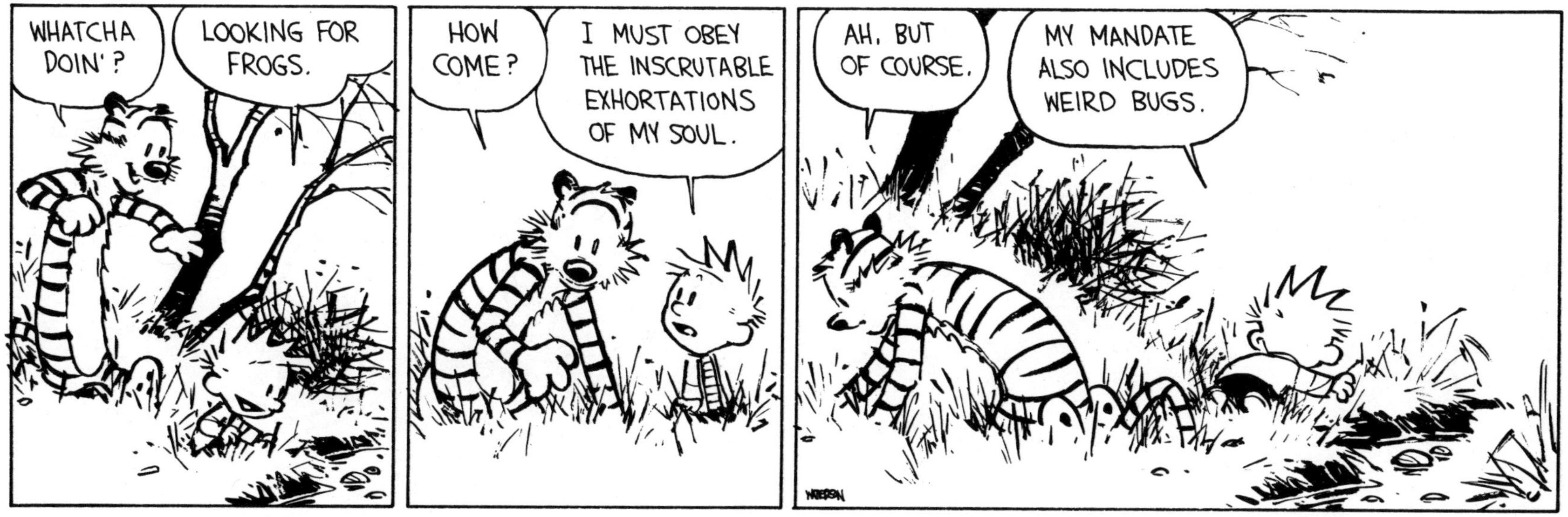
WHATCHA DOIN'?
LOOKING FOR FROGS.
HOW COME?
I MUST OBEY THE INSCRUTABLE EXHORTATIONS OF MY SOUL.
AH, BUT OF COURSE.
MY MANDATE ALSO INCLUDES WEIRD BUGS.

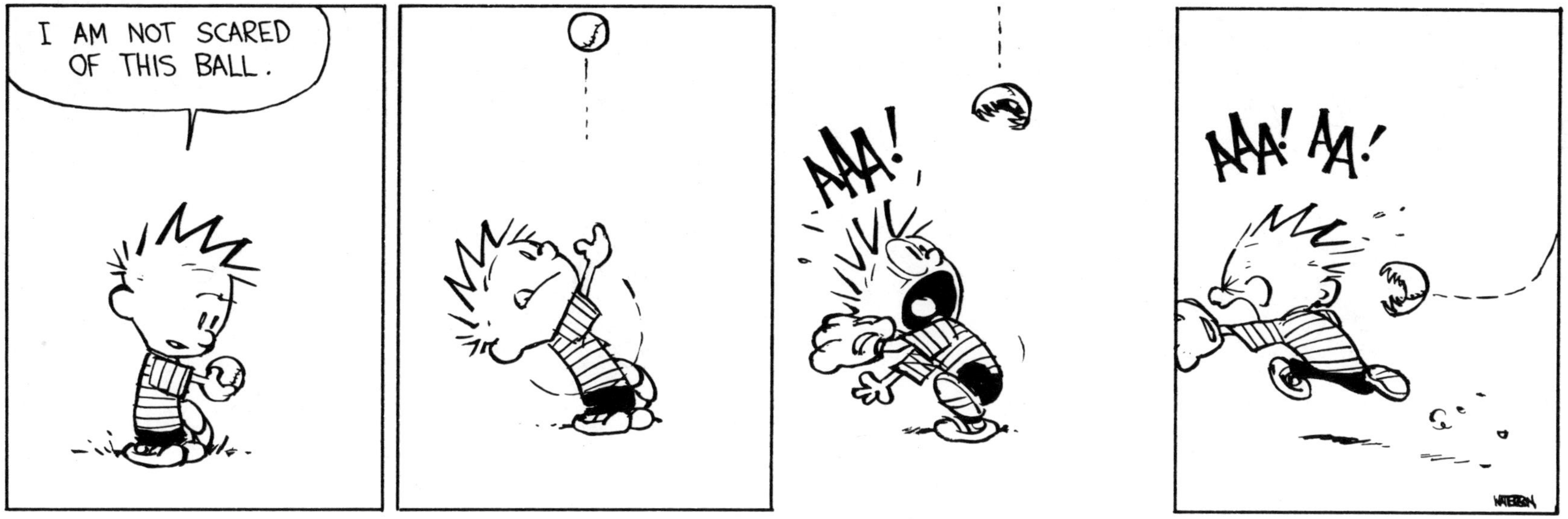
I AM NOT SCARED OF THIS BALL.
AAA!
AAA! AA!

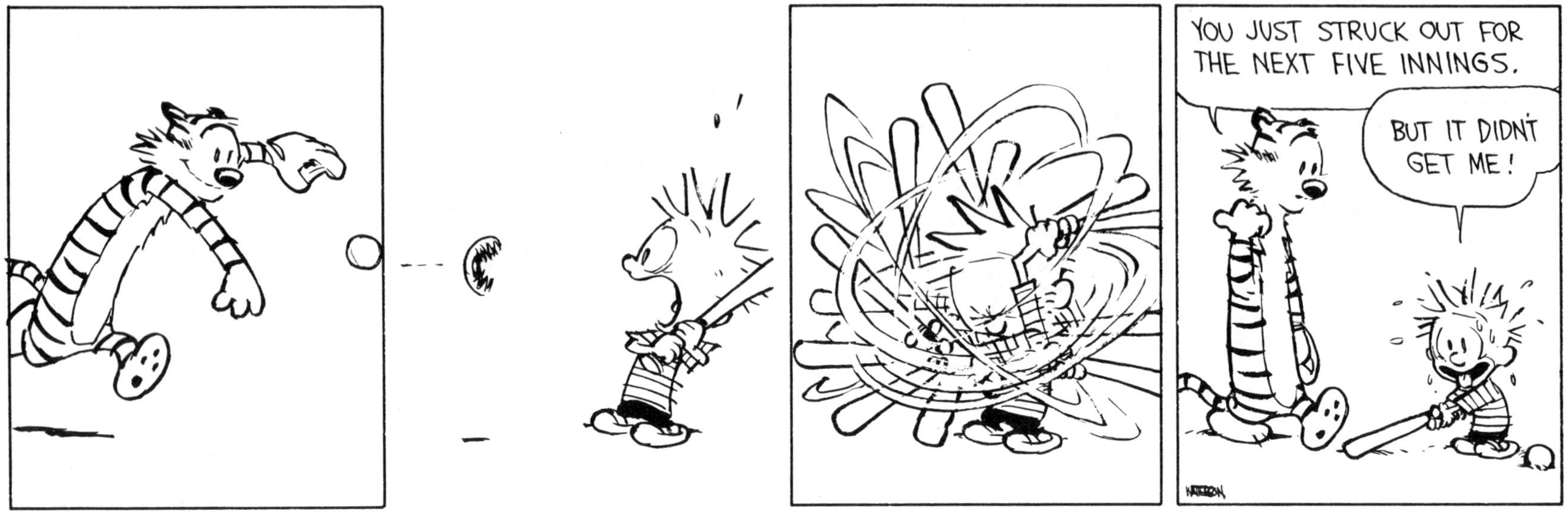
YOU JUST STRUCK OUT FOR THE NEXT FIVE INNINGS.
BUT IT DIDN'T GET ME!

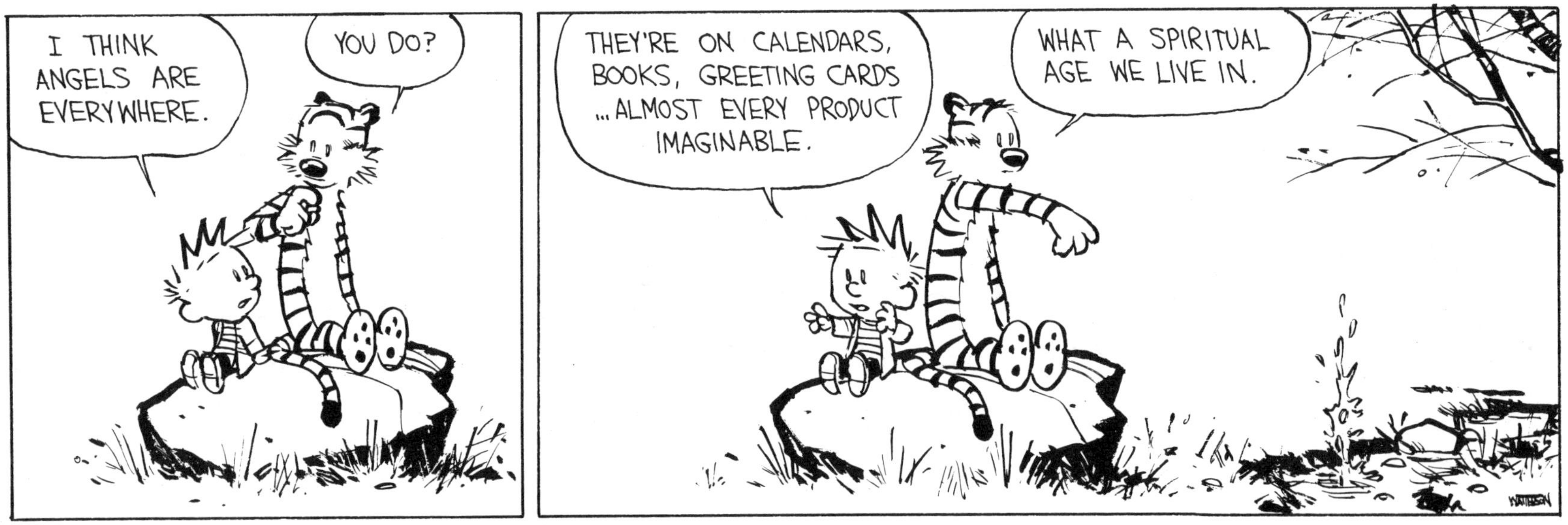
I THINK ANGELS ARE EVERYWHERE.
YOU DO?
THEY'RE ON CALENDARS, BOOKS, GREETING CARDS ...ALMOST EVERY PRODUCT IMAGINABLE.
WHAT A SPIRITUAL AGE WE LIVE IN.

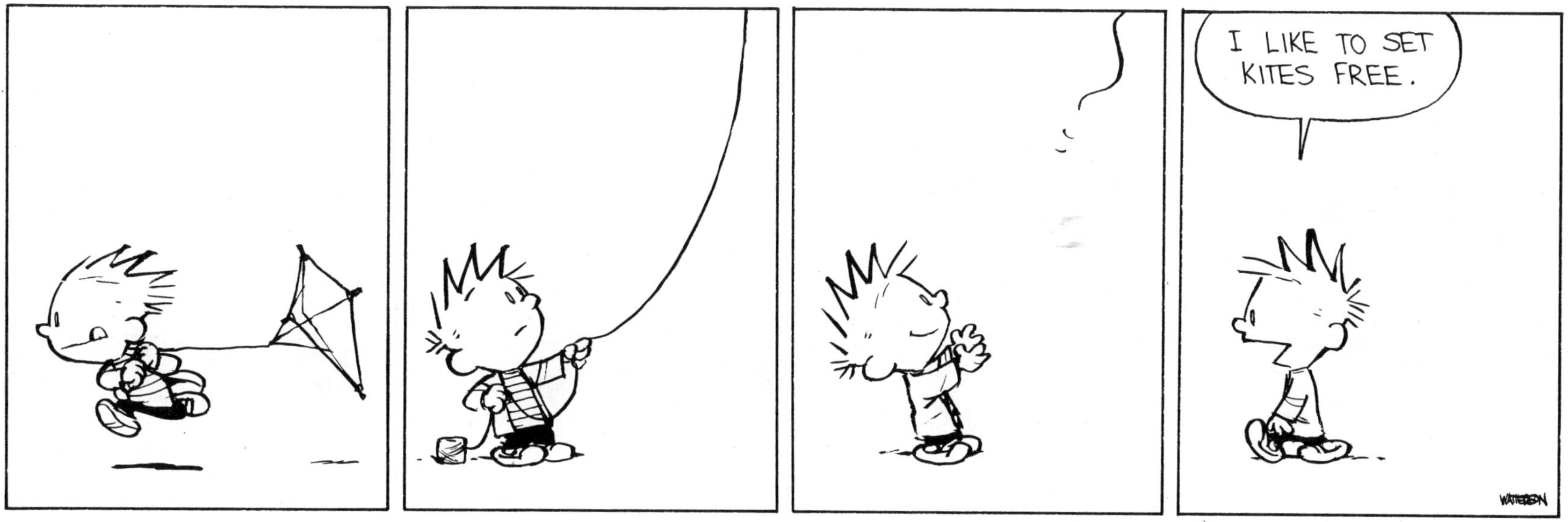
I LIKE TO SET KITES FREE.

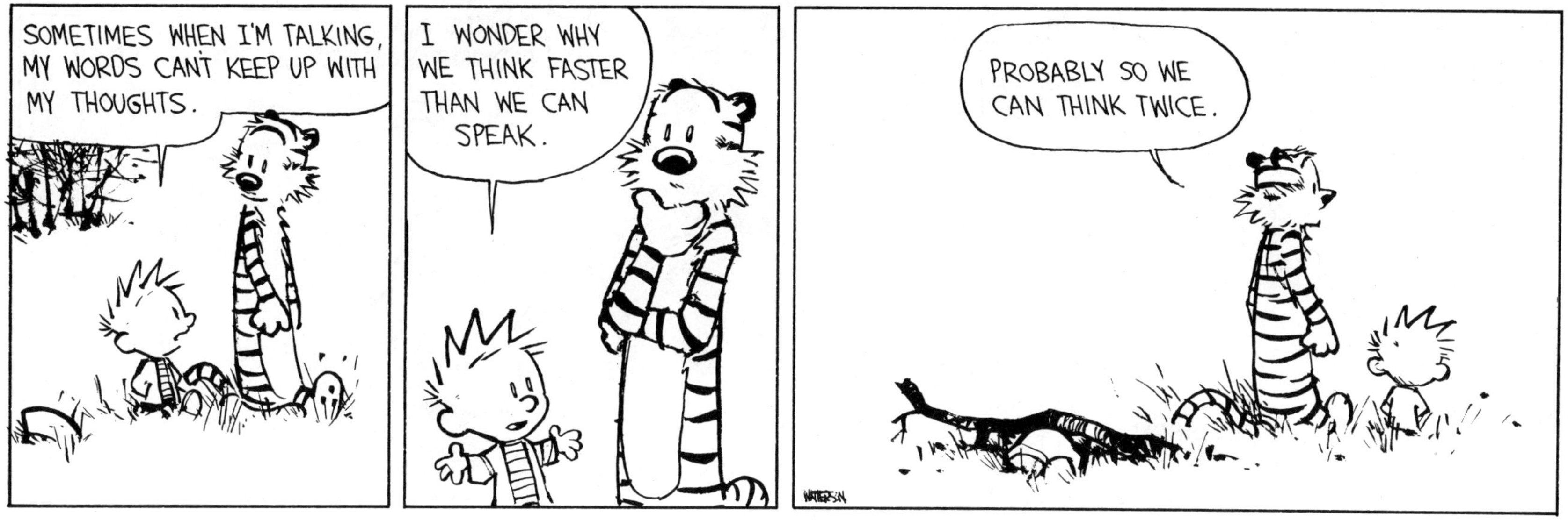
SOMETIMES WHEN I'M TALKING, MY WORDS CAN'T KEEP UP WITH MY THOUGHTS.
I WONDER WHY WE THINK FASTER THAN WE CAN SPEAK.
PROBABLY SO WE CAN THINK TWICE.

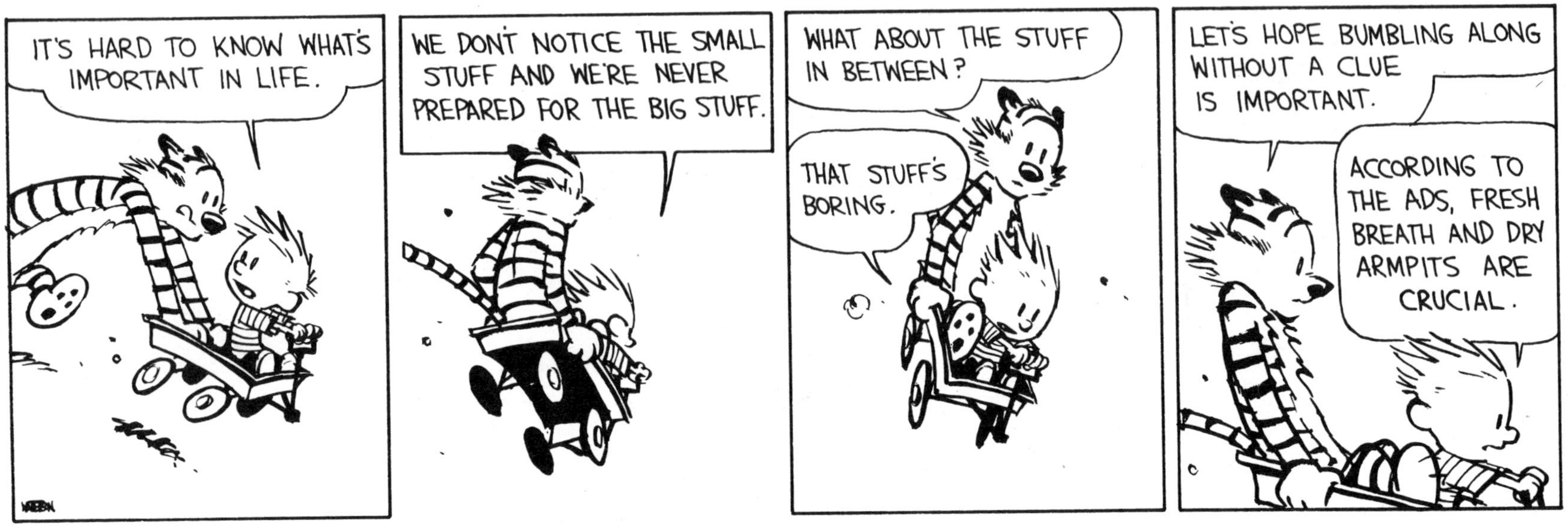
IT'S HARD TO KNOW WHAT'S IMPORTANT IN LIFE.
WE DON'T NOTICE THE SMALL STUFF AND WE'RE NEVER PREPARED FOR THE BIG STUFF.
WHAT ABOUT THE STUFF IN BETWEEN?
THAT STUFF'S BORING.
LET'S HOPE BUMBLING ALONG WITHOUT A CLUE IS IMPORTANT.
ACCORDING TO THE ADS, FRESH BREATH AND DRY ARMPITS ARE CRUCIAL.

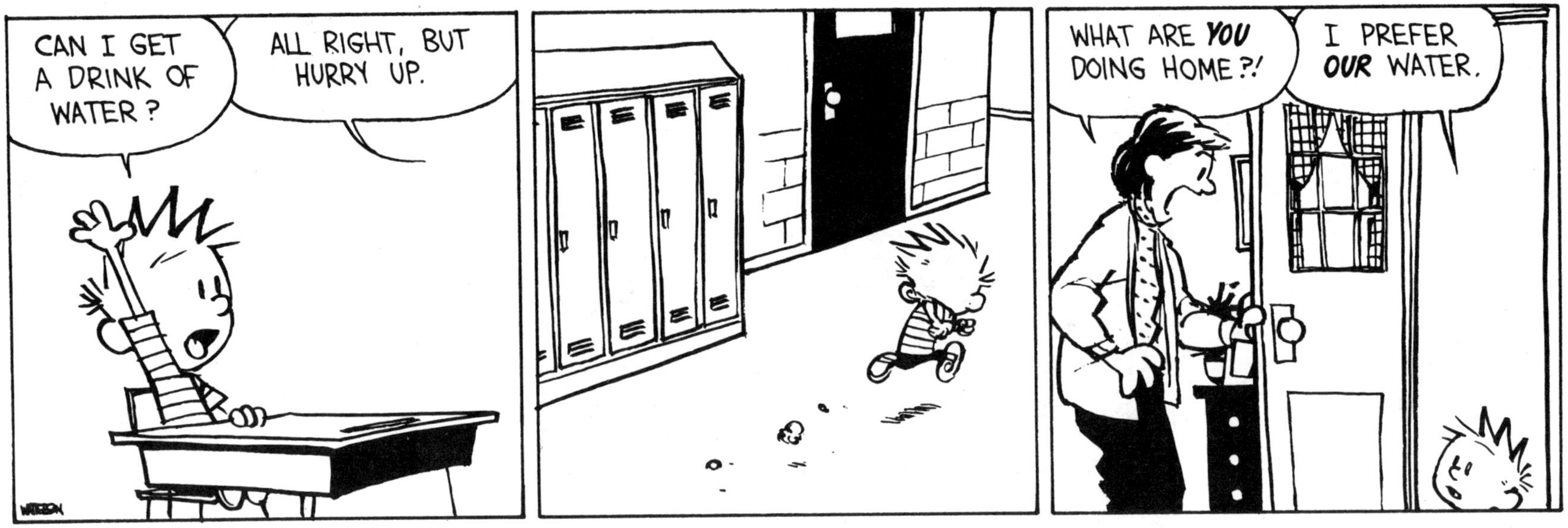
CAN I GET A DRINK OF WATER?
ALL RIGHT, BUT HURRY UP.
WHAT ARE **YOU** DOING HOME?!
I PREFER **OUR** WATER.

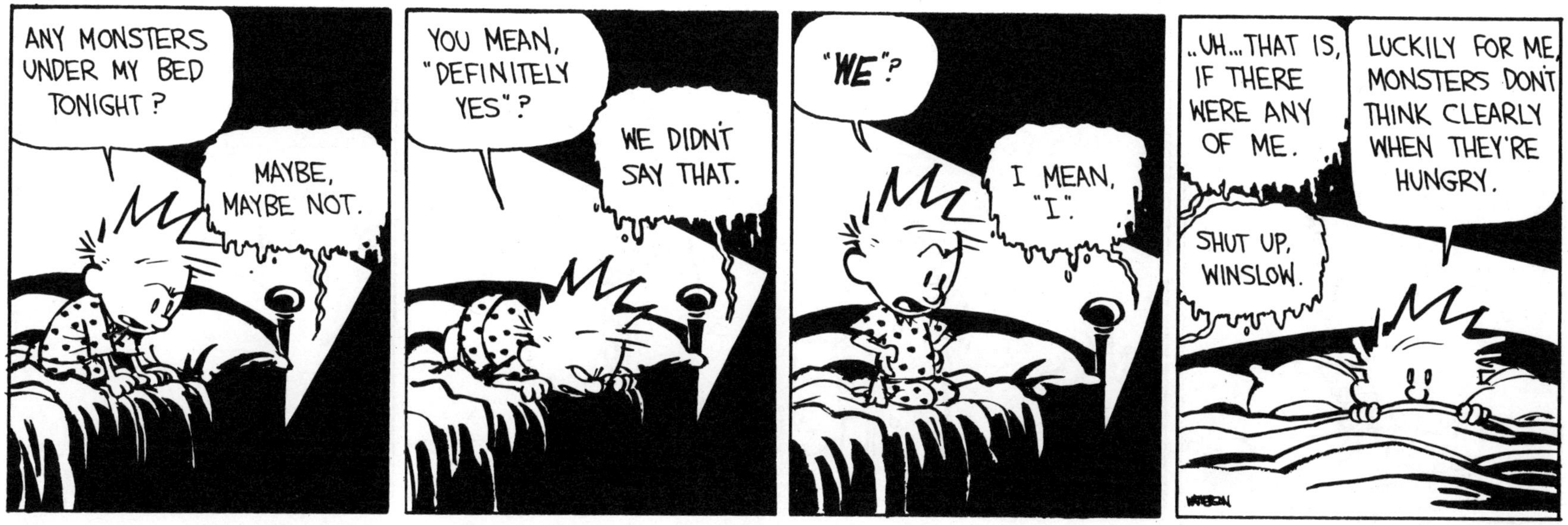
ANY MONSTERS UNDER MY BED TONIGHT?
MAYBE, MAYBE NOT.
YOU MEAN, "DEFINITELY YES"?
WE DIDN'T SAY THAT.
"WE"?
I MEAN, "I".
..UH...THAT IS, IF THERE WERE ANY OF ME.
SHUT UP, WINSLOW.
LUCKILY FOR ME, MONSTERS DON'T THINK CLEARLY WHEN THEY'RE HUNGRY.

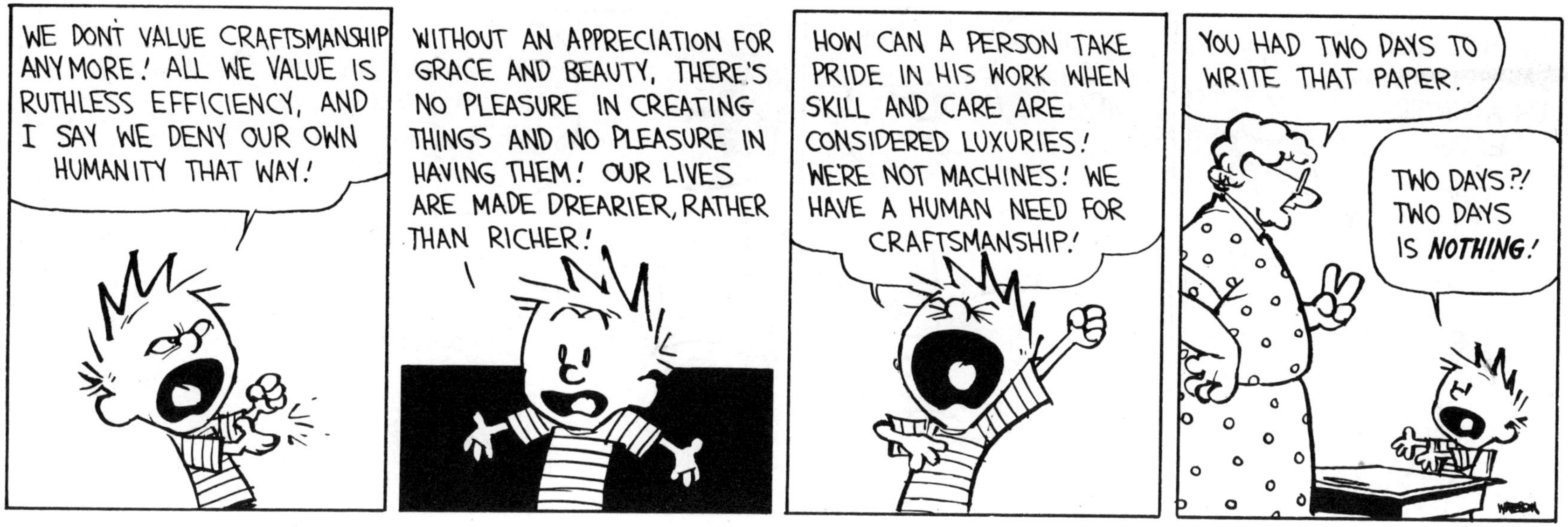
WE DON'T VALUE CRAFTSMANSHIP ANYMORE! ALL WE VALUE IS RUTHLESS EFFICIENCY, AND I SAY WE DENY OUR OWN HUMANITY THAT WAY!
WITHOUT AN APPRECIATION FOR GRACE AND BEAUTY, THERE'S NO PLEASURE IN CREATING THINGS AND NO PLEASURE IN HAVING THEM! OUR LIVES ARE MADE DREARIER, RATHER THAN RICHER!
HOW CAN A PERSON TAKE PRIDE IN HIS WORK WHEN SKILL AND CARE ARE CONSIDERED LUXURIES! WE'RE NOT MACHINES! WE HAVE A HUMAN NEED FOR CRAFTSMANSHIP!
YOU HAD TWO DAYS TO WRITE THAT PAPER.
TWO DAYS?! TWO DAYS IS NOTHING!

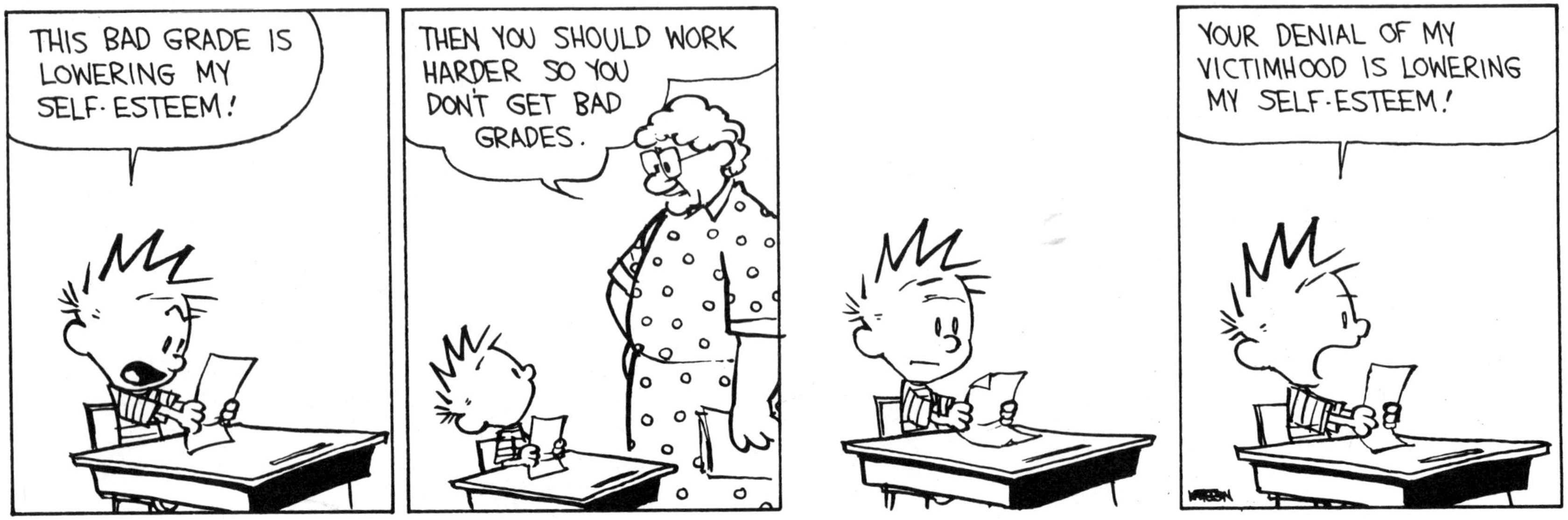
THIS BAD GRADE IS LOWERING MY SELF-ESTEEM!
THEN YOU SHOULD WORK HARDER SO YOU DON'T GET BAD GRADES.
YOUR DENIAL OF MY VICTIMHOOD IS LOWERING MY SELF-ESTEEM!

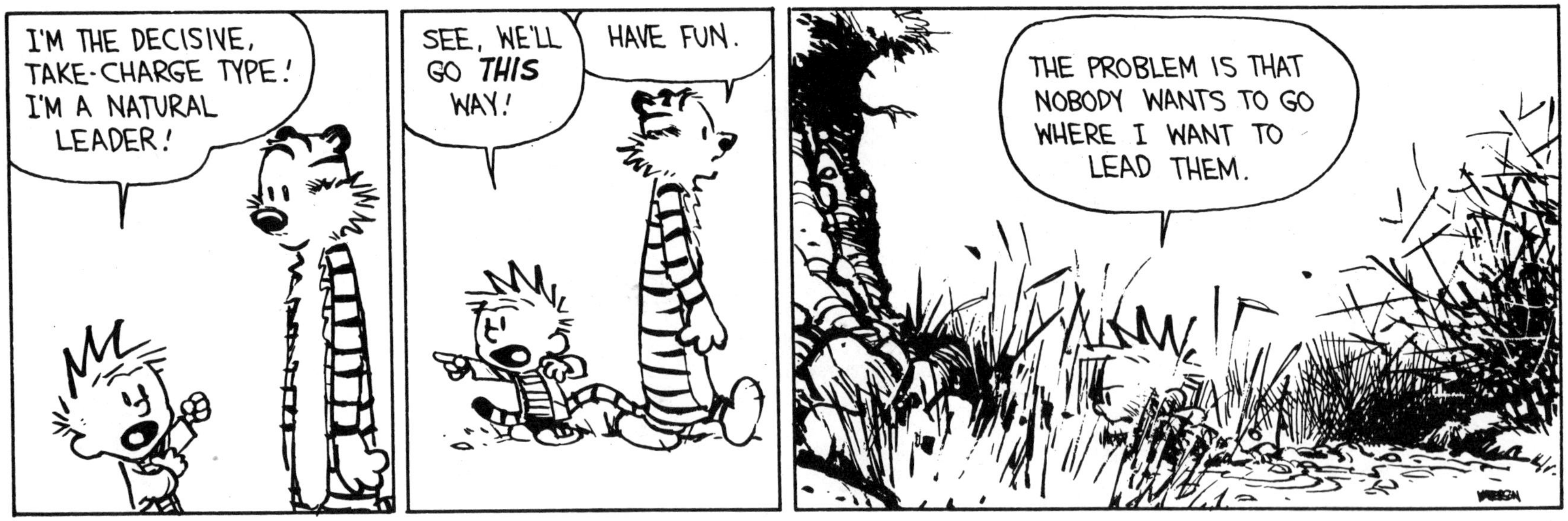
I'M THE DECISIVE, TAKE-CHARGE TYPE! I'M A NATURAL LEADER!
SEE, WE'LL GO **THIS** WAY!
HAVE FUN.
THE PROBLEM IS THAT NOBODY WANTS TO GO WHERE I WANT TO LEAD THEM.

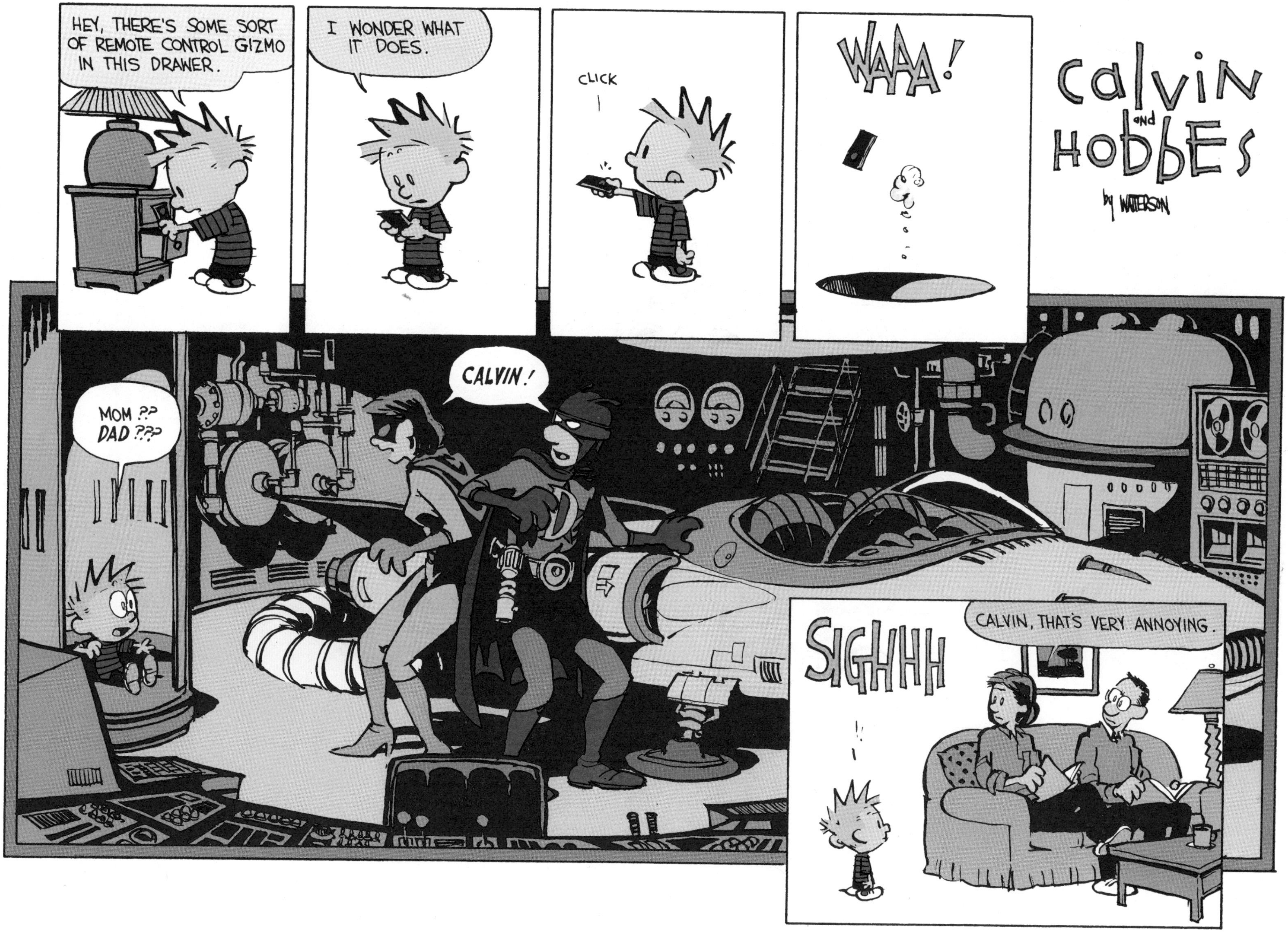
HEY, THERE'S SOME SORT OF REMOTE CONTROL GIZMO IN THIS DRAWER.
I WONDER WHAT IT DOES.
CLICK
WAAA!
Calvin and HOBBES
by WATTERSON
MOM ?? DAD ???
CALVIN!
SIGHHH
CALVIN, THAT'S VERY ANNOYING.

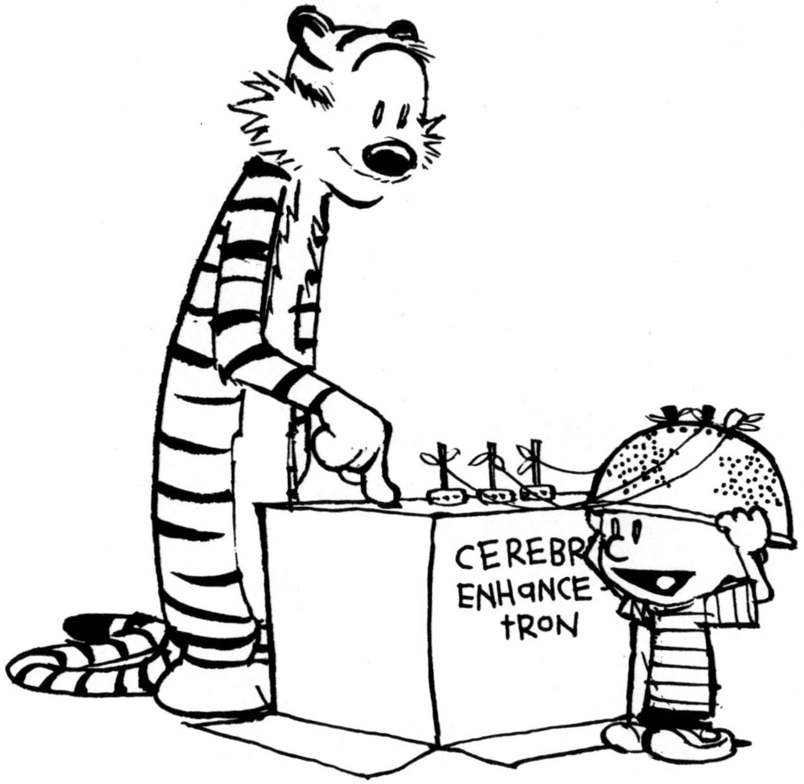
CEREBRIC ENHANCE-TRON